To Peter,

In acknowledgement of your
years at Ashgate Hospice Board.

All the very best for the future.

David   18 July 2019

D1797580

Basque Politics Series

No. 13

FIRST DRAFT EDITION

Bitter Justice

The Penitentiary of El Puerto De Santa María and Its Basque Dimension, 1936–1949

David Lyon

Center for Basque Studies

University of Nevada, Reno

This book was published with the generous financial assistance of the Basque government

Basque Politics Series, No. 13
Series Editor: Xabier Irujo

Center for Basque Studies
University of Nevada, Reno
Reno, Nevada 89557
http://basque.unr.edu

Copyright © 2016 by David Lyon
All rights reserved. Printed in the United States of America.
Book design: Juan San Martin
Cover Photo: Aerial view of El Puerto de Santa María, courtesy of Patrimonio Historico del Ayuntamiento de El Puerto de Santa Maria. Jose Ignacio Delgado

Library of Congress Cataloging-in-Publication Data

Names: Lyon, David, 1935- author.
Title: Bitter justice : the penitentiary of El Puerto de Santa Maria and its Basque dimension, 1936-1949 / David Lyon.
Description: Reno, Nevada : Center for Basque Studies, University of Nevada, Reno, [2017] | Series: Basque politics series ; No. 13 | Includes bibliographical references and index.
Identifiers: LCCN 2017019381 | ISBN 9781935709800 (pbk. : alk. paper)
Subjects: LCSH: Political prisoners--Spain--El Puerto de Santa María--History--20th century. | Basques--Spain--El Puerto de Santa María--History--20th century. | Prisons--Spain--El Puerto de Santa María--History--20th century. | Spain--History--Civil War, 1936–1939--Prisoners and Prisons. | Spain--Politics and government--1939-1975.
Classification: LCC DP269.65 .L96 2017 | DDC 365/.94688--dc23 LC record available at https://na01.safelinks. protection.outlook.com/?url=https%3A%2F%2Flccn.loc. gov%2F2017019381&data=01%7C01%7Cdmontero%40unr.

Contents

Introduction   11

1 The Penitentiary of El Puerto de Santa María   25

2 A Basque Dimension within El Puerto de Santa María   57

3 Collective Memories of Basque Relatives of the Prisoners
  in the Penitentiary of El Puerto de Santa María
  between 1936 and 1949   97

4 Case Studies of Prisoners in the Penitentiary of
  El Puerto de Santa María   135

5 The Penal Policy of the Franco Regime:
  Charges, Sentences, Transfers, and Release Conditions
  of Prisoners in El Puerto de Santa María   199

6 The End of the Odyssey   231

Bibliography   243

Acknowledgments

Preparation for this project has led to an eventual outcome that has taken a considerable time in the making. I am indebted to a large number of people in Spain and the United Kingdom for advice and information that has enabled me to complete this work. During a six-year period, I have established communications with many people, mostly in Spain. My thanks to them all, but I am unable to mention everyone concerned. However I make no apology for my list of acknowledgements taking up more space than perhaps is usual in view of this help.

The idea of researching this topic arose as a result of an initial discussion in June 2005 with Manuel Ravina Martín, Director of the Provincial Historical Archive of Cádiz.[1] He has been of enormous help and has spared me invaluable time over the years and made available the categorized data of prisoners in the penitentiary of El Puerto de Santa María during the years 1936–1949. Other help in Andalusia has come from Luis Carlos Gómez, Director of the Provincial Historical Archive of Huelva and Ana Becerra Fabra of the Municipal Historical Archive of El Puerto de Santa María.

---

1. Manuel Ravina Martín now moved to other Directorship. Replaced by Manuel Cañas Moya as Director, who also assisted.

The advice of Andalusian historians Fernando Romero Romero (Villamartín) and José Luis Gutiérrez Molina (Seville) has been invaluable.

As the focus of research moved to the Basque Country, I received help from the then two Basque National Archives that included important guidance from Eduardo Jauregi of the Sabino Arana Fundazioa in Artea[2] and Roberto Kerexeta of Irargi, the Centro de Patrimonio Documental de Euskadi/Euskadiko Dokumentu Ondarearen Zentroa in Bergara.[3] María González Gorosarri of Mallabia and Andoni Barrera of Durango, both members of Durango 1936 Kultur Elkartea, opened many doors. In the case of María, she not only facilitated access to her own extended family and friends who had relatives in El Puerto de Santa María, but also to other descendants of prisoners via an interview with the Basque newspaper Deia. These interviews were crucial to my research as it enabled me to make contacts that hitherto were not open to me. My undying gratitude to these Basque relatives who have so generously given me personal and intimate details about their families. Without them there would not have been the all important chapter on the prisoners' experiences from a human and personal angle. The names of the prison relatives included:

María González Gorosarri (Mallabia), María Asunción Gerediaga Barramendi (Durango), Yolanda Echaburu Alzaa (Berriz), Jabier Gorosarri (Berriz),

José Arrondo Uriarte (Durango), Joxemari Mendizábal (Donostia-San Sebastián),

Julene Miren Pujana Bolibar, (Otxandio), José Luis Arrondo Uriarte (Durango), Martín Aurrekoetxea Unzueta (Bilbao), Joseba Arruza Goitia (Mungia), Arantzazu Garay (Bilbao), Joseba Andoni Bikandi Arana (Loiu), María del Carmen Ruiz de Aguirre (Amorebieta), Irantzu Bustinza Ruis de Aguirre (Galdakao), Galder Unzalu Etxabe (Zarautz), Begona Torrontegui Aguirre (Maruri), Rafa Mendibil Sobrón (Urduña), Mikel ArietaAraunabeña (Erandio), Kepa Gorosarri (Durango).

My particular thanks to Irantzu Bustinea of Galdakao who has provided me with so much information (which included a hitherto hidden diary of her grandfather who was a prisoner in El Puerto between 1938 and 1940). Her mother, María del Carmen Ruiz de Aguirre of Amorebieta, also wrote me an invaluable letter about her father and I had a very help-

---

2. Archives now moved to Goaz Museum, Bilbao with Marian Moreno, Director, who also assisted.
3. From January 2014 this archive was moved to the Euskadiko Artxibo Historikoa-Archivo Histórico de Euskadi (Historical Archive of the Basque Country) in the center of Bilbao.

ful meeting with them both in Mungia. In our correspondence Joxemari Mendizabal Sarasua of Donostia-San Sebastián has answered detailed questions arising from his book on Basque prisoners, which mentions that a very close relative of his was a prisoner in El Puerto. The historians Pedro Barruso Barés (Donostia-San Sebastián) and Gutmaro Gómez Bravo (Madrid) have always been extremely helpful and supportive. My thanks also to Jesús Gutiérrez Arosa.

In the United Kingdom I am especially grateful to Paul Preston who generously gave me his time and priceless advice at the outset of my research and who helped me to make invaluable contacts. Other thanks go to Julius Ruiz for constructive advice on the interpretation of the maze of collective trials that helped my understanding of prison files and Peter Anderson for his guidance on locating the whereabouts and identities of Basque priests in Carmona. My biggest debt is to Mary Vincent my supervisor at Sheffield University who constantly offered me guidance, direction, and sense of purpose without which my postgraduate research material would not have been utilized to maximum effect. The advice of her colleague, Miriam Dobson, has also been most welcome. Although the observations of Stuart Christie covered a different prison and a period slightly outside the remit of this research, I welcomed his views from a practical standpoint as a prisoner of Franco between 1964 and 1967. Encouragement and advice from other areas of Sheffield University with interests in Spain was received from Toni Ibarz and Bob Brittain whilst Chris Jones, the University Library Systems Manager has always been unfailingly helpful. Finally I should like to express my thanks to Terence Daniel Lynch, a retired UK tribunal judge who was able to offer an interesting comparative insight on the military tribunals of Franco.

The research is concluded with regret in that not only will I be bidding farewell to a very old friend, but also because I have realized that I have been unable to use much of material painstakingly extracted from the Cádiz archives.

None of the above are responsible for the views expressed and errors, where they might exist, are totally mine. This also applies to any possible errors of the Basque names and places of Basque prisoners from the lists of penitentiary files of El Puerto (where they have originally been entered in Spanish).Finally I express my thanks to my wife Diana, both for her endless efforts here and in the very many visits to Andalusia and the Basque Country. Without her help (and patience) this work would not have been possible.

Introduction

Un muerto en España está más vivo que en ningún sitio:
hiere su perfil como el filo de una navaja barbera.

Federico García Lorca

The idea of carrying out a research project on the prisons of Franco began as a result of a casual conversation in June 2005 about the Spanish Civil War with the then director of the Provincial Historical Archive (Archivo Histórico Provincial) in Cádiz.[1] He mentioned that his archive had recently cataloged a considerable new batch of Civil War prison files relating to a large nearby penitentiary, El Puerto de Santa María.[2] He informed me that to the best of his knowledge, nobody had researched this material, which was available to the public.

I embarked on the project expecting to concentrate on prisoners from the Cádiz area, as El Puerto was the largest nearby prison. Although there was a large local intake from Cádiz province to El Puerto (2,400), attempts to contact any relatives of prisoners from the area proved unsuccessful. Further investigation established that there were an almost equally large number of prisoners from the Basque Country; this partially altered the focus of my research.

---

1. Henceforth AHPC/PSM Legajos 29246–29474.
2. Henceforth El Puerto.

The prison files revealed that, out of 5,479 inmates in the peak year of intake in 1940, some 2,178 were from the Basque Country.[3] This led to an unforeseen decision to visit Basque archives in Artea and Bergara.[4]

During my visit there I made some invaluable Basque contacts in Durango that led to communication with some relatives of prisoners in El Puerto. This included María Gorosarri, who introduced me to several people who had relatives in El Puerto;[5] and this resulted in an interview with the Basque newspaper *Deia*.[6] As a result, some twenty people contacted me from Erandio, Loiu (Lujua), Mungia (Munguía), Bakio (Baquio), Amorebieta, Durango, Otxandio (Ochandiano), Urduña (Orduña), the Txorierri Valley and Zarautz. All were willing to communicate with me and to talk about the experiences of their family members, who had been in El Puerto between 1937 and 1943.[7]

These contributions were highly valid, invaluable sources that were complementary to the archive material obtained elsewhere and made it come to life. An awareness of the difficulties of persuading relatives to talk about the Spanish Civil War was an important factor and their contribution ensures that the impact of imprisonment of Basque soldiers and their families by the Franco regime is recorded for posterity.

The focus of this research concentrates on issues arising from a large penitentiary in Andalusia between 1936 and 1945, with a Basque dimension. My investigation into individual prison files, in archives in both Cádiz province and the Basque Country, enabled me to take a comparative approach suggesting that Basque prisoners might have been treated more unfavorably than prisoners from Cádiz. A further analysis of the charges, sentences, and conditions of release confirmed my views that these were more stringent for Basque prisoners. El Puerto was also best

---

3. AHPC/PSM Legajos 29246–29476.
4. Other archives have been used to give further information on the position of Basque prisoners in Andalusia during and after the Spanish Civil War: Archivo Histórico Provincial de Huelva: la Prisión Provincial de Huelva (Henceforth AHPH/PPH), Signaturas 07516/021–07620/032; Archivo Histórico Municipal de El Puerto de Santa María (AHPC/PSM); and Centro Municipal de Patrimonio Histórico de El Puerto de Santa María (Henceforth CMPH/PSM).
5. Interviews in Durango and Berriz, October 6 and 7, 2009.
6. Interview with Iban Gorriti of *Deia*, Durango, October 10, 2009.
7. In some cases this proved particularly fruitful. For example Irantzu Bustinza (granddaughter) from Galdakao and María del Carmen (daughter) from Amorebieta allowed me to see a prison diary of their grandfather/father. And Joxemari Mendizabal Sarasua (nephew) from Donostia-San Sebastián answered my queries concerning Basque prisoners' diaries mentioned in his book, *Gudaris y rehenes de Franco (1936–1943). Diarios de José Manuel Mendizabal "Mañul", José Luis Lasa y Fernando Agirre* (Irún: Alberdania, 2006).

placed to afford a fuller picture of the Basque dimension in this context since it contained more Basque prisoners than all the other Andalusian prisons added together.

This work examines five important interrelated issues, before arriving at a conclusion. First, an examination of the background of El Puerto prison including conditions and treatment of its inmates; second, a review of the condition of the Basque prisoners with an analysis of the origins of and particular responses to their experiences; third, a presentation of collective memories of Basque relatives of the prisoners, relating to their life before, during, and, perhaps as important, the way they were treated after their return to their communities;[8] fourth, case studies that include a diversity of charges and a wide range of different categories of "offenders"; fifth, an analysis of any inconsistencies of sentences, charges, and release conditions that affected Basque and Cádiz prisoners.[9] The conclusion highlights these irregularities and discrimination against those convicted from the Basque Country.

The Francoist policy of incarceration of political enemies was one of the major aspects of repression during the Civil War and the early rule of Franco, taken here as the period 1936–1949;[10] "crimes were considered political for the purposes of allowing a military tribunal to be held in each case."[11] The National Defense Council declared martial law in the rebel Nationalist[12] zone on July 28, 1936.[13] Any kind of resistance left all liable to trial by military tribunals for the crime of military rebellion, in which the maximum sentences were either death or imprisonment for thirty years. By virtue of a charge such as *rebelión militar* (military rebellion) or *adhesión a la rebelión* (support for rebellion) or simply *rebelión*

8. Helen Graham writes that for many "the Spanish Civil War still had years, indeed decades to run". See *The Spanish Republic at War, 1936–1939* (Cambridge: Cambridge University Press, 2002), 425. This view was often reflected in the treatment of released prisoners.

9. The archives contained in AHPC/PSM contained Civil War sentences and charges from eighteen different military tribunals, reflected in the El Puerto prison intake from 1936–1943.

10. The imprisonment of political prisoners during and immediately after the Civil War was a direct outcome of Francoist policy.

11. Michael Richards, *A Time of Silence: Civil War and the Culture of Repression in Franco's Spain, 1936–1945* (Cambridge: Cambridge University Press, 1998), 78.

12. The word Nationalist here refers to the terms *Nacional* or *Nacionales* which derive from the *Moviento Nacional* (National Movement), an umbrella organization for different groups supporting Franco and the military uprising of 1936. It is not to be confused with the nationalists of the Basque Country and Catalonia who opposed Franco.

13. *Boletín Oficial De la Junta de Defensa Nacional*, July 30, 1936.

(rebellion) the alleged "crimes" were de facto political since the Defense Council ruling of July 28, 1936 categorized them as representing a direct challenge to the state.[14]

This rationale was reinforced by the Nationalist military prosecutor in the Basque Country, Eugenio Fernández Asiain, who wrote that "rebellion consisted of the defense of the Republican regime."[15] Even Ramón Serrano Suñer confessed later that "this was to turn justice on its head."[16] The framework of the Bellón Commission and the *Causa General* (an extensive process of judicial investigation) [17]was accompanied by coercive legislation such as the Law of Purging the Publicly Employed;[18] the Law for the Repression of Freemasonry and Communism;[19] and the Law of Political Responsibilities.[20] These acts, allied to those of security, criminalized the activities of many under martial law that lasted until 1948. Helen Graham writes that,

Where we see Francoism going further is in what they did to the defeated. There is a startling uniformity about the degradation and humiliation inflicted upon hundreds of thousands of Republican prisoners after the end of the military conflict . . . [they] spent time in what historians now term the penal universe of Francoism . . . Those confined were subject to a sustained and brutal attempt to reconfigure their consciousness and values.[21]

As shown in table I.1 the effects of Nationalist incarceration of polit-

---

14. Gutmaro Gómez Bravo, *El exilio interior. Cárcel y represión en la España franquista, 1939–50* (Madrid: Taurus, 2009), 15.

15. Eugenio Fernández Asiain, *El delito de rebelión militar. Estudio sistemático del delito, comentado, concordado y anotado* (Madrid: Instituto Edit. Reus, 1943), 13.

16. Ramón Serrano Suñer, *Entre el silencio y la propaganda, la Historia como fue. Memorias* (Barcelona: Planeta, 1977), 220–21, 244. The illegal uprising by the Nationalists on July 17, 1936 was carried out against the constitutionally elected government of the day. A "self defense" military intervention became the major "legal" expression of legitimacy with martial law declared with a resolve "to enforce its responsibilities in such solemn times." The Nationalist Bellón Commission duly "established the illegitimacy of the legal government" in 1939 with the help of the Causa General, established in 1940 to provide evidence of the "criminality"of the domestic government.

17. They were retrospective attempts to justify the mid July 1936 rising and establish the illegality of the Republic. The right had questioned the February 1936 General Election result in Spain. Above all, they sought to retrospectfully justify the use of martial law and military tribunals instead of civil courts. This explains the absurd length of prison sentences and the widespread use of collective trials referred to later in this book.

18. *Boletín Oficial de Estado* (Henceforth, *BOE*), February 14, 1939.

19. *BOE*, March 2, 1939.

20. *BOE*, March 22, 1939.

21. Helen Graham, *The Spanish Civil War: A Very Short Introduction* (Oxford: Oxford University Press, 2005), 84, 129.

ical enemies are illustrated by the enormous increase in prison population from 1931–1933 as compared to number of inmates between 1940 and 1941.[22] Some historians considered that "87 percent of prisoners with higher sentences of between 12 to 30 years were political"[23]

Table I.1. Number of prisoners incarcerated by Nationalists in 1931, 1933, 1940 and 1941. Instituto Nacional de Estadístico, 1922–42.

1931	10,386
1933	8,640
1940	270,719
1941	233,373

In addition to the use of prisons, Nationalist policy involved incarceration of political prisoners in concentration camps, labor battalions, and military workshops. Javier Rodrigo illustrates the very considerable impact that concentration camps made between 1936 and 1942, with eighty-nine opening and closing in 1939; he also estimates that there were 188 such camps in this six year period.[24] The following map shown in figure I.1 gives an idea of the conversion of Spain into an immense prison in this period and gives an indication of the deployment of different types of detention establishments.[25]

One of the main functions of concentration camps was to categorize prisoners. In 1937, they were divided into five categories that determined whether they were usuable by Nationalists: 40 percent were Nationalist supporters; 20 percent were doubtful; 15 percent could be rehabilitated; 10 percent were criminals; and 10 percent were liberals. The remainder were unclassified. In total, 35 percent were considered suitable for reeducation or forced labor. These included the two categories of doubtful (20 percent)

22. Instituto Nacional de Estadístico, Período 1858–1997: INEbase Historia Anuario, Población Reclusa
Existencia en 1 de enero, años 1922 a 1942.
23. Casanova in *Morir, matar, sobrevivir* (Barcelona: Crítica 2002) 25, cites the publication *El Livre Blanc* (Paris 1953); Ricard Vinyes analyses this in detail in "Territoris de càstig" in *Noticia de la negra nit* (Barcelona 2001) 43-55.
24. Javier Rodrigo, "Internamiento y Trabajo Forzoso: Los campos de Concentración de Franco," *Hispania Nova. Revista de Historía Contemporánea*, 6 (2006). Online journal.
25. Españoles Encarcelados. Based on information extracted from Javier Rodrigo *Cautivos. Campos de concentración en la España franquista 1936–1947* (Barcelona: Crítica, 2005) and José Manuel Sabín, *Prisión y muerte en la España de la postguerra* (Madrid: Anaya & Mario Muchnik, 1996).

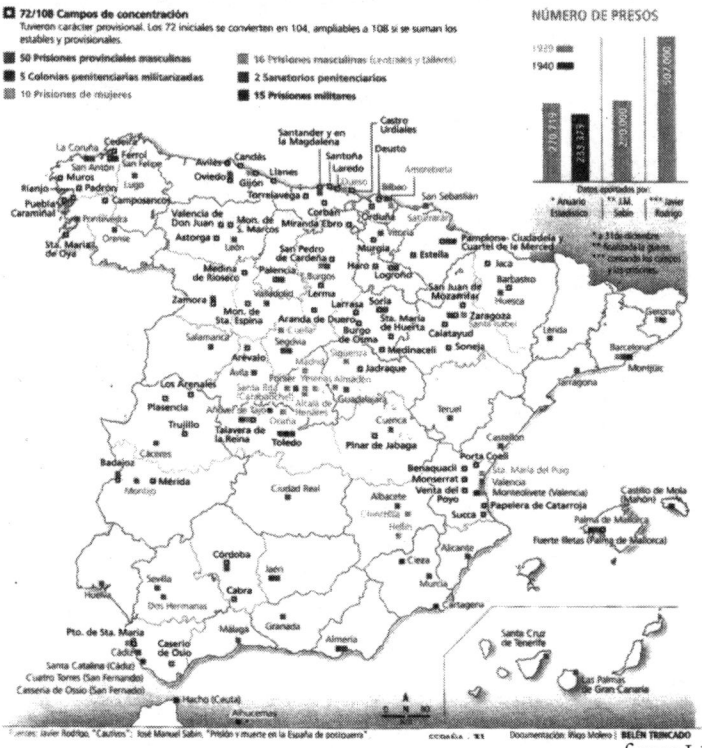

figure I.1

and those that might be influenced (15 percent).[26] James Matthews writes about "recycling" prisoners and estimates that, by the end of 1937, the Nationalists had taken some 107,000 prisoners. This involved the posting of almost 59,000 straight to Nationalist units with some 30,000 to labor battalions.[27] In all probability the total number affected in the postwar period included some 500,000 concentration camp prisoners with some 150,000 shot for what were perceived to be clear "political causes."[28]

Part of the Nationalist policy of imprisonment of political prisoners involved the "cleansing of Spain," which involved social control, violence, indoctrination, purification, and constant coercion, including "reeduca-

---

26. Rodrigo, *Cautivos*, 70–71.
27. James Matthews, *Reluctant Warriors: Republican Popular Army and Nationalist Army Conscripts in the Spanish Civil War, 1936–1939* (Oxford: Oxford University Press, 2012), 203–4.
28. See Rodrigo, "Internamiento y Forzoso. Los Campos de Concentración de Franco," *Revista de Historia Contempránea*. Número 6 (2006) 5-6.

tion and re-catholicization." Redemption was all important and "aimed at isolating individuals in order to break the strong solidarity among political prisoners."[29] Máximo Cuervo Radigales, director of prisons, wrote in the journal *Redención* of "the importance of the spiritual and political redemption of prisoners in order that they might be integrated into the bosom of Spain."[30] This accorded with Franco's views when he stated "we must carry out the slow task of redemption and pacification, without which the military occupation will be largely useless."[31] There are a variety of publication dates ranging from 1993 to 1995. My copy is the 1995 edition from UK Fontana Press, an imprint of Harper Collins who published in 1993. Reeducation involved daily political indoctrination that necessitated compulsory Fascist salutes and the singing of Nationalist and Fascist anthems. The Redemption of Sentences through work scheme provided the Nationalists with cheap labor and extended to prison workshops. The first of these was at Alcalá de Henares, opened by José Agustín Pérez del Pulgar, a Jesuit priest, in August 1939.[32] He argued that penitence involved "a change of psychology, moral state, and social conditioning."[33] Two of the best examples of forced labor in large public ventures were the Valle de los Caídos (Valley of the Fallen), a large public monument honoring those who had fought and died for Franco;[34] and the Guadalquivir Canal.[35] The work done by prisoners attracted a very small reduction of sentence and payment for their families.

The Francoist policy of imprisonment assumed a role that went far beyond the merely punitive and used mass incarceration as a device to remove political opponents from circulation. In the case of Basques, this policy involved their transportation to remote places many miles from their homes. Andalusian prisons were a popular destination, with jails including El Puerto, Seville, Granada, and Huelva, allegedly totaling some four thousand Basque prisoners.[36] A diary of some Basque prisoners re-

29. Gutmaro Gómez Bravo "The Origins of the Francoist Penitentiary System, 1936–1948," *International Journal of Iberian Studies* 23, no. 1 (2010), 11.
30. Máximo Cuervo Radigales, Director of Prisons, in *Redención*, 1, April 1, 1939.
31. Paul Preston, *Franco: A Biography* (London: London: HarperCollins, 1995), 241.
32. Sabín, *Prisión*, 188–97.
33. José Agustín Pérez del Pulgar, *La solución que España da al problema de sus presos políticos* (Valladolid: Librería Santarén, 1939), 1.
34. See Daniel Sueiro, *La verdadera historia del Valle de los Caídos* (Madrid: Sedmay, 1976).
35. See Gonzalo Acosta Bono, José Luis Gutiérrez Molina, Lola Martínez Macias, and Ángel del Rio Sánchez, *El canal de los presos (1940–1962): Trabajos forzados: de la represión política a la explotación económica* (Barcelona: Crítica, 2004).
36. Sabino Arana Fundazioa: el penal de El Puerto de Santa Maria. A confidential report by a visiting Basque delegation in this prison, July 1939. GE-244-01. Henceforth

fers to an incident concerning their behavior in a prison chapel that resulted in a threat of further removal to the Canary Islands.[37] In the case
of Juan Ajuriagerra, a member of the Bizkaian Provincial Council of the
PNV (Partido Nacionalista Vasco, Basque Nationalist Party), and one of
the negotiators of the Pact of Santoña, he was actually transferred to the
Canary Islands from Burgos prison in 1942. "Prisoners from Spanish jails
who were considered to have 'deviated' could be relocated to Burgos; convicts who attempted escape were often immediately transferred to Chinchilla penitentiary [in Albacete], famous for its brutal conditions."[38] In the
same way some prominent political prisoners were subjected to adverse
prison conditions allied to illness that led to their death, as was the case of
Julián Besteiro in Carmona prison in 1940.[39]

Imprisonment for political prisoners might lead to execution or
death. One witness speaks of two thousand prisoners shot at Ocaña (Toledo) prison;[40] in Segovia (Castile and León) 195 men simply died in prison in 1936.[41] Matilde Eiroa San Francisco considers that 710 executions
took place in Málaga prison between 1939 and 1942;[42] while in 1937 "at
least" 389 died of maltreatment in Santander.[43] In addition, according to
Julián Casanova, in 1940, "there were more than 20,000 women political
prisoners."[44]

The Nationalist policy of imprisoning Republicans[45] deemed as "political enemies," both during and immediately after the Civil War, was used
indiscriminately and capriciously. Lengthy sentences for a large number
of ill-defined "crimes" were handed down by military tribunals that operated almost independently until the early 1940s; they frequently ignored

---

SAF/PSM/CONF/7/39.

37. Mendizibal, *Gudaris y rehenes de Franco (1936–1943)*, 208.
38. Gómez Bravo, "The Origins of the Francoist Penitentiary System," 13.
39. Besteiro was President of the UGT and President of the Congress of Deputies and a
    supporter of Casado in his last ditch rising in March 1939 against Negrín.
40. Sergio Vilar, *Protaganistas de la España democrática. La oposición a la dictadura 1931–
    1969* (Paris: Ediciones Sociales, 1969), 227.
41. Paul Preston, *The Spanish Holocaust: Inquisition and Extermination in Twentieth-Cen-
    tury Spain* (London: HarperPress, 2012), 201.
42. Matilde Eiroa San Francisco, *Viva Franco. Hambre, racionamiento, Falangismo. Mála-
    ga, 1939–42* (Málaga: M. Eiroa San Francisco, 1995), 246–47.
43. Preston, *The Spanish Holocaust*, 438.
44. Julián Casanova, "Las caras del terror," in *Morir, matar, sobrevivir: La violencia en la
    dictadura de Franco*, ed. Julián Casanova, Francisco Espinosa, Conxita Mir and Fran-
    cisco Moreno Gómez (Barcelona: Crítica, 2002).
45. The term Republicans is used here (and throughout the book) in a general sense to
    refer to people who were loyal to the Spanish Republic, the legitimate government of
    the day.

tariffs recommended by the Nationalist administration. For the great majority of Civil War prisoners, the imprisonment ended with parole; the latter commenced on September 28, 1938, and was concluded by October 1945 (with the exception of those convicted for "blood crimes").[46] Chapter 5 includes examples of widely different conditions of sentences and release, between Cádiz province and the Basque Country. There is also a comparison between those prisoners who were sentenced for "political crimes" and those for "nonpolitical crimes." In many cases Basque prisoners were detained for up to a year longer than those prisoners from Cádiz province. On release, liberty proved to be tenuous and released prisoners were always subjected to additional surveillance.[47]

The actual number of Republican prisoners who were considered to be "political" was always contentious. Carme Molinero cites Ricard Vinyes who argues that Franco believed these prisoners were not political "but maladjusted criminals, not resistance fighters, but bandits."[48] Eiroa San Francisco writes that "official records show that at the end of 1942, of 124,423 prisoners held, 80 percent were detained for crimes of rebellion."[49] On March 15, 1943 the outgoing Minister of Justice, Estéban Bilbao, admitted to 75,000 political prisoners, referring only to prisons and not those in labor battalions and military prisons. The figure did not include many political prisoners who had been classified as common criminals.[50] Later, on March 24, 1945 in a meeting between Franco and the US Ambassador Norman Armour, when the latter asked about the thousands of political prisoners in Spanish jails, Franco insisted that there were only 26,000.[51] (Military rebellion continued to be regarded as a political offense and was not treated as a civilian crime until May 3, 1963, following the execution of the Communist Julián Grimau the month before).[52]

In my view, the penitentiary of El Puerto was typical, albeit with two caveats. One, it served as a large isolationist prison for more Basque prisoners than all the other Andalusian prisons. Second, apart from jails in Barcelona and Madrid, El Puerto was one of the larger prisons in Spain in January 1942, according to the Spanish National Statistics Institute (Insti-

---

46. *BOE*, December 20, 1945.
47. Mirta Núñez Díaz-Balart, *Los años del terror: la estrategia del dominio y represión del General Franco* (Madrid: La Esfera de los Libros, 2004), 82. Also see chapter 4.
48. Carme Molinero, Margarida Sala, and Jaume Sobrequés, eds., *Una inmensa prisión. Los campos de concentración y las prisiones durante la guerra civil y el franquismo* (Barcelona: Crítica, 2003), xx.
49. Eiroa San Francisco, *Viva Franco*, 263.
50. Preston *Franco*, 527.
51. Ibid., 526.
52 See Manuel Ballbé, *Ordén público y militarismo en la España constitucional 1812–1983* (Madrid: Alianza Editorial, 1983), 420–27.

tuto Nacional de Estadístico de España, see table I.2).[53] A summary of the prison population at this time gives an idea of the comparative standing of El Puerto in Spain. The town of El Puerto de Santa María had fallen almost immediately to the Nationalists on July 19, 1936; this meant that the local penitentiary was a constant factor in Nationalist penal policy.

Table I.2. Large prisons ranking in size based on information available in 1941. *Anuario Estadístico de España*, 1942.

Madrid	12,955
Barcelona	11,093
El Puerto	5,069
Zaragoza	4,996
Toledo	4,978
Valencia	4,666
Jaén	4,426
Burgos	4,399
Murcia	4,282
El Dueso (Santander)	3,368

Work on the Francoist repression has been led by historians such as Paul Preston, Michael Richards, Julián Casanova, Francisco Espinosa, Conxita Mir, Francisco Moreno Gómez, and Mirta Núñez Díaz-Balart.[54] Research on earlier work has already appeared on prisoners in *Libro Blanco sobre las cárceles franquistas 1939–1976* by Ángel Suárez, and studies by Ronald Fraser, Tomasa Cuevas, J.M. Sabín, Santos Juliá, and Ricard Vinyes.[55] The later depiction of Spain as "one big prison" by Carme Moline-

---

53. "La clasificación de la población reclusa existente en las prisiones centrales y las prisiones provinciales en 1 de enero,"*Anuario Estadístico de España, Instituto Nacional de Estadística de 1941 a 1950, Población reclusa, Justicia, V1, V11 clasificación de la población reclusa existente en las prisiones centrales and provinciales de enero 1942.* The exact nomeclature of prisons is as shown in the *Anuario Estadistico* of 1941 to 1950.

54. Paul Preston, *The Politics of Revenge: Fascism and the Military in Twentieth-Century Spain* (London: Unwin Hyman, 1990); *Franco*; "The Crimes of Franco," Study Day, BFI Southbank, January 19, 2008; *The Spanish Holocaust*. Richards, *A Time of Silence*; *Morir, matar, sobrevivir*, ed. Casanova, Espinosa, Mir, and Moreno Gómez; Núñez Díaz-Balart, *Los años del terror*.

55. Ángel Suárez, *Libro blanco sobre las cárceles franquistas 1939–1976* (Paris: Ruedo Ibérico, 1976); Ronald Fraser, *Blood of Spain: The Experience of Civil War 1936–1939* (London: Allen Lane, 1979); Tomasa Cuevas, Presas, *Mujeres en las cárceles franquistas* (Barcelona Icaria 1985); Sabín, *Prisión y muerte en la España de postguerra*; Santos Juliá, Julián Casanova, Josep María Solé and Tomás Villaroya, *Víctimas de la guerra civil* (Madrid: Temas de Hoy, 1999); Ricard Vinyes, *Irredentas: Las presas políticas y sus hijas en las cárceles de Franco* (Madrid: Temas de Hoy, 2002).

ro, Margarida Sala, and Jaume Sobrequés in 2003 opened Pandora's Box.[56] This momentum allied to the Law of Historical Memory in 2007 also gave rise to more research affecting penal policy.[57] Among others this included work by Gonzalo Acosta, José Luis Gutiérrez, Lola Martínez, Javier Rodrigo, Julius Ruiz, Gutmaro Gómez Bravo, and Peter Anderson. [58]

Some prisoners' files of this Andalusian penitentiary have been complemented by evidence from their relatives. This considerably aided my research, which in turn relates to questions that are still being raised in Spain. *El pacto de olvido*, the agreement to forget, accepted by most parties during the period of transition after the death of Franco in 1975, is now being questioned. For many in Spain the whereabouts and proper burial of their relatives remains unfinished business.[59] Some still do not know of the location of the prisons that held their relatives. Many of the younger generation want to know more of the happenings of the Civil War.[60] This curiosity even extends to some of the smaller towns of *España profunda*, deepest Spain, of the 1930s.

The Association for the Recuperation of Historical Memory has also generated a climate since its foundation that has led to a demand for more documentation and evidence in many parts of Spain; this has also involved exhumations. [61]There are now regular forums, exhibitions concerning past events, many concerning a focus on missing persons, their whereabouts and circumstances concerning illegal executions.[62] In one

56. Molinero, Sala, and Sobrequés, eds., *Una inmensa prisión* (
57. A fairly recent development in 2007 involved the Spanish Parliament passing The Law of Memory. It formally denounced the Franco regime, ordered the removal of all symbols of the old regime from the streets, buildings, and mandated local authorities to unearth mass graves from the Civil War.
58. Acosta Bono, Gutiérrez, Martínez Macías, and del Rio Sánchez, *El canal de los presos (1940-62)*; Rodrigo, *Cautivos*; Julius Ruiz, *Franco's Justice: Repression in Madrid after the Spanish Civil War* (Oxford: Clarendon Press, 2005); Gómez Bravo, *El exilio interior*; "The Origins of the Francoist Penitentiary System, 1936-1948," 5-21; Peter Anderson, *The Francoist Military Trials: Terror and Complicity, 1939-1945* (New York: Routledge, 2010); "Singling Out Victims: Denunciation and Collusion in the Post-Civil War Francoist Repression in Spain, 1939-45", *European History Quarterly* 39, no. 1 (2009), 7-26; "In the Interests of Justice? Grass-roots Prosecution and Collaboration in Francoist Military Trials 1939-45", *Contemporary European History* 18, no. 1 (2009), 21-44.
59. See Paloma Aguilar, *Memoria y olvido de la guerra civil española* (Madrid: Alianza Editorial, 1996).
60. This curiousness may well have contributed to the rise of new political parties in Spain such as Podemos.
61. Since the banning of Baltasar Garzón, (human rights judge), from acting as a judge on May 14, 2010, it could be argued that the drive for exhumations of Spanish Civil War graves has lost its impetus.
62. For example, the Durango 1936 Kultur Elkartea was founded in 2007 as an association

notorious Andalusian case, Francisco Ochoa Cossi, a former mayor of El Puerto de Santa María and last President of the Diputación Provincial (provincial council) of Cádiz, disappeared under unknown circumstances, probably executed on August 16, 1936.[63] The matter is still of considerable local interest.

In Andalusia many of the records kept in municipal cemeteries of those killed in the first few days of the rising in July 1936 have simply disappeared. In the case of archive documentation of the provincial prison of Seville, records were kept of prisoners during the Republic and the summer of 1936. Details of victims of the first stage of the repression were controlled by the Military Delegation for Public Order in Seville, which drew up lists of prisoners to be shot every day.[64] Unfortunately some of these records were destroyed. In the case of Cádiz, which fell in a few days, Francisco Espinosa writes of the early trials: "We received no information from what might have been the report of the examining judge, the composition of the court, the defense case, factors that determined the sentence and its confirmation . . . the outcome of the appeal and places of execution, all without any legal communication that might be used for inscription purposes."[65]

Missing documentation even presented problems to the Franco regime itself, so much so that, in 1945, it appointed a special investigation tribunal of three military judges of the First Military Region (with jurisdiction in Madrid and beyond). Its remit was to investigate the whereabouts of 481 documents relating to sentences, without which parole applications could not be processed. The documents were not all located successfully and two years later some twenty-eight had still not been found.[66] There was large-scale purging of thousands of archives from 1965 to 1985 (partly stopped by the Law of Archives 1985), the destruction of many Falange archives, the disappearance of documents of provincial po-

---

that tries to trace relatives and holds meetings and ceremonies to pay homage to those lost in the Spanish Civil War. At one of their meetings which was held in Durango on October 26, 2012, Benita Uribarrena Bollain, a survivor of the bombing of Durango in April 1937 was present. Email from María González, February 19, 2013.

63. See Jesús Narciso Núñez Calvo, *Francisco Ochoa Cossi: 1898–1936. El último Presidente de la Diputación de Provincial de Cádiz en la Segunda República. Una muerte esclarecer* (Cádiz: Diputación Provincial de Cádiz, 2005).

64. Allegedly in Seville the Enforcement Officer received files marked 'X-2' on the files of prisoners to be executed. Email from Fernando Romero Romero, March 1, 2012.

65. Francisco Espinosa, *La Justicia de Queipo: Violencia selectiva y terror fascista en la II División en 1936: Sevilla, Huelva, Cádiz, Córdoba, Málaga y Badajoz* (Barcelona: Crítica, 2006), 43.

66. Ruiz, *Franco's Justice*, 123.

lice, prisons, and Civil Governors, "inadvertent" losses and cases in which some town councils sold archives as waste paper for recycling.[67] For example, in 1977 in Catalonia, Rodolfo Martin, Minister of the Interior at the Civil Guard (Guardia Civil) established a paramilitary force charged with police duties who were ordered to destroy most of the Falange files and the large archive of the National Movement of Barcelona;[68] most of the documentation was incinerated discreetly.[69] Some progress was made in June 2006 when Spain signed an agreement with the Red Cross to acquire copies of 80,000 documents held in Geneva, with particular interest in lists of prisoners. Information about prisoners in the Civil War is now dispersed over many archives in Spain, in a variety of conditions, and is not always easy to access. In my experience the attitudes of the archivists range from friendly and open to excessively bureaucratic or simply obstructive. A relatively recent article in the newspaper *El País* highlights very well some of the problems that Spanish historians still encounter.[70] Some provinces have lost more archives than others, but their destruction was not uniform. There were other difficulties in which archives were reputed to exist but were not yet cataloged as in Castile La Mancha with information about the prison of Ocaña; even the Cádiz archives have not yet been able to catalog all Civil War prisoners in El Puerto between 1937 and 1943.

In the case of Cádiz, the Provincial Historical Archive contains information relating to the prisoners in El Puerto in which documents of over five thousand inmates imprisoned for alleged Civil War crimes in the period 1936–1943 were recently cataloged in February 2008. But even here there is no guarantee that every prisoner has a documented file. In some cases where prisoners were transferred, their files went with them. This means that the records of these prisoners would be kept at the prison where they were eventually released.[71] This may explain the existence of index cards (*fichas*) of Civil War prisoners in the new prison, El Centro Penitenciario Puerto 1, 2, and 3 near Sanlúcar de Barrameda, transferred on closure of the original El Puerto prison in 1981. In cases in which Basque prisoners were transferred from El Dueso (Santoña) to El Puerto,

---

67. Political Affairs Comittee, Parliamentary Assembly, Council of Europe, doc 0737, paras 78–79, March 4, 2005.
68. Josep Benet, *El País*, December 23, 2004.
69. Information confirmed by local residents Juan Luis and David López. Allegedly, a disused oven in Poblenou in Barcelona was used for incineration purposes.
70. José Andrés Rojo, *El País,* June 2, 2008.
71. Information from the director of the Provincial Historical Archive of Cádiz and the archivist of the Municipal Archive of Santa María.

a fair number of Basque files are held in the Cádiz archives. Other prison files are either illegible or simply contain such sparse information that they serve no research purpose.

There is still more information about the prison of El Puerto in the archives in Cádiz that has yet to be cataloged. [72] Much depends on the priorities of the archivist. Notwithstanding, the Provincial Historical Archive in Cádiz has an unusual number of workable documents of individual prison files in 1936–1949, not always common in Spain.[73]

There are now relatively few men alive who were prisoners in El Puerto between 1936 and 1949: this research is in part a memorial to them and the many prisoners who were imprisoned (and died) fighting for the legitimate government of Spain.

---

72. In my experience even where cases have been catalogued, it does not automatically follow that each prisoner has been included in the list of prisoners for that area. This has applied to both lots of prisoners on the Cádiz and Basque Country lists. The only possible remedy here has been to search through individual box numbers where each prisoner has a separate file number.

73. For the purpose of this project, information has been facilitated by a concentration of prison files for those mainly sentenced between 1936 and 1939, available in the Cádiz archives. Files relating to those convicted under the Law of Political Responsibilities in February 1939 are in the Archivo Histórico Nacional (National Historical Archive, Madrid), the Centro de la Memoria Histórica (Center for Historical Memory, Salamanca), and in the Tribunal de la 2ª Región Militar (Court of the Second Military Region, Seville).

1

The Penitentiary of El Puerto de Santa María

Mejor quisiera estar muerto,
que preso para toda la vida,
en ese penal del
Puerto de Santa María.

"If this still does not meet your requirements, I would like the whole of
the wording to be worked in to the beginning of the chapter".if it does, I
would like the rest of the ballad included in the beginning.

—Popular Flamenco ballad

The prison of El Puerto de Santa María served as a large and important institution in the penal system until the old prison was closed in 1981. This
study concentrates on the years 1936–1949, a period during and shortly
after the Spanish Civil War. There were many ballads relating to Franco's
prisons during and after the War, a well-known Flamenco ballad suggests
how prisoners viewed El Puerto (figure 1.1), with death preferable to imprisonment there. Even as late 1946, the director of the prison, Ramón
Caballero wrote to the captain general of the Second Military Region
complaining about the difficult inmates. He considered "that the prison
population was the worst in Spain . . . during his first year, the disciplinary
board had to impose 230 [disciplinary] *sanciones* of confinement to cells."[1]

This chapter investigates some common aspects of the prisoners'

---

1.   Gómez Bravo, *El exilio interior*, 151.

Figure 1.1

collective experiences. Three key themes have been chosen: (1) the experience of the prisoners and the living conditions in El Puerto; (2) the background of the prisoners, taking into consideration educational, social, and geographical factors; and (3) the treatment of the prisoners, with reference to starvation, denial of religious sustenance, and the implementation of the death penalty.

The background of the prison is fundamental in that El Puerto, at first sight a large local prison, proved to be a mix of local inmates and those from the Basque Country. The religious issue is highlighted by the presence of a large contingent of devout Catholics from the Basque Country; their treatment in the matter of provision of facilities for religious worship illustrated the inconsistency of their jailers in their approach to what was a matter of fundamental importance to some of the prisoners.

El Puerto operated as a prison between 1886 and 1981. Known as *"El Saco"* or "the sack." This is simply an expression indicating a confinement of space. The prison was located on the outskirts of El Puerto de Santa María, on the banks of the River Guadalete. It was eight kilometers (five miles) away from Cádiz by sea across the bay or some twenty-one kilometers (thirteen miles) by road, near a railroad station on the Cádiz to Seville route. Jerez de la Frontera is also nearby, readily accessible by road. The two then adjoining streets were Isidoro Rodríguez and Avenida de la Victoria.

Originally built in the sixteenth century by the Dukes of Medicaneli, the building had a checkered life. Earlier it was donated to a religious order; previous uses included that of a hospice, convent, and monastery, the Monasterio de la Victoria becoming a prison in 1886. Perhaps as an omen of things to come, one of the early administrators was Julio Millán Astray, father of the founder of the Spanish Legion. His son José was later concerned with the rise of Franco, who was his second-in-command and field commander of the Legion. The legacy of the pattern of extreme violence within the penitentiary of El Puerto was illustrated by the killing by a prisoner of Astray's predecessor, Manuel García Torres, in February 1898.[2]

In the aftermath of their victory in 1939 the Nationalists adopted a punitive policy of large-scale imprisonment of their defeated opponents and El Puerto had an important role to play in this respect during the Spanish Civil War off 1936–1939 and in the immediate postwar period. Julián Casanova writes about "half a million people being crowded into prisons and concentration camps";[3] while Carme Molinero draws attention to "Vengeance . . . the [Franco] regime exerted all [possible] punitive action against the prisoners."[4] As Chapter 5 illustrates, the large amount of movements of prisoners both in and out of Andalusia is relevant to denote the relationship of El Puerto to other prisons in the area;[5] (Table 1.1 denotes the standing of El Puerto in Andalusia in January 1941, based on 1940 data.)[6] By 1943 virtually all prisoners of war had been released, unless they had been imprisoned for "blood crimes." In order to appreciate the status of El Puerto, it is helpful to review its importance in the prison system of the province of Cádiz and Andalusia as a whole in 1940.

Table 1.1 indicates the comparative importance of prisons in Andalusia in relation to the intake of prisoners.[7]

2. Manuel Martínez Cordero, *El Penal de El Puerto de Santa María 1886–1981* (Cádiz: Diputación de Cádiz, 2005), 33–34.
3. Julián Casanova, *The Spanish Republic and Civil War*, trans. Martin Douch (Cambridge: Cambridge University Press, 2010), 332.
4. Molinero, Sala, and Sobrequés, eds., *Una Inmensa Prisión*, xix.
5. Daniel Gatica Cote, "Una cárcel de posguerra: La prisión central de El Puerto de Santa María en 1940: Los prisioneros gaditanos," *Revista de Historia de El Puerto de Santa María*, sumario no. 35 (2005), 8.
6. See table I.2 for an indication of the national standing of El Puerto in 1941–42.
7. Gatica Cote, "Una cárcel de posguerra," 8.

Table 1.1. *The larger prisons within Andalusia in 1940.*
Revista de Historia de El Puerto de Santa María, sumario 35 (2005).

Prison	Number of prisoners
Prisión Provincial de Málaga	8,523
El Puerto de Santa María	5,479
Cárcel Córdoba	4,000
Prisión Provincial de Jaén	3,991
Prisiones de Almería	1,537

After 1939 El Puerto became one of the more important national penitentiaries, disregarding the arrangements made for the imprisonment of soldiers in the late surrenders that took place in Valencia and Madrid. Of its 5,479 inmates in 1940, over 2,100 were Basque while some 28 percent inmates were drawn from the mountains around Ronda.[8] This area was one the bulwarks of rural anarchism in Andalusia as may have later been reflected in its prison population. For example, anarchism was very prevalent in Grazalema (taken after four days of fighting on September 15, 1936), Montejaque (which had an anarchist mayor in the 1930s), Benaoján, and El Gastor (where a short lived Republic existed in the latter). There were also other prominent anarchist groups in Villamartín, Alcalá de los Gazules, Olvera, Sanlúcar de Barrameda, and La Línea de la Concepción. Civil registers of the Sierra de Cádiz identify 15 percent of the victims, who were from El Gastor.[9] Out of sixty-three mountain prisoners, seventeen were from Grazalema.[10] There were also 16 percent from the Jerez de la Frontera countryside where there were as many as four anarchist groups in 1936.[11] Within the Sierra de Cádiz, some nine prisoners from Torre Alháquime, south of Olvera, were shot by Nationalists in July 1937 while in El Puerto prison.

Figure 1.2 shows the security arrangements within the prison of El Puerto itself. The protective barriers to the entrance to individual cells give some idea as to the relations that existed between the prison guards and inmates. These obstacles acted as a safeguard for guards against attack by prisoners when the former were delivering food to them in over-

---

8. Ibid., 9–10.
9. Fernando Romero Romero and Pepa Zambrana Atienza, "La represión en El Gastor durante la Guerra Civil," *Almajar* 3 (2007), 151–58.
10. See Diego Caro Cancela, *La Segunda República en Cádiz. Elecciones y partidos políticos* (Cádiz: Diputación Provincial, 1987), 94–5.
11. José Luis Gutiérrez Molina, *La idea revoluciónaria: El anarquismo organizado en Andalucía y Cádiz durante los años trienta* (Madrid: Madre Tierra, 1993), 159.

Figure 1.2

crowded, ill ventilated cells. Even today the visitor is struck by a sense of foreboding when visiting the old cells that still remain, in which the heat is overpowering and ventilation extremely poor and in which prisoners were limited to a cell of approximate measurements of 250 cm (8 feet) in width x 350 cm (11.5 feet) in length.[12] Normally accommodating one prisoner per cell before the war, they were used for three inmates in the period 1937–44 and sometimes more in the worst year in 1940.

The climate in this part of Spain was always a constant enemy of the prisoners and an adverse factor in their living conditions. The location of the prison (not very far away from Cape Trafalgar) laid it open to strong winds from the Levante in the summer and frequent downpours in the winter. In fact the location of El Puerto de Santa María makes it vulnerable to the Atlantic at all times.

---

12. Visits to the old prison of El Puerto on June 11 and 12, 2008.

The proximity of salt marshes and ever-present, persistent mosquitoes in the hot summers of Andalusia made the prison a very considerable health risk. Once a prisoner became ill, his chances of survival were greatly reduced.

Medical facilities during the period of 1936 to 1949 were always basic. The prison hospital of El Puerto was divided into three main areas, described in a confidential report written by a visiting Basque delegation in July 1939.[13] One ward dealt with prisoners suffering from tuberculosis, had forty-four patients, and was always fully occupied. There was an annex with fifteen patients, with a waiting list; applicants continued to live alongside non-tubercular patients. The second ward for general medicine and surgery had forty-nine beds, with an annex of nine beds, intended for the most serious surgical cases. The third ward, with a capacity for seventeen patients, was devoted to the chronically sick. There was constant demand for the beds, and one of the major problems was isolating tuberculosis patients.

This proved to be impossible as they came from greatly overcrowded cells and those who were ill came to hospital wards that were only marginally better. There was a constant danger of infection, with a shortage of the most basic medicines of aspirin and iodine. All beds in the wards were without sheets and many had neither blankets nor pillows. These often had to be brought from home, especially difficult where relatives were traveling from the Basque Country. Prison visits were formally permitted only twice a year during festival days on September 24, *el día de la Merced*, the feast day of the Virgin of Mercy and the patron saint of prisons. This was followed some three months later by a permitted visit on January 6, *el día de Reyes*, the Epiphany or Three Kings' Day.[14]

It is disturbing to read in the confidential Basque report that the treatment given by the official prison doctors was either nil or negligible. The constant shortage of medicine was partly offset by either voluntary subscriptions or drugs sent in individual parcels from home. However

---

13. Sabino Arana Fundazioa: el penal de El Puerto de Santa María. A confidential report by a visiting Basque delegation on the situation of Basque prisoners in el penal de El Puerto de Santa María, July 1939. GE-244-01. (Henceforth SAF/PSM/CONF/7/39). A copy of this report was also sent to R.C. Stevenson, British consul in Bilbao. The report was made initially to the PNV and Basque government. This document was transferred to the Irargi Central del Patrimonio Documental Euskadi/Euskadiko Dokumentu Ondarearen Zentroa, Gobierno Euskadi/Eusko Jaurlaritza, in May 2009. (Henceforth CPDE/PSM). Email from Eduardo Jauregui, Coordinator of the Nationalism Archive, Sabino Arana Foundation, January 22, 2013.
14. In mid winter this must have made travelling extremely difficult for Basque Country relatives in view of the weather and road conditions.

when either came to the notice of the prison controllers, they were often suppressed on the grounds that it was contrary to prison rules. It appears that, on one occasion, a prison medical official (who had not completed his medical course) simply confiscated part of the contents of the packages sent from home in order to supplement already scarce prison medical supplies. In another case he refused to sign the voucher authorizing entry, on the grounds that had he done so, the village would know that the prison was without medicines. In other cases, supplies were refused, even although the prisoners had already paid for them at the pharmacy in the village. It appears that most of medical treatment afforded seems to have come from the Basque prisoners who were doctors.

There were about one hundred cases per day that required medical or surgical attention. Here again equipment was negligible and the tanks sterilizing water did not work. Any surgical equipment in good order was the personal property of the prisoner doctor, who acted as head of the surgical ward. It seems that there were even cases of the surgeon having to convert pairs of white socks into operating gloves. Bandages and dressings were only available at intervals and were sometimes unsterilized. Cleanliness was virtually impossible. Aftercare was greatly limited where the diet of recuperating prisoners was insufficient to enable them to fully recover. Meat was not available to them and part of the recuperation diet could consist of one fish slightly bigger than a sardine, if the patient was fortunate.

Although the report relates to the situation of the Basque prisoners, it also reveals general conditions in the prison.[15] The report enables the reader to acquire a picture of the problems of survival in which prisoners had to contend not only with the attitude of the jailers, but also with the continual problem of hunger, which was to worsen within the next few years. The Basque report of 1939 placed great emphasis on the horrific health problems of the inmates of this prison:

> The problem was fearful. Places where prisoners slept lacked ventilation. Gross overcrowding made breathing difficult, despite all windows being permanently open. They slept on straw or maize mattresses with a maximum space of 45 cm [18 inches] . . . those with wider mattresses had to share. During sleep prisoners were compressed together: body on body, mouth to mouth . . . illnesses became much more contagious, worsened by an unbelievable number of mosquitoes, lice, fleas, bed bugs, and flies. Everything

---

15. Ibid.

contributed to an incredible degree of filth. Prisoners could not wash their blankets and mattresses owing to a water scarcity, allied to places to wash them, and access to hot water.[16]

Unfortunately there are no statistics relating to the number of prisoners who died within a year of release, but several relatives indicated that medical conditions affected availability to work afterward (see Chapter 3). This is unsurprising, given the conditions revealed in the report:

> Normally the prison might have 800 to 1,000 inmates. Now there were 5,400. Skin and lung diseases abounded, foot problems were common, and scabies was rife, as was direct contagion. Illnesses of respiratory tracts also abounded. Tuberculosis caused most deaths, was common, with few isolation facilities. There was a special type of illness, leaving those affected as weak as if they had suffered typhoid fever. This often resulted in prisoners suffering temperatures of 40°C [104°F] or more, thus leaving them prostrate. Recovery was impeded by bad diet. This type of influenza adversely affected the lungs, necessitating convalescence. Many inmates were generally run down, lacked appetite, and suffered from stomach ailments and nervous problems. The most single medical complaint, bronchitis, amounted to 40 percent of those treated . . . The prison diet consisted of a spoonful and a half of vermicelli soup, a spoonful and a half consisting of garbanzos or lentils in a bad condition (when there was oil it was often sour); there is no meat; all food insipid and of the worst quality; the lentils were mixed with a large amount of millet and other seeds; the food lacks protein and nutrition.[17]

Figure 1.3 gives some idea of the overcrowded dining conditions that existed in the prison. Although informative, this photograph and several others would have been shown for propaganda purposes.

In addition to the high death rates caused by tuberculosis between 1939 and 1942 (36.44 percent) there was also heart failure (12.71 percent). Other diseases included pneumonia, meningitis, cancer, gastric ulcers, and nephritis.[18]

---

16. SAF/PSM/CON/7/39, 7. This short extract highlights the dreadful conditions in El Puerto. Salient public health issues have been extracted and translated by the writer.
17. Ibid.
18. Gatica Cote, "Una cárcel de posguerra," 18.

Figure 1.3

The fact that there were five times as many prisoners in El Puerto in 1940 as in 1935 caused horrific congestion. Clearly the 270 cells were not nearly enough to accommodate all prisoners, and some twenty additional areas were adopted for prisoners' confinement. This proved to be highly unsatisfactory and the lack of facilities made living conditions extremely difficult. For example, there were no more than four shower areas with fifty-seven faucets for the entire prison population. There was only one urinal and one lavatory in one of the larger *brigadas* (prisoners' confinement areas) with 309 prisoners.[19] The vast majority of prisoners had to work, again in severely overcrowded and substandard conditions.

Figure 1.4

19. Martínez Cordero, *El Penal de el Puerto de Santa María 1886–1981*, 154.

This is illustrated by figure 1.4 showing the prison workshop around the year 1940.

Another Basque report by a former inmate who went by the name of "Verdes" concerned prison conditions in March 1940.[20] Here again, although this information referred to conditions experienced by Basque prisoners, it also serves as a highly revealing account of prison conditions in general. It mostly complements the other Basque report on the prison, albeit eight months later (see also figure 1.5):

> On arrival there were 1,500 prisoners, today there are 4,196, although there were 4,446 inmates at times. Prisoners slept in cells, confined areas, corridors, and passages in conditions that were barbarically overcrowded, arousing visions of Dante's Inferno. Each prisoner has a space of 40 cm by 170 cm. Filth and putrefaction abounded, with an unbearable stench and focus of infection that was richer than any bacteria cultivated in a laboratory.[21]

The victorious Nationalists believed that when the Republic lost the war, the Republican prisoners lost whatever rights they may have had before July 1936. This was enforced by the Nationalist penal system and "Two and a half years later, the decision of the regime to ignore the Geneva Convention on prisoners of war, ensured that the prisons and camps which held hundreds of thousands of Republicans would become what one of them called 'cemeteries for the living.'"[22] Conditions in the prisons were not made easier by the fact that many of the prison warders were former Nationalist soldiers who received these appointments as a sinecure for service to the *Patria*. All of the prison guards in El Puerto carried automatic pistols when on duty and although there were rumors of violent deaths, there appeared to be only two recorded examples of the violence that lurked beneath the surface. One case involved the assassination of the

---

20. SAF/PSM/ANON/3/40. The archive classification is ANV, Fondo Verdes, DP-0740-03. Fondo Verdes refers to the surname of a former inmate of El Puerto who compiled this document. No further information is available other than that he was then a Basque nationalist prisoner in Seville provincial prison. The report was submitted to the authorities of the PNV and the Basque government. It complements the content of the Basque delegation of July 1939, SAF/PSM/CON/7/9. Email from Eduardo Jauregi, Coordinator of the Nationalism Archive, Sabino Arana Foundation, January 22, 2013.
21. SAF/PSM/ANON/3/40.
22. Preston, *The Spanish Holocaust*, 507.

prison administrator Manuel García in 1898 by a disaffected prisoner;[23] the other was that of a prisoner, José Luis Hidalgo, aged twenty-five from Morón. He was a member of the CNT (Confederación Nacional de Trabajo, National Workers' Confederation, an anarchosindicalist labor union) who had been imprisoned for the possession of explosives. On October 6, 1936 he was involved in an altercation with a soldier, who then proceeded to shoot him in the head. Despite the attentions of the prison doctor, Dr. Ruiz Guzmán, Hidalgo died.[24] An indication of relations between prisoners and guards is indicated by the entrance to individual cells; specifically, particular care was taken by guards to leave food in the carousel of revolving bars at the entrance to each cell (see figure 1.2).

Figure 1.5

23. Martínez Cordero, *El Penal de El Puerto de Santa María 1886–1981*, 35–36.
24. Ibid., 146–47.

The economic situation in Spain in the early 1940s meant that much of the population outside was also on the verge of starvation with 1940, 1943, and 1945 being years of intense famine.[25] This prompted the intervention of the Rockefeller Foundation in 1941 with a nutritional survey of the situation in Puente de Vallecas.[26] Although this study related to Madrid, it indicated that the problem of hunger affected other areas than Andalusia. This was reflected in the living conditions of prisoners all over the country, especially in the winter of 1940–41, a year of widespread starvation in Spain.[27] In Córdoba there were 502 deaths from hunger and deprivation.[28] There was also a typhoid epidemic in 1941 that affected the provinces (and prisons) of Madrid, Málaga, Seville, Granada, Melilla, Valencia, and Cádiz. El Puerto prison also suffered a high mortality rate, with the average age of death at around forty-eight in 1941.[29] Chronic overcrowding, allied to the severe shortage of preventative medicine, was always a contributory factor. Records demonstrate that there were 318 deaths from nonviolent causes between April 1939 and July 1942; in 1941 some 134 prisoners died of causes within this category between February and July (see table 1.2).[30] The testimony of one prisoner there, Rafael Sánchez Guerra, a member of Segismundo. Casado's National Defense Council, affirms that in March 1941 there were seventy-eight deaths from hunger in El Puerto.[31] He also refers on several occasions to the terrible specter of hunger that had already cast its sinister shadow over the whole prison, where many fell victim to malnutrition.

Gómez Bravo writes:

> The months of February and March of 1941 were terrible. In the penitentiary of El Puerto de Santa María, for example, the diet consisted of (poor grade) vegetation with vinegar, because the

25. Laura Inés González-Zapata et al., "Famine in the Spanish Civil War and Mortality from Coronary Heart Disease: A Perspective from Barker's Hypothesis," *Gaceta Sanitaria* 20, no. 5 (2006), 360-67.
26. See Isabel del Cura and Rafael Huertas, "Public Health and Nutrition after the Spanish Civil War: An Intervention by the Rockefeller Foundation," *American Journal of Public Health* 99, no. 10 (October 2009), 1772–79.
27. The *BOE*, April 15, 1943, contains a description of the food rationing system prevalent after the Civil War.
28. Francisco Moreno Gómez, *Córdoba en la posguerra. La represión y la guerrilla, 1939–1950* (Córdoba 1987) 237.
29. Gatica Cote,"Una cárcel de posguerra," 16.
30. Ibid. Also see table 1.2.
31. Rafael Sánchez Guerra, *Mis prisiones* (Buenos Aires: Claridad, 1946), 69–87.

price of spinach during these months was between four and six pesetas per kilo. The relentless increase of prices led to a shortage of basic food in an already very poor diet.[32]

Table 1.2. Percentage of yearly nonviolent deaths, 1939–1942.
Revista de Historia de El Puerto de Santa María, sumario 35 (2005).

Year	Number of nonviolent deaths	Total number of nonviolent deaths as a % between 1939 and 1942
1939	20	6.29
1940	38	11.29
1941	194	61
1942	66	20.76
Total	318	

In the immediate aftermath of the Spanish Civil War the prison population increased enormously. For example, in the town of El Puerto de Santa María in 1940, almost 20 percent (5,479) of the total population was composed of prisoners in the local penitentiary. By 1945 the town population was 28,312 inhabitants, including fewer than 5 percent (1,255) imprisoned. The origin of the prison inmates is highlighted by evidence available from the Padrón General de Habitantes (local census) of 1940.[33] At maximum intake estimated figures indicate that there were 2,365 (43.16 percent) from Andalusia, with 3,064 (55.92 percent) from elsewhere, the vast majority of them, 2,171 (39.6 percent), from the Basque Country, and 50 (0.91 percent) from abroad. Interestingly, one of the relatives of a Basque prisoner in 1940, on being interviewed, talked about his father telling him that there were "several Russians who were prisoners with me in El Puerto" (see figure 3.1).

A study of typical prisoners from Cádiz in El Puerto in 1940 indicates that they were male, aged between thirty-six and thirty-seven, married, with a standard of literacy.[34] Many of the findings of Daniel Gatica Cote coincide with those of Francisco Cobo Romero for the provincial prison of Jaén, in which the prisoners were "male, between thirty-seven and thirty-eight, with a rural background and a lowly social class."[35] I find myself

---

32. Gómez Bravo, *El exilio interior*, 97.
33. Archivo Histórico Municipal de El Puerto de Santa María, Padrón General de Habitantes, 1940 (Henceforth AHM/PSM/PGH/40). 1940 Legajo 2276, 1945 Legajo 2278.
34. Gatica Cote, "Una cárcel de posguerra," 10.
35. Francisco Cobo Romero, *Conflicto rural y violencia política: el largo camino hacía la dictadura, Jaén 1917–50* (Jaén: Universidad de Jaén, 1998), 339–40.

in agreement with these joint findings with the exception of the comment about the standard of literacy; my research into prisoners' files in Cádiz province revealed a not insignificant minority stamped "*mala educación.*" This caused me to doubt that all prisoners from this area, most of who were agricultural workers, had a standard of literacy. Socioeconomic patterns were tightly controlled by large landowners in Andalusia. These patterns also revealed the civil status of the typical prisoner from the Cádiz area in El Puerto in 1940: 58.19 percent of prisoners were married, 40.52 percent were single, and 1.29 percent were widowed.[36]

The files of prisoners confirmed agricultural work as an important occupation, but show how the prison intake was drawn from a surprisingly wide range of Spanish society.[37] The net of imprisonment was spread not only over combatants, but people with a background that could scarcely be deemed to constitute a security risk to the *Nuevo Estado*, the so-called New State.

The range of occupations represented in table 1.3 undoubtedly affected the response to imprisonment. The considerable numbers of Basque prisoners reflected the heavy industrial occupations (including those in mining and the iron and steel industry) of Bilbao with Altos Hornos de Vizcaya constituting the biggest iron and steel producer in Spain. An attendant experience of labor union membership probably explained the Basque ability to organize within prison. Although there was some industrial presence from the docks of Cádiz, the prison intake from this area was mainly agricultural. In both the Basque Country and Cádiz province, the majority of those in El Puerto were sentenced as defeated soldiers. It may be of interest to note that while there were nine prisoners from Cádiz sentenced for the "crime" of Freemasonry, only one from the Basque Country fell into this category.

---

36. AHM/PSM/PGH/40 Legajo 2276.
37. AHP/PSM. Legajos 29257–29296, 29308–29319, 29347, 2952–2953, 29357.

Table 1.3. Details of the occupations extracted from prison files of El Puerto. Archivo Histórico Provincial de Cádiz.

Profession	Public Service	Industry/Commerce	Trades	Unskilled
Teacher	Nurse	Brewer	Tinsmith	Agricultural labourer
Accountant	Sailor	Stationer	Carpenter	Stoker
Quantity Surveyor	Soldier	Salesman	Painter	Waiter
Lawyer	Train Driver	Ironmonger	Riveter	Street cleaner
Draughtsman	Railway worker	Sales representative	Cabinetmaker	Stallholder
Journalist	Health worker	Naval machinist	Electrician	Cart driver
Musician	Guardia Civil	Miner	Stone mason	Newspaper seller
Photographer	Guardia de Asalto	Panel Beater	Baker	Tinker
Actor/Director	Postman	Clerk	Tailor	Salt extractor
Student	Municipal Employee	Interior decorator	Bricklayer	
	Politician	Moulder	Engraver	
	Trade Union Organiser	Gunsmith	Locksmith	
		Metalworker	Furniture polisher	
		Cooper	Cobbler	
		Bank worker	Plumber	
		Foundry worker	Fisherman	
		Lathe operator	Chauffer	
		Coachbuilder		
		Industrial worker		
		Storekeeper		

There is an important aspect of prison life that has yet to be mentioned: namely that concerning religious sustenance and pastoral care, sometimes denied or reluctantly offered by the prison authorities in El Puerto. This resulted not only in a clash of expectations regarding religious provision, but also questions the commitment of the regime as a defender of Catholicism. This appears to have had a demoralizing effect on Basque prisoners.

Basque prisoners noted the absence of religious observances: there was one Mass in a small dark room, without a priest on festive days. Even in cases of grave illness, the chaplain was absent. Where he attended, it was to present Francoist propaganda. There was a "spiritual welfare of prisoners association" that organized two or three discussions with a priest. The aftermath left a feeling of pessimism, affecting the Catholics far more than nonbelievers (see figure 1.6).[38]

Figure 1.6

The Basque prisoners arrived around January 20, 1938 and met Father Gutiérrez Silva, a Jesuit, who was in charge of family visits to prisoners. He did not permit these visits unless proper bureaucratic formalities had been observed. One of these involved confession. If convinced of religious worth, the following week the priest returned, having obtained the

38. SAF/PSM/CON/7/39.

names of other prisoners who wanted to confess. But the sacraments did not reach many people and the Basque prisoners spoke to Father Gutiérrez Silva, who appeared sympathetic. Nothing happened. They made the same request to Father Arjona, another Jesuit, who came to the prison several times instead of the other priest. He thought that it would be an excellent idea to celebrate a Mass with Communion in the prison, outside normal regulations. The only difficulty he foresaw was the shortage of priests. He showed that the problem could be resolved easily, celebrating one of the two masses. But months went by and nothing improved.

This attitude is very interesting, bearing in mind the pressure that the Franco regime placed on all inmates to submit to "purification through religion" during their time in prison. Indeed, in order to obtain parole via *condicional libertad*, prisoners had to have completed a course of religious instruction. Michael Richards observes that the Nationalist penal policy included a philosophy of redemption by work "The 'Christian missionary state', led by Franco, 'redeemer of prisoners', could grant this mercy once 'spiritual atonement and repentance' had been demonstrated . . . 'Moral redemption' would come through work as the offender 'recognised the damage caused to society and to his own family.'"[39] Within the prison there was pressure to sing daily patriotic songs and submit to religious instruction allied to Nationalist propaganda. Photographs show full attendances at the prison chapel and religious festivals were the very few days that the prisoners could have family visits. During the *Fiesta de la Merced* there were religious and arts celebrations that lasted three days. It could be that, on being asked to provide more religious sustenance, the prison authorities felt that they were being subjected to unacceptable pressure by the Basque prisoners. The authorities may have felt that to satisfy these prison demands would reduce the service that the local priest gave to his parishioners. However, as the report indicates, this Basque pressure was to prove successful.

The day of San José arrived and a prisoner wanted to take Communion and requested a confessor. The response was that they would have to offer everybody confession. The director was informed that there were three hundred prisoners requiring Communion, but they were told that there were insufficient priests. Communion was offered for the most devout twenty worshippers. The Basque prisoners considered this absurd, withdrawing their request. Later the priests arrived, and 314 prisoners took Communion.

---

39. Richards, *A Time of Silence*, 80. See also Franco, *Palabras del Caudillo 19 abril 1937-7 diciembre 1942* (Madrid 1943) 85.

...since the prisoners requested Father Gutiérrez Silva not to
send priests that talked exclusively about politics, the priests did
not return. The day of Corpus Christi, arrived . . . there were
three sick, bedridden prisoners wanting to take Communion.
The parish priest said that a chaplain could only be available at
7:30 am the following day. The prison Inspector insisted that
getting the prisoners ready so early was problematical (although
the prisoners had to get up at 5:45 am in order to take a shower).
The parish priest said it was unusual to take Communion on the
day of Corpus, that sick prisoners did not need to take it because
they had done so at Easter, and there were only three of them.[40]

This episode reflects the different religious practices that existed
in the Basque Country and Andalusia, which may also account for the
different expectations of pastoral provision within this prison.[41] Hugh
Thomas writes that "Basque priests claimed that, in 1936, almost all the
agricultural population of Guipúzcoa, Álava, and Vizcaya and over half of
those in industrial areas . . . were practising Christians."[42] There were far
fewer parish priests in Andalusia, where many regarded the priests as enemies of the Republic. Certainly the prison priests were highly unlikely to
share the Basque expectations of provision of pastoral care, although one
of them was not from Andalusia. Padre Jorge Loring, a Jesuit priest from
Barcelona, served at this prison between 1941 and 1946.

Apparently this particular incident ended successfully with an appeal
to the religious conscience of the prison priest.

One patriotic Basque prisoner said that the charity of Christ
extended to all Christians, particularly where the person was
sick and imprisoned . . . the parish priest promised to bring
Communion to the three sick prisoners at 8:30 am. This was
done . . . nevertheless a chaplain never visited the sick bay, even in
grave medical cases identified by the prison doctors. Disposal of
corpses was carried out without a chaplain or anything religious,
in dilapidated coffins, without upholstery or any kind of basic

---

40. SAF/PSM/CON/7/39.
41. For variations of religious practices at this time see Frances Lannon, *Privilege, Perse-
    cution and Prophecy: The Catholic Church in Spain, 1875–1975* (Oxford: Clarendon,
    1987); William J Callahan, *The Catholic Church in Spain 1875–1998.* (Washington,
    DC: Catholic University of America Press, 2000).
42. Hugh Thomas, *The Spanish Civil War* (London: Penguin, 1977), 87.

finish. Finally the coffin had a crude wooden cross. (All of this must have been a cause of great distress to Christian families of the prisoners).[43]

It appears that the prisoners were frequently promised (incorrectly) that there would be two chaplains allocated to the prison, and that when they arrived, the spiritual needs of the prisoners would be satisfied; problems remained because the chaplains wanted to limit Mass to Sundays. On various Saturdays, on the eve of solemn fiestas, the Basque prisoners had wanted to confess, but a priest was unavailable. Confessions had been heard on Sundays, with the clergy limited for time, and prisoners had to confess at great speed, standing in the square. The penal authorities had demonstrated that the Spanish clergy had not responded to these prisoners' needs. A young priest had started to come to the prison but this stopped. It seems that the problem could easily have been solved giving two hours a week to the prison population.

Figure 1.7 gives an indication of the importance of religion to some prisoners in El Puerto. It was one of the very few activities that prison guards and prisoners shared together. A reasonable surmise is that many of the prisoners waiting to receive the Holy Sacrament were Basques.

Figure 1.7

43. SAF/PSM/CON/7/39.

The second Basque report of 1940 and the photograph raise the question again of Mass being used for Francoist propaganda.[44] As has already been mentioned, this was an issue of considerable concern to some of the Basque prisoners there. There is a reference to a priest of Seville, Don Laureano Tobar, holding his arms high and shouting "*Gora España*" (Long live Spain, in Basque) and concluding his service with a shout of "*Viva Franco*" instead of "*Ave María Purísima.*" Another case cited involved a Dominican priest, who while addressing some four thousand prisoners in El Puerto about the sacrament of confession, eulogized the deeds of the Spanish Foreign Legion. He referred to them as "brave and heroic legionnaires" and "the bridegrooms of death" (*los novios de muerte*). These comments were regarded as particularly insensitive as many of the Basque prisoners might well have certainly shared the view that the Legion was "composed in large part of fugitives and criminals [with] its ranks . . . indoctrinated with a cult of virility and slaughter."[45] To hear a Catholic priest praising the Nationalist elite force (with its long associations with Franco) renowned for slaughter in Badajoz and elsewhere was deeply disturbing to the many Basque prisoners who were Catholics. A not dissimilar situation appears to have taken place on Maunday Thursday in April 1939 in Burgos prison, where Basque prisoners, some of whom made up the prison choir, reacted badly to a Father Bolinaga using Mass to highlight the crimes of the Republic. The prisoners felt that that the priest had abused his authority, without any dignity, simply because he was wearing a cassock.[46]

There is also an allegation that the prison chaplains in El Puerto had secret instructions from the Controller of Prisons.[47] Allegedly they were told that if they encountered any prisoners who had been wrongly condemned, instead of listening to their complaints, they should try to inculcate in them a spirit of Christian resignation. In this way the prisoners could accept the situation as an expiation of their sins and refrain from troubling the prison authorities. Many of the prisoners felt that these particular priests had abused their religious status, and considered them to be agents of the regime. This reaction may be explained by Gerald Brenan, who was of the view that parishioners could expect certain behavior from

---

44. SAF/PSM/ ANON/3/40.
45. Antony Beevor, *The Battle for Spain: The Spanish Civil War, 1936–1939* (London: Penguin, 2006), 56.
46. Mendizabal, *Gudaris y rehenes de Franco (1936–1943)*, 286.
47. SAF/PSM/CON/7/39.

their priests. "[Basque] Catholicism . . . is modern; if one wishes to see monks who are not engrossed in political propaganda, well-educated clergy, unfanatical bishops, this is the part of Spain where one is most likely to find them."[48] The Basque delegation also reported (to the Basque government-in-exile, the PNV, and the British consul in Bilbao) that the director pressured the prisoners into contributing to the cost of purchasing an image of the *Virgen de la Merced* (patron saint of prisoners), arguing that other prisons had done something similar.

Many of the observations of the two Basque reports were very perceptive;[49] the response of the prison authorities here indicates a greater interest in presenting an appearance of the importance of religion, as opposed to the genuine provision of religious sustenance to their prisoners. Nevertheless, the question of religion was probably more important to some of the Basque prisoners than the rest of the inmates. The issue emerged as a matter that put the professed Christian principles of the penal authorities to the test. It raises interesting issues about the role of prison chaplains in the jails of Franco; the evidence would tend to confirm a continuation of the role that the majority of Catholic priests played in Andalusia, where they were regarded as allies of the large landowners, the Civil Guard, and the Army.

The imprisonment of defeated Republicans, drawn from numerous occupations and from different parts of the country, added a great variety to prison life. To illustrate the kind of prisoner behind the occupations I have chosen six. They include a lawyer and ex president of Catalonia (Luis Companys), an actor/director from Madrid (Cipriano de Rivas), a labor union organizer from Andalusia (Carlos Zimmerman), a journalist from Catalonia (Juan Lladós Virós), an actor and politician from Madrid (Rafael Sánchez Guerra), and a lathe operator and extremely prominent Basque politician (Ramón Rubial).[50]

Luis Companys was imprisoned by the Alejandro Lerroux administration in 1934 for his part in proclaiming the existence of a Catalan state

---

48. Gerald Brenan, *The Spanish Labyrinth: An Account of the Social and Political Background of the Civil War* (Cambridge: Cambridge University Press, 1960), 97.

49. SAF/PSM/CON/7/39. The Basque delegation report of July 1939 concerned the situation of Basque prisoners in El Puerto. It mainly contained references to accommodation, including sanitary, medical, and prison hospital facilities, diet, and religious provision (including access to priests). SAF/PSM/ANON/3//40. This report of 1940 by a former prisoner is not so systematic; it largely devotes itself to prisoners' conditions and the way priests conducted services and complements the Basque delegation report.

50. Information confirmed by archivist of AHM/PSM and Centro Penitenciario 1 at the Sanlúcar complex, June 20, 2008.

within the Spanish Republic.[51] This falls outside the Civil War period, but he has been included in view of the fact he was one of the most prominent inmates of this prison. He was convicted of rebellion and sentenced to thirty years' imprisonment on June 6, 1935 by the Constitutional Rights Court (Tribunal de Garantias), by ten votes to eight. Companys was initially imprisoned aboard the prison ship "Uruguay" in the Port of Barcelona, and then transferred to El Puerto on August 14, 1935 at the age of fifty-two. He was imprisoned with two Catalan advisers, Juan Luhí and Juan Comerera. A reporter from *El Mundo Gráfico* wrote about his conditions and treatment in the penitentiary.[52] Companys was allowed books and documents in his cell, with access to the press. Clearly the treatment and conditions were far different from those imprisoned during the Civil War, if only on the grounds that there were far fewer prisoners in 1935 as compared to 1940. Companys was released after the Popular Front victory in February 1936 and restored to his position as President of the Generalitat (the Catalan government). He went into exile in France in February 1939 after the fall of the Republic, and was later handed over by the Vichy Government to the Gestapo. Extradited to Spain in August 1940, Companys was shot by the Franco regime at Montjuic on October 15, 1940.

The actor and arts director Cipriano de Rivas Cherif was originally condemned to death, later commuted to thirty years' imprisonment for *adhesión a la rebelión*. Records show that he was transferred to El Puerto from Madrid provincial prison at the age of forty-nine on January 23, 1941.[53] On June 8, 1942 he was transferred to the Prisión del Fuerte in Pamplona-Iruñea, Navarre, and eventually released on March 16, 1946. Cherif was a highly unusual prisoner in that he was related to the President of the Republic, Manuel Azaña. His younger sister, Dolores, had become Azaña's wife, so Cherif was the brother-in-law of the official leader of Spain. He had collaborated with Azaña in running a literary magazine, and had been Spanish consul in Geneva at the League of Nations. In addition he was a poet, actor, and director of the Spanish theater company, *Escuela Nueva*.

The labor union organizer was Carlos Zimmerman Ruiz, from Andalusia, sentenced to thirty years' imprisonment for *adhesión a la rebelión*. Records show that he was imprisoned at the age of thirty-nine on November 25, 1940.[54] He was transferred from the Granada provincial prison

51. Brenan, *The Spanish Labyrinth*, 291–92.
52. *Mundo Gráfico*, August 21, 1935.
53. Information confirmed by archivist of AHM/PSM, June 20, 2008.
54. Ibid.

and was moved from El Puerto on November 30, 1942 to the prison at Valencia, where he was "placed at the disposition of the *Juzgado militar no.12.*" Zimmerman came from San Roque and was an important anarchist leader in Andalusia.[55] He served as secretary of the Seville branch of the CNT and was active in promoting industrial action in the province.

The journalist was the Catalan Juan Lladós Virós, initially condemned to death and later commuted to thirty years' imprisonment on August 16, 1938 at the age of thirty-two.[56] Lladós Viros came to El Puerto from the provincial prison of Santander, leaving the former on December 9, 1938 for the Centro Penitenciario Militar de Dos Hermanas in Seville. It would be true to say that the Franco regime took a close interest in newspapers and journalists, particularly in those areas that had experienced Republican control for an extensive period during the war. For example, the Catalan newspaper *La Vanguardia* was forced to change its name to *La Vanguardia Española*. The 1938 Press Law had also resulted in other journalists being imprisoned in El Puerto, including José María Deu, correspondent of *Redición*.

The actor and director Rafael Sánchez Guerra, from Madrid, was accused of *rebelión militar*, and sentenced to thirty years' imprisonment on January 9, 1941, aged forty-two.[57] Indicted with Besteiro, he was member of Casado's Defense Junta in 1938, came to El Puerto from the Cuellar prison after serving time in Madrid prison, and was released on parole (*libertad condicional*) on January 9, 1941. Sánchez Guerra had an extremely varied and unusual background as a journalist. As a Catholic Republican politician he was deputy for Jaca in the Spanish Parliament at the age of twenty-three; he also served as a soldier in Africa, where he was wounded and decorated with the *Medalla Militar* or Military Medal. In the early days of the Republic he was Secretary General of the President's Office, a post that he relinquished on the resignation of President Niceto Alcalá-Zamora in 1936. Sánchez was President of Real Madrid Football Club from 1935 to 1939, and was also a councilman in Madrid where he remained until March 28, 1939. Imprisoned for twenty-six months, he finally spent time in three jails, including El Puerto; on his release he wrote several books on his experiences there (some of his comments are quoted earlier). He also became a minister under José Giral in the Republican government-in-exile in France.

The lathe worker and subsequent leading Basque politician was

55. Gutiérrez Molina, *La idea revolucionaria*, 67, 106.
56. Information confirmed by the archivist of AHM/PSM, June 20, 2008.
57. Ibid.

Ramón Rubial Cava, probably the most important political organizer in El Puerto during this period. He was accused of *rebelión* and sentenced to thirty years on June 14, 1939 at the age of thirty-four. Rubial was transferred to El Puerto from Bilbao prison and was also detained in Aranjuez prison near Madrid on May 21, 1942.[58] He had a previous history of political activity and joined the apprentices' division of the metalworkers section of the UGT (the Unión General de Trabajadores, General Workers' Union) in Bizkaia (Vizcaya) at age of fourteen. He was later imprisoned in 1934 on charges of sedition by the Lerroux government for his work on behalf of the Revolutionary Movement of Erandio. In July 1936 he joined the "Mateos" group that became the First Battalion of the Socialist Militias; he later reached the rank of lieutenant. He then joined the Fifth Battalion (Madrid) that operated in Eibar, Gipuzkoa. Toward the end of the war he was involved in the Fifteenth Brigade (Santander), but was captured in Bilbao on November 1, 1937.

Later, on being interviewed about conditions in El Puerto prison in 1986, Rubial said: They put us in these horrible cattle wagons and transported us to the penitentiary of El Puerto de Santa María. In the first few days we were imprisoned in terrible conditions—with seven prisoners in cells that usually accommodated two . . . the worst of this was the food. . . We were usually offered very weak soup made with strands of vegetation that they had gathered in a truck from a nearby area. People were dying of hunger.[59]

The arrival of Rubial in May 1939 in El Puerto brought a different dimension to the life of the prisoners, which in a small part made the stark and brutal regime of the penitentiary more bearable. Indeed, activists in Spanish prisons were to prove a contributory factor in Franco's decision to reduce the prison population as overcrowding led to political unrest. This political and social organization in El Puerto was driven by two Basque socialist prisoners, Rubial and Gorostiza [60]two Asturians, Avelino Cadavieco and José Fuentes, and José Congil from Santander. The cabal was led by Rubial, who was president of an organization of some three thousand prisoners. Among others it included members of the UGT, the PSOE (Partido Socialista Obrero Español, Spanish Socialist Workers' Party),

---

58. Ibid.
59. Ramón Rubial Fundazioa, *Historia y Memoria*, "Cárcel y Represión Franquista 1937–56," para. 3.3 out of 3.7, at www.ramonrubial.com/03_represion3.asp. Accessed February 20, 2010.
60. There were two Gorostizas in El Puerto. Both were from Bizkaia. One was Modes Gorostiza Goicoecha from Bilbao and the other was Teodoro Urquidi Gorostiza from Ochandiano. The former had a longer sentence. See also Chapter 6.

and the JSU (Juventudes Socialistas Unificadas, United Young Socialists). This cohesiveness assisted prisoners separated from their families, strangers in prison, who faced an uncertain future. Help was given in writing letters home, passing messages from one prison to another, and laying the foundation for the PSOE on their release (although the party was largely inactive in the 1940s and was illegal until after 1975). These kinds of actions built up a collective spirit inside the prison and helped to recover lost morale. This organization was built on a mutually dependent network with delegate responsibility for different areas in the prison. Rubial described this structure in El Puerto between 1939 and 1942 as follows: "The socialist organization in El Puerto was well structured. Divided into cells, controlled by four prisoners with delegated powers, the brigades operated in each one of the five courtyards that constituted the prison, they in turn were coordinated by the director general of the courtyards."[61]

Inevitably, the activities of the cabal were discovered (in October 1940). The organization was dismantled: armed guards surrounded the prisoners in the yard, and the prison director threatened them with severe consequences if the identity of the organizers was not revealed. Rubial accepted full responsibility, thus avoiding punishment for his companions. He was transferred to another prison in Cádiz and sentenced to another fourteen years' imprisonment; released in 1956 on *libertad condicional*, he continued as an underground organizer for the PSOE and the UGT. He found it difficult to get work, eventually obtaining employment as a lathe operator in a friend's workshop. Rubial was again detained for his part in a strike in Bargas, Toledo (Castile La Mancha), in 1967, later resuming his political career, first becoming senator for Bizkaia in 1977 and then first President of the Consejo General Vasco (Basque General Council, the post-Franco pre-autonomous administrative authority for the Basque Country that existed between 1978 and 1980) in February 1978. He served as President of the PSOE and Vice President of the Senate. Amazingly, for a former inmate of the penitentiary of El Puerto, he lived to the age of ninety-two. There is now a statue of Ramón Rubial outside the Guggenheim Museum in Bilbao, on the side that abuts the river. Before leaving important Basque prisoners in El Puerto, mention should be made of a leading Basque bertsolari and poet, Balendin Enbeita. The prison file is rather unclear and inconclusive but confirms an admittance to El Puerto in August 1938 and release on May 1941.

---

61. Ibid., "Cronologia carceleria," para. 3.3 out of 3.7. Accessed February 20, 2010. Also see José María Benegas, *Ramón Rubial. Reflexiones* (Madrid: Pablo Iglesias, 2011), 69–121, 203–235.

No chapter on prisons during this period would be complete without reference to penal involvement in carrying out death sentences as decreed by the Franco regime. Military tribunals arrived at decisions that would be ratified by Franco until May 1940; hereafter such decisions were taken by captains general on the recommendation of the Judge Advocate.[62] Once a decision to execute had been reached, it would be passed to military governors who would then pass it on to prison governors for implementation. There may have been cases in which some guards enjoyed passing on the news; in the case of El Puerto it was sometimes relayed to

Figure 1.8

inmates in the large parade ground area within the prison (figure 1.8).

The accuracy of information about the number and identity of people shot by both sides in prison during the Civil War is difficult to verify. During my research into prisoners' files between 2008 and 2011 in the Provincial Historical Archive, I found that material relating to prisoners shot by Nationalists in El Puerto from 1936 to 1940 was clearly stated in the documents held in this Cádiz archive.[63] But as has been stressed before, even this archive does not contain all documents of prisoners during this period as some material is yet to be processed. This must inevitably

---

62. Ruiz, *Franco's Justice*, 102. Ruiz states that this decree issued by the Presidencia de Gobierno on May 25 1940 does not appear in the official Boletín del Estado or the Diario Oficial de Ejército. The case that Ruiz puts forward of concealment is more or less supported by Preston in *Franco*, 226 where he shows that *Franco goes to enormous lengths to conceal his casual cruelty in his responsibility for sentencing people to death.

63. SAF/PSM Legajos 29247, 29248, 29249, 29250, 29255, 29259.

contain information relating to other executed prisoners.

Table 1.4. Executions in El Puerto. Provincial Historical Archive of Cádiz

Name	Age/ Status / Origin	Date Executed
Pedro Pérez Álvarez	32, married, agriculture, Torre Alháquime	July 2, 1937
Antonio Jiménez Amaya	26, single, agriculture Torre Alháquime	July 2, 1937
Antonio Vega Caballero	34, married, agriculture Torre Alháquime	July 2, 1937
Antonio Morales Jiménez	33, single, agriculture Torre Alháquime	July 2, 1937
Roque Morales Geva	55, married, agriculture Torre Alháquime	July 2, 1937
Pedro Marín Salguero	38, married, agriculture Torre Alháquime	July 2, 1937
Diego Medina Guerra	33, married, agriculture Torre Alháquime	July 2, 1937
Juan Medina Guerra	36, married, agriculture Torre Alháquime	July 2, 1937
Fernando Barriga Galán	32, married, agriculture Torre Alháquime	July 2, 1937
José Moreno Romero	22, single, agriculture El Gastor	Oct. 5, 1937
Gaspar Moreno Romero	31, n/k, agriculture El Gastor	Oct. 5, 1937
Fernando Moreno Paradas	n/k Olvera	Mar. 26, 1938
Diego Castro Leo	n/k Olvera	Mar. 26, 1938
Juan López Macías	32, married, tailor San Fernando	Mar. 26, 1939
Manuel Tinoco Rodríguez	36, single, n/k Jerez	Mar. 28, 1939
José Serrano Pérez	n/k Cádiz	Mar. 28, 1939
Alfonso Barranco Morales	35, married, day laborer San Roque	Mar. 28, 1939
Sebastián León López	36, married, chauffer Castellar	Mar. 28, 1939
José María León López	33, married, chauffer Castellar	Mar. 28, 1939
Pedro Gallardo González	30, married, bank clerk La Línea	Mar. 28, 1939
Anastasio Tomay Damián	25, single, salesman La Línea	Mar. 28, 1939
Juan Rubio Benítez	37, widower, stallholder San Roque	Mar. 28, 1939
Enrique Moreno Chicana	n/k Granada	Mar. 28, 1939
Miguel Vallejo Vera	n/k Peñarrubia	Nov. 9, 1939

The death lists compiled by an association titled Foro por la Recuperación de la Memoria de El Puerto de Santa María (Forum for Recovering Historical Memory about El Puerto de Santa María) includes sources such as the Municipal Archive of El Puerto de Santa María, the register of the municipal cemetery of El Puerto de Santa María, and the register of burials in common graves. In some cases there is a match with details of prisoners shot in El Puerto. But this is not so in all. As far as prisoners from Torre Alháquime shot in the penitentiary are concerned, a further cross reference has been made to an article by Gonzalo Acosta Bona and Francisco Romero Romero.[64]

An example is provided of some of the names of prisoners executed in the prison of El Puerto between 1937 and 1939 (see table 1.4).[65] They are the only figures than I can definitely substantiate.[66] In all likelihood the total figure may very well have exceeded this. Information concerning lists and whereabouts of those shot (and buried) by the Nationalists during the period 1936–39 is constantly changing. The Foro por la Recuperación de la Memoria de El Puerto de Santa María claims that many more prisoners were executed from the El Puerto penitentiary than originally thought and offers a provisional list of around three hundred prisoners shot in "El Saco" between 1936 and 1939.[67] Sebastián Guzmán Martín believes eleven prisoners from Chipiona were shot;[68] whereas Jesús Núñez Calvio, Mercedes Rodríguez Izquierda, Fernando Romero Romero, and Pedro Pablo Santamaría Curtido indicate that thirteen from Rota were shot.[69] Nobody

64. Gonzalo Acosta Bono and Francisco Romero Romero, 'La recuperación de la memoria histórica: cancelar una deuda con el pasado', in "Todos Los Nombres, Todas las Fosas: Dos Proyectos para La Recuperación de la Memoria Histórica en Andalucía," *Aljamar. Revista de Historia, Arqueología y Patrimonio de Villamartín y la Sierra de Cádiz* 3 (2006), 134–140.

65. AHPC/PSM. Legajos 29247, 248, 249, 250, 254, 255, 259.

66. Ibid. Also see Fernando Romero Romero, *Socialistas de Torre Alháquime: de la ilusión republicana a la tragedia de la Guerra Civil 1931–1946* (Torre Alháquime, Cádiz: Ayuntamiento de Torre Alháquime; Ubrique, Cádiz: Tréveris, 2009), 81–134.

67. Information retrieved from www.forumperlamemoria.org/?LISTADO-DE-FUSILA-DOS-PROCEDENTES. Accessed February 3, 2014. Also see Archivo Histórico de El Puerto de Santa María, San Luis Gonzaga, Legajos 1842 and 2810. Record of executions from August 13, 1936–November 30, but gaps in information in 1937, 1938, and part of 1939. And Mapas de Fosas de Cádiz-Financiado de Justicia y Administración Pública de la Junta de Andalucía 2007–2009: Cádiz (1.1) and El Puerto de Santa María (1.2).

68. Email from Fernando Romero, September 17, 2012; Sebastián Guzmán Martín, *Luces y Sombras de la historia de Chipiona. Segunda República, Guerra Civil y represión militar* (Chipiona: Ayuntamiento de Chipiona, 2007).

69. Jesús Núñez Calvio, Mercedes Rodríguez Izquierdo, Fernando Romero Romero, and

from Chipiona or Rota is included in table 1.4.

Nine notorious cases relate to prisoners from Torre Alháquime in El Puerto prison, all of whom were shot on July 2, 1937. At the time, Torre Alháquime had a population of 1,200 while nearby anarchist groups in Arcos de la Frontera, El Gastor, Olvera, Ronda, Setenil de la Bodegas, Benaoján, and Montejaque made the area a target for General Gonzalo Queipo de Llano, commander of the Nationalist Army of the South.[70] From the spring of 1937 in Grazalema, Setenil de la Bodegas, Villamartín, Espera, and Arcos de la Frontera there were local executions. There were transfers to different prisons in Andalusia including Casena de Osio de San Fernando, the provincial prison of Cádiz, and the District Prison of Jerez de la Frontera. Yes. It also applies to the neighbouring towns of Vejer de la Frontera and Arcos de la Frontera.. But in many cases they are simply referred to as Jerez, Arcos and Vejer but that is not their full title.. Here they awaited ratification of the death sentences. Torre Alháquime was one of the areas with executions in El Puerto.[71] Figure 1.9 shows four photographs of those executed from the area while in this prison.[72]

The background of those executed from Torre Alháquime amply illustrates the kind of prisoner selected under the "justice" of Franco.[73] They included the Socialist mayor Pedro Alvarez, a town councilman Pedro Marín Salguero, and the alleged militant socialists Fernando Barriga Galán, Juan Medina Guerra, Antonio Jiménez Amaya, Antonio Vega Caballero, Roque Morales Geva, and Antonio Morales Jiménez. The last two were father and son. This was not all the hardships that the families of the executed prisoners of El Puerto had to face. For example, after Juan Medina Guerra was shot, his widow Dolores Gámez Parra had to manage not only with the loss of her husband, but also had to leave Torre Alháquime with all her children when her house was burned down.

The enforcement of the death penalty in the penitentiary of El Puerto is well described in the case of the Torre Alháquime executions. There was previous correspondence with the municipal judge of El Puerto de Santa María advising him of the confirmation of sentences and listing the names of prisoners to be shot. They were to be shot at 6 am, when they

Pedro Pablo Santamaría Curtido, *Memoria rota. República, Guerra Civil y Represión en Rota* (Rota, Cádiz: Ayuntamiento de Rota, 2008).

70. Gutiérrez Molina, *La idea revolucionaria*, 158–165.

71. Romero Romero, *Socialistas de Torre Alháquime*, 158–203.

72 Fernando Romero Romero, "Torre Alháquime 1936: A todos se les aplicó el bando de la guerra," *Cuadernos Para El Diálogo* 39 (March 2009), 27, 28, 30.

73. Romero Romero, *Socialistas de Torre Alháquime*, 158–203. These extracts contain further personal details of the executed prisoners.

Figure 1.9

were taken from the prison chapel (where they were offered some kind of religious sustenance) to the back of the town cemetery. This was to be in the fourth yard (or space) near the railroad line on the route to Sanlúcar. The following people would be required to be in attendance: the military commander of the town, Don Carlos Rivera Mallaina, a detachment of infantry based in the town, a company of *Carabineros* (border guards), representatives of the Falange Española (the official fascist political party) and Nationalist militia, and a Civil Guard squad. The prisoners were shot by the Civil Guard squad and all buried in two common graves, alongside others, in the fourth yard. Death was certified by the forensic doctor Don Luis Bootellos Campos.

Another of the executed prisoners in El Puerto in 1936 is closely associated with an unsolved death of perhaps the most prominent Republican politician in the province of Cádiz, Francisco Ochoa Cossi. This has remained unresolved for seventy-three years. The prisoner from El Puerto prison who was executed was his brother, Eduardo Ochoa Cossi, shot on August 18, 1936. Married, he was the father of five very young children. But he had four brothers, one of them Francisco Ochoa Cossi, last president of the Diputación de Cádiz and first Republican mayor of El Puerto de Santa María.[74] Detained early on in the Civil War by the Nationalists, Francisco disappeared and his body has never been found. His friend José María Fernández Gómez, mayor of Puerto Real, was detained at the same time. Here again his body has never been found. It is widely believed that they were both shot, probably around the same time as Eduardo Ochoa Cossi.

This chapter has been an attempt to give the reader some appreciation of the life of the inmates who were prisoners of war under the early regime of Franco. Their everyday struggles involved dealings with: "Transfers, lice, cold, thirst, humiliation and punishments. .These were the main experiences of the prisoners... the sickness: a crucial aspect in order to appreciate their daily life since, no matter how you look at it, that was the main cause of mortality."[75]

The prison of El Puerto was one of the largest Nationalist prisons in Andalusia and an important contributor to the penal system of Franco, in which survival often involved trial by ordeal. Any evaluation of the information obtained from the individual files of the inmates and their individual experiences should be interpreted within this context.

---

74. See *Diario de Cádiz*, April 30, 2003.
75. Rodrigo, *Cautivos*, 160.

2

A Basque Dimension within El Puerto de Santa María

Venceréis, pero no convenceréis.
Venceréis porque tenéis sobrada fuerza bruta;
pero no convenceréis, porque convencer significa persuadir.
Y para persuadir, necesitáis algo que os falta: razón y derecho.

—Miguel de Unamuno,
Basque Rector of Salamanca University at his last public meeting on

This chapter seeks to reflect a Basque dimension that emerged from the large number of prisoners from the Basque Country who were imprisoned in El Puerto between the years 1936 and 1943. In order to achieve this objective, there has been a focus on five different, but related, areas: (1) the Basque political and economic situation between 1900 and 1936; (2) the origins and imprisonment of Basque captives destined for El Puerto (July 1936–September 1937); (3) a comparison with reception prisons en route to El Puerto (September 1937–April 1938); (4) Basque prisoners in El Puerto (April 1938–January 1943); and (5) repression and response (during and after release from prison).

Although the sections have been dealt with separately, some aspects may overlap. They have been included as part of the background for completeness.

The Basque Political and Economic Situation between 1900 and 1936

A very brief account of Basque politics at that time helps to give an indication of the allegiances most probably held by the great majority of the Basque prisoners in El Puerto. One of these major allegiances almost certainly would have been to the Basque Nationalist Party (the PNV).

From 1917 to 1931, it controlled the majority of parliamentary seats of the Basque Country. However, the creation of the new Spanish Republic on April 14, 1931 did not immediately lead to a spirit of cooperation.

The last Spanish general election results in 1936 before the outbreak of the Civil War provided a good example of the likely allegiances and established loyalties of the Basque prisoners. For example, the Secretary of the Basque Government in London, Jose Ignacio Lizaso, gave his interpretation of the outcome of this General Election in 1936 in his letter to Katharine Stewart-Murray, Duchess of Atholl, a British Member of Parliament.

> The possibility for victory here was either Left or the Basque Nationalists . . . Franco had little support in the Basque Country . . . the single deputy elected was a señor Oriol, of the Álava who owned large numbers of estates and pressured his workers to vote for him . . . in Bilbao city the Popular Front combination of Republicans, Socialists, Communists and the C.N.T, gained 4 deputies as compared to 2 for the Basque Nationalists. This was a result of support from industrial workers and non Basques . . . there was also an important sector in the Basque Country who were disinterested in politics, but who are devout Catholics.[1]

In Araba (Álava) however, it would be expected to return a majority of right-wing candidates. In the case of Navarre, there was an even larger right-wing vote in 1936; later, its Carlist militiamen, the *Requetés*, were in particular an extremely supportive recruiting area for the army of Franco. Helen Graham draws attention to the problematic nature of Basque politics at this time with her observation that:

> While the PNV was an influential force, the politically divided nature of the Basque region i.e. the strong influence of the traditionalist Carlist right] . . . meant that it was not hegemonic. The PNV's influence was predominant in the province of Vizcaya. But in its capital, Bilbao, the PNV had to struggle against the PSOE.[2]

---

1. Letter to Duchess of Atholl, MP, from José Ignacio Lizaso, Basque National Council, London, undated, CPDE/PSM.
2. Graham, *The Spanish Republic at War, 1936–1939*, 31n14.

Further tensions existed between the Basque CNT and the PNV, in which the PNV was zealous in seeking Basque military and political control. Problems also existed between those from the commercial and professional classes and large industrialists. The professional classes were likely to support the Republic in the interests of Basque autonomy while the large industrialists were most likely to support Franco in view of their previous economic cooperation with Madrid banking system. Many of these viewpoints would be represented among the Basque prisoners in El Puerto. Here, the prisoner power groups lay between Basque Nationalists and a left-wing base of Socialists, Communists, and the CNT in the early 1940s.[3] They were to cause the prison authorities some problems.

The problem of religion and religious provision was to raise its head in the prison of El Puerto and is a recurrent theme in this work. This problem of religion (albeit in a somewhat different form) was replicated in Basque dealings with the Nationalists outside the prison gates. Mary Vincent observes that "Nowhere were the convulsions of Catholic politics more apparent than in the Basque Country."[4] The Basques had been described as "Soviet Separatists" by some; part of "*la horda roja*" by others; the archbishop of Burgos called Basque priests "the dross of Spanish clergy, in the pay of the reds"[5]

This approach was also pursued by other senior Spanish clergy, who publicly condemned all Basque Catholics who supported the Basque cause. This attitude was reinforced by the attitude of the Nationalists to Basque clergy. For example, an informative but undated document simply headed *Sacerdotes Vascos Fusilados* (Executed Basque Priests, obtained from the Basque Archive in Bergara) lists some sixteen named Basque priests, aged between twenty-four and sixty-four, shot by Nationalists, almost all without trial.[6] This contrasts very markedly with the treatment afforded to the priests elsewhere in Nationalist Spain. It should also be noted that the PNV assigned chaplains to Basque battalions.

---

3. AHPC/PSM Legajos 29258–29476. Four hundred left-wing and Basque nationalist prisoners were transferred on December 14, 1938 to Seville. Also see SAF/PSM/ANON/3/40. Rubial, the prison PSOE organizer, was transferred out in late October 1940.
4. Mary Vincent, *Spain 1833–2002: People and State* (Oxford: Oxford University Press, 2007), 195. Also see Lannon, *Privilege, Persecution and Prophecy*, 197–213. 251–52.
5. Beevor, *The Battle for Spain*, 225.
6. CPDE/PSM /PSM, "Sacerdotes Vascos Fusilados." Undated.

Origins and Imprisonment of Basque Captives Destined for El Puerto (July 1936–September 1937)

At the outbreak of war on mainland Spain on July 19, 1936, the Basque provinces split into two different camps. In Navarre and Araba, General Emilio Mola was able to count on enthusiastic support from Carlist *Requetés* and the rebellion there was successful, although support from these two provinces was not uniform. The Basque prisoners in El Puerto from Araba and Navarre were quite widely scattered in these provinces.[7] Prison documents indicate that there was only one prisoner from each of the twenty-five (Araba) and thirty-two (Navarre) small towns and villages (see table 2.1).

This gives the impression that Republican support in both provinces was dispersed, despite enormous pressure to support the Nationalists. Interestingly, one of the postcards from an inmate of this prison comes from one of the small villages, Oion (Oyón), in Araba. In particular, individuals from small villages will have been under tremendous pressure to change their allegiance; if not soldiers, they will also have been easy to denounce as they will have been very well-known. On the other hand, Bizkaia and Gipuzkoa (Guipúzcoa), with the corroboration of the PNV, supported the Republic (table 2.2). In these areas the Local Defense Committees of the Popular Front assumed power, in some cases before the PNV took control. In Durango (Bizkaia), one of the members of the Defense Committee was Ángel Gorosarri Gojenola, a civilian who was imprisoned in El Puerto (see chapter 4).

In order to provide a background of Basque prisoners in El Puerto, two comparative extracts are provided from the documents of the Historical Archive in Cádiz and the Spanish National Statistics Institute, 1940 census.[8] They include places of origin and their population (where obtainable) in relation to larger and smaller areas of population. At the same time, these areas are also related to prisoner intake. This statistic is not offered as absolute, bearing in mind the prison archives still necessitate further classification. It is provided to give the reader a flavor of the origin and numbers of the Basque prison intake in 1940.

---

7.   AHPC/PSM Álava Legajos 29258–29453. Navarra Legajos 29256–29440.
8.   Instituto Nacional de Estadística de España, *Censo de la población de España 1940*.

Table 2.1. Prisoners from the largest Basque cities and towns in 1940.
Instituto Nacional de Estadística de España, Censo de la población de España.

Province	Place of origin	Population in 1940	Prisoners
Bizkaia	Bilbao	195,186	195
Gipuzkoa	Donostia-San Sebastián	109,000	64
Bizkaia	Barakaldo	36,335	34
Araba	Vitoria-Gasteiz	49,752	22
Gipuzkoa	Eibar	11,772	21
Bizkaia	Portugalete	10,613	16
Bizkaia	Galdakao	7,101	16
Bizkaia	Abanto-Zierbena	9,576	15
Gipuzkoa	Arrasate-Mondragón	8.645	13
Bizkaia	Ortuella	5,688	12
Bizkaia	Durango	8,797	11

Table 2.2 includes any place that supplied more than eleven prisoners. Towns providing between three and eleven prisoners included seventy-two from Bizkaia, twenty-five from Gipuzkoa, nine from Navarre, and ten from Araba. While there were prisoners in El Puerto from all over Bizkaia, if the areas of Greater Bilbao are included, the total intake from that area amounts to something like 350 prisoners. These areas included Barakaldo (Baracaldo), Getxo (Guecho), Portugalete, Galdakao (Galdácano), Abanto-Zierbena (Abanto y Ciérvana), and Ortuella (as part of Greater Bilbao). In Gipuzkoa, Donostia-San Sebastián with its larger population and active CNT support constituted the major resistance of this province. However, Donostia-San Sebastián fell early, on September 13, 1936; while the fall of Bilbao did not take place until almost a year later, on June 19, 1937. Some Basques moved from Gipuzkoa to Bilbao for a variety of different reasons.

Table 2.2. Prisoners from the smallest Basque towns and villages in 1940.
Instituto Nacional de Estadística, Censo de la población de España

Province	Town / Village	Prisioners	Population
Navarre	Etxarri	1	102
Navarre	Orbaizeta	1	486
Araba	Alegria-Dulantzi	1	596
Araba	Gesaltza Añana	1	628
Araba	Oion	1	1,163
Navarre	Pitillas	1	1,237
Bizkaia	Ermua	1	1,411
Navarre	Etxarri Aranatz	2	1,634
Navarre	Leitza	1	1,679
Araba	Aramaio	4	1,765
Navarre	Atarrabia	1	1,913
Araba	Amurrio	2	1,945

Other very small towns and villages supplied between one and three prisoners to the penitentiary of El Puerto: there were twenty-nine from Araba, thirty-five from Navarre, forty-nine from Gipuzkoa, and sixty-two from Bizkaia. Examples of the small towns and villages in question in Araba and Navarre are cited below in the footnote.[9] In contrast, Republican support was scattered very lightly across Araba, although in Navarre, there were a few areas of Republican resistance. Loyalties were complex. The small town of Ermua, with a population of 1,411, had been the only place in Bizkaia to come out against the proposed Basque statute of autonomy in 1932. Perhaps more importantly, it had also been the only town

9. AHPC/PSM PSM Legajos 29246–29258. Includes examples of scattered Republican support (1–3 persons).   Araba: Agurain (Salvatierra), Alegria-Dulantzi, Amurrio,, Aramaio (Aramayona), Arespalditza (Respaldiza), Artziniega (Areniega), Aretxabaleta (Arechavaleta), Baranbio (Barambio), Barriobusto-Gorrebusto, Beluntza (Belunza), Buradon Gatzaga-Salinillas de Buradón, Elvillar-Bilar, Elgea (Elguea), Izarra, Lagran, Legutio (Villareal), Lezama, Luiaondo (Luyando), Marieta, Maroño, Olaeta, Olano, Puentelarrá-Larrazubi, Salinas de Añana-Gesaltza Añana, Saratxo (Saracho), Soxo (Sojo). Navarre: Abaurregaina (Abaurrea Alta), Aguilar de Códes, Aizkoa (Azcona), Allo, Altsasu (Alsasua), Arbizu, Atarrabia (Villava), Bargota, Buñuel, Cascante, Corella, Etxarri (Echarri), Fitero, Irunberri (Lumbier), Iturmendi, Leitza (Leiza), Lerín, Lizarra (Estella), Luzaide (Valcarlos), Murchante, Olazti (Olazagutía), Orbaizeta (Orbaiceta), Pamplona-Iruñea, Pitillas, Sansol, Sesma,Tutera (Tudela), Viana, Villafranca. I have deleted the name places questioned. The names originally come from the archives at Cádiz.

in Bizkaia to come out in favor of Franco's Nationalists. Nevertheless, one of its local residents was imprisoned in El Puerto for supporting the Republic. In the case of Pamplona-Iruñea, in Navarre, a recruiting center for General Mola, a similar situation arose in that there were three Republican supporters imprisoned in El Puerto. The situation was extremely difficult for them and their families on release from prison as was the case for all other Republican prisoners in Nationalist areas.

By September 1936, the Basques had formed around forty infantry battalions of up to 750 men in each. Antony Beevor writes: "The Basque nationalists established a very rigid control with their paramilitary militia, the Euzko Gudarostea, which excluded left-wingers and non-Basques."[10] However, both the UGT and the CNT formed their own battalions to fight in the army corps of Euzkadi (the Basque Country). Some of the Basques who were to become prisoners in El Puerto had been members of the Basque units like the Loyola, Kirikiño, Araba, Arana Goiri, Amuategui, and Rebelión de la Sal Battalions. Basque agents started to buy arms from abroad and were even able to buy Czech military equipment from German agents in Hamburg.

Military operations commenced in the Basque Country in late July 1936. The Battle of Irun was the critical battle of the campaign of Gipuzkoa and its capture on September 5, 1936 cut off Gipuzkoa and Bizkaia from French support. Donostia-San Sebastián was captured just over a week later on September 14. Figures provided by Michael Richards suggest that "nearly 1,000 executions took place in [Santander] in the first three months of the Nationalist [victory] . . . In spite of Franco's pledge that 'those [Basques] who surrender to our credo have nothing to fear', within a month of the fall of the city [Bilbao] in June 1937, nearly a thousand leftists and Basque Nationalists had been executed and a further 16,000 imprisoned."[11]

In some cases imprisonment was accompanied by fines of 10,000 pesetas or more and confiscation of property, thereby making it extremely difficult for families of prisoners to live. Basque children were evacuated to a number of countries, with 4,000 sent to the United Kingdom alone. Most had returned by 1941. Other Basque refugees fled to other parts of Spain and France and further afield, with sizeable evacuations in 1937. Luis Núñez Astrain, born and died in Donostia, was editor of the (now defunct) Basque daily newspaper *Egin* from the 1980s until 1998, esti-

---

10. Beevor, *The Battle for Spain*, 104.
11. Richards, *A Time of Silence*, 41–42.

mates that up to 150,000 Basques had left by 1937;[12] Jesús Alonso Carballés considers that some 130,000 refugees had left by March 1937.[13] In addition, the speaking of the Basque language, Euskara, was prohibited and incurred severe penalties (figure 2.1).

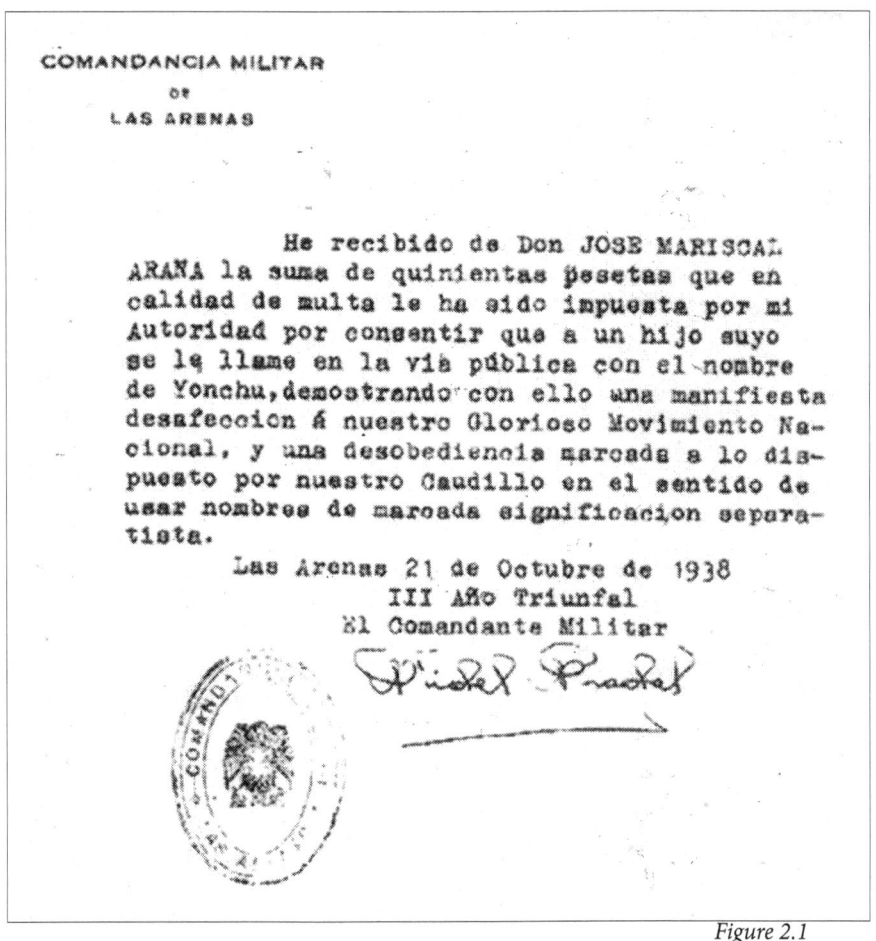

Figure 2.1

The new monarchist mayor of Bilbao, José María de Areilza, had been condemned to death, escaped, and became mayor on July 1, 1937. His speech on the fall of Bilbao epitomized the views of the victorious Nationalists toward the Basque Country:

12. Luis Núñez Astrain, *The Basques: Their Struggle for Independence* (Cardiff: Welsh Academic Press, 1997), 78.

13. Jesús J. Alonso Carballés, "El Primer Exilio de los vascos 1936–1939," *Historia Contemporánea* 35 (2007), 683708. Also see Juan Bautista Vilar, *La España del exilio: Las emigraciones políticas españolas en los siglos XIX y XX* (Madrid: Síntesis, 2006).

No negotiated peace . . . [instead] The Law of War, hard, virile, unyielding, inexorable. There have been victors and the vanquished. United Spain has triumphed, that is the Traditionalist Spanish Falange. The nightmarish evil called the Basque Country has been defeated forever, as has the socialism of Prieto and the imbecilic philosophy of Bizkaia.[14]

Areilza's speech is triumphant in the extreme and he adopts a vengeful tone as he attacks the Basque Country and the socialism of Prieto and Bizkaia in particular. For Areilza there were clearly only two types of Spaniards after the termination of the Civil War: the victors and the vanquished. Redemption was promised from "the red scum in the service of Moscow" and "the Bizkaian nationalist scum in the service of separatism." This illustrates and explains the repressive climate that the defeated Basques had to encounter, as enforced in the prisons and in the region as a whole. Francoist repression was strongest in areas in which Basque nationalist consciousness was strongest. In the cases of Bizkaia and Gipuzkoa, foral privileges were withdrawn but in Araba and Navarre they were not.

My research in the Basque Country with relatives of prisoners in El Puerto left me in no doubt that a key aspect of repression was the Nationalist determination to ensure that families also suffered economic hardship indefinitely (see Chapters 3 and 4). As a result of imprisonment, everyday law-abiding people were impoverished, criminalized, and stigmatized, sometimes suffering permanent loss of health or even worse, allied to the devastation of their families.

Not only was the fall of Santander in late August 1937 one of the most decisive events of the Spanish Civil War, but it also placed enormous pressure on prison accommodation. The massive surrender of some 50,000 prisoners involved many *gudaris* (Basque soldiers), some of whom would eventually end up in the penitentiary of El Puerto. Rodrigo considers that:

The fall of Santander was, of its kind, the most massive and important surrender of all the Civil War . . . the unilateral surrender of the Basque nationalist battalions signified such a disaster involving its own interests as to considerably weaken the Republican northern front . . . the death sentences that they asked for, according to Italian sources were 510.[15]

---

14. Quoted in Carlos Fernández, *Antología de 40 años (1936-1975)* (Sada, La Coruña: Edicios do Castro, 1983), 41.
15. Rodrigo, *Cautivos*, 59.

This large-scale surrender meant that prisoners were placed in nearby penal establishments. Subsequent trials were often mass affairs conducted by military tribunals. The outcome was either death or, in the main part, a thirty-year sentence for "rebellion" in a variety of penal establishments. The Nationalists had failed to respect the terms agreed with the Italians in the Pact of Santoña. After the non-observance by Franco of the Pact of Santoña, Beevor believes that "Basque soldiers were taken off British ships . . . at gunpoint. Summary trials followed and a large proportion of officers and many soldiers were executed."[16] It is hard to locate an exact figure but between July 18 and August 13, *La Gaceta del Norte* reported ninety-three Basques executed.[17]

A Comparison with Reception Prisons en route to El Puerto (September 1937–April 1938)[18]

Many Basques were initially imprisoned (or executed) in Burgos, the Larrinaga prison in Bilbao, Laredo, Castro-Urdiales, and El Dueso in Santoña (the latter three all in Cantabria). In the case of the prison of El Dueso, there exists an undated document from the Basque archives in Bergara that lists thirty-three named Basque prisoners as having been executed in that prison.[19] Twenty were soldiers, of whom eleven were officers. All with one exception (an eighteen-year-old from Bilbao) were alleged to have had some form of connection with the PNV (the Basque Nationalist Party), the UGT (the Socialist labor union), the CNT (an anarchosindicalist labor union), the BBB (the Bizkaian provincial committee of the Basque Nationalist Party), or the JSU (United Youth Movement of Socialists). They were part of the Rosa de Luxemburgo, Meabe, Morteros de Euskadi, Rusia, and Amayur Battalions.

Notwithstanding, El Dueso (Santoña) in Cantabria was the major initial prison for many Basques (mainly *gudaris*), who were then transferred to Andalusian jails. An extract from the diaries of *Gudaris y Rehenes de Franco* gives an idea of a Basque intake from Gipuzkoa in October 1937.[20] Some fifty-seven officers were named in Basque units, in the Loyola, Su-

---

16. Beevor, *The Battle for Spain*, 238.
17. *La Gaceta del Norte*, July 18–August 13, 1937.
18. A few Basque priests may have passed through the reception prisons for the *gudaris* but the former generally went to the prison at Carmona. They have been included to illustrate the different manner in which Basque priests were usually dealt with by Franco.
19. CPDE/PSM, Prisioneros de Santoña, "Condenados a muerte," undated.
20. Mendizabal, *Gudaris y rehenes de Franco (1936–1943)*, 212–14.

karieta, Itxarkundia, Aralar, Amayur, Saseta, Padura, Igenieros no. 2, Bolivar, and Lenago-il Battalions. In the cases of the San Andrés, Itxarkundia, and ANV2 Euzko Indarra Battalions; the commanding officers were imprisoned in El Dueso.

Figure 2.2 illustrates the indoctrination that followed. Once imprisoned, the Basques and other Republican prisoners had to observe due obeisance to the regime responsible for what was an illegal incarceration, whether in the prison of El Dueso or El Puerto.

Figure 2.2

This is the kind of forced response that appears to have been quite common in the jails of Franco. A Basque officer who was a prisoner in El Dueso, Santoña, confirms this practice. "We came out every day in order to sing *Cara al Sol* [the Falange anthem] in front of the flag. One day a prisoner said '*Viva a la República*' and on the following day they shot him in front of the rest of the prisoners."[21] Failure to render homage resulted in punishment (see Chapter 4). Prisoners were compelled to sing *Cara al Sol* and *Oriamendi* (the Carlist anthem), in the knowledge that both had the status of a national anthem. The former refers to a "United Spain," while the latter contains the words "when the red berets (the Carlist militia, the *Requetés*) enter Madrid." Both anthems could be guaranteed to give considerable offense to Republican, and especially Basque, prisoners. The practice whereby prisoners were compelled to sing the Falange an-

---

21. Rodrigo, *Cautivos*, 59.

them appears to have been quite widespread. Basque prisoners also mention that this applied to the concentration camp of San Pedro de Cadeña, where "*el trata era similar al de Dueso: Cara al Sol con el brazo en alto*" (the treatment was similar to that of Dueso: Cara al Sol with your arm raised [in salute]).[22]

The experiences in El Dueso gave many prisoners a foretaste of what was to come later in El Puerto. A revealing insight to conditions in El Dueso and later Larrinaga prison is provided by Robert P. Clark. He reports that:

> Conditions in El Dueso during this period defy description. Prisoners were put together in groups of forty in cells of not more than thirty square meters with no running water and no toilet facilities. Food consisted of small portions of bread and soup, with sardines on occasion. Prisoners were forced to participate in ceremonial exercises centering on rendering the ritualistic fascist salute, and singing the Spanish national anthem; refusal to do so brought beatings and deprivations.

In October the tempo of beatings, torture, and forced confessions increased. And then, on October 15, the dreaded executions for rebellion began.[23] This kind of treatment is confirmed by Rafael de Gárate, a prisoner who kept careful records of the executions in his diary. "From December 1937 to July 1938, 241 men were executed in Larrinaga. In June 1938 . . . 1,014 of Larrinaga's 2,437 prisoners were condemned to death. In July, 600 of these (including Gárate) were sent to the penal prison in Burgos, where treatment was much worse."[24]

This extract gives a good example of the kind of reception that defeated Basques might expect to receive elsewhere. Even where they survived execution, they often had to deal with prison guards who realized that they were dealing with prisoners on behalf of Nationalist leaders who urged "exemplary punishment." Moreover, many of the custodians were not just prison guards, they were former Nationalist soldiers who had diametrically opposite political views to those of their captives. The example had been clearly set by the leader of the *Nuevo Estado*, who openly pur-

---

22. Mendizibal, *Gudaris y rehenes de Franco (1936–1943)*, 109.
23. Robert P. Clark, *The Basques: The Franco Years and Beyond* (Reno: University of Nevada Press, 1979), 83-84.
24. Ibid. Also see Rafael de Gárate, *Diario de un condenado a muerte* (University of Virginia 1974).

sued a policy of revenge and punishment toward the defeated.

The diary of Fernando de Aguirre from Ibarra, Gipuzkoa, records the problems Basque prisoners encountered when traveling to the penitentiary of El Puerto:

> We were treated like pigs in cattle wagons. In the three days traveling we were not allowed to leave these wagons for ANYTHING . . . El Puerto de Santa María was far away . . . We do not believe that we ever visited our brother Joshe Mari in this prison. You have to realize that this journey was very long and extremely awkward.[25]

Not only were conditions often abominable in prisons at the other end, their traveling arrangements were not unlike those of cattle. The actual distance between Bilbao and El Puerto de Santa María is 498 miles, but a travel route now by car varies from 566 to 616 miles, depending on the route taken. The vast majority of relatives could never afford the transport costs of visits that were only permitted a few times a year. At that time many of the roads in the Basque Country were no more than narrow winding mountain passes, almost impassable in winter.

Basque (and other) prisoners could be threatened with a transfer to an even more remote situation in the event of perceived breach of discipline. Fernando Aguirre (already quoted) had already been found guilty of *auxilio a la rebelión* (aiding the rebellion), with a sentence of twelve years' imprisonment. He had been a sergeant in the Second Section of the First Company, "Aitzol," was eventually admitted to the penitentiary of El Puerto on August 24, 1938, and released on August 19, 1940. In this instance he refers to an incident in the prison of El Dueso, prior to his transfer to Andalusia. This incident took place in the chapel when some Basque prisoners were reported for singing in Euskara, possibly *Eusko Gudariak*, an anthem of the Basque army. They were threatened with a transfer to the Canary Islands but thanks to the intercession of some nuns, this threat was lifted. [26]Other prisoners were not so fortunate and one Basque prisoner, Juan Ajuriagerra, a qualified engineer, was transferred to a prison in the Canary Islands for refusing to cooperate in the reconstruction of the Alcázar of Toledo. He was president of *Bizkai Buru Batzar* (Bizkaian Provincial Council of the PNV), and was partly responsible for negotiating the Pact of Santoña on behalf of the PNV in August 1937 with

25. Mendizabal, *Gudaris y rehenes de Franco (1936–1943)*, 208.
26. Ibid., 208.

the Italians. His transfer to the Canary Islands would have made the long journey for visiting relatives from the Basque Country almost impossible, as it also involved a maritime trip. The cost and time would have made this a most effective repressive instrument available to the prison authorities, to be used against prisoners who would not cooperate. According to José Manuel Mendizabal, the threat of a transfer to the Canary Islands was often made, but was infrequently carried out.[27] In the case of Ajuriagerra, the Nationalist prison authorities clearly decided to make an example of him in view of his standing in the Basque Country.

This absence of modern communications in the Spain of the 1930s could well mean that the train journey from the north to the south could last up to three days, with inevitable stops on the way. All this led to a greater likelihood that the long journey would bring additional misfortune to the transported prisoners. This was indeed the case as far as the comrades of Marcelo Usabiaga were concerned. Usabiaga, aged ninety-two at the time of the interview and a former Basque soldier, was one of the El Puerto prisoners of that period still alive. Another incident provides a good example of the tribulations and dangers faced by Basque prisoners in transit. Some fifty-seven Basque prisoners were killed in a mysterious train accident on the November 19, 1937 at Alanís de la Sierra near Seville. The whereabouts of all the bodies remains a mystery and is currently under investigation. The only living survivor of the train crash was Romualdo Royo from Getxo, also over ninety-years-old at the time of being interviewed. The writer of the article in *El Diario Digital*, Carmen Barreiro, states that Royo had a prodigious memory. Royo remembers the sinister night as if it were yesterday:

> I am sure because the crash stopped my watch. The train was taking us from Laredo to the University of Deusto, from there to Zaragoza and then to Seville. On arriving at the station of Cazalla de la Sierra, they changed the order of the wagons in which prisoners were traveling. We continued toward Alanís, where the train crashed into another locomotive. Four of my neighbors were saved, with eighteen survivors in total. A detachment of soldiers led by a Captain Garrote took the survivors to the prison at Seville. Nobody told us of the possible causes. Absolutely nothing.[28]

---

27. Ibid., 335.
28. *El Diario Digital*, March 29, 2000. Highly unusual outcome of an interview with an over 90-years-old former prisoner of El Puerto who appears to have been particularly lucid.

Before transfer to Andalusian prisons, the majority of Basque prisoners had already gotten a foretaste of things to come during their placements in nearby penal institutions. Overcrowding was widespread as is well illustrated by the position in some of the nearby prisons in July 1938 (see table 2.3): Many stories of hardship relate to Basque prisons and Basque prisoners. On July 16, 1937, Félix Padín, a militant anarchist and a lieutenant in the Durruti Battalion, was captured in Urbi (Bizkaia) and transferred to a prison in Vitoria-Gasteiz with forty prisoners to a cell. There he could scarcely move.[29] The other case involved José María Otxoa, an officer of the Basque Army, who was imprisoned with one thousand Basque soldiers on September 4, 1937 in the penitentiary of El Dueso, Santoña. Even where a defense was provided it was often of a very low caliber, was of a group nature, and was curtailed by time. For example, Otxoa considered that his defense was provided by a second lieutenant who "spoke garbage." Groups of twenty-five prisoners here were sentenced to *reclusión perpetua*, life imprisonment.[30]

Table 2.3. Examples of overcrowded prisons in northern Spain July 1938. *Cautivos*, Rodrigo[31]

	Prisoners	Capacity
Santoña (Infantería)	3,518	1,500
Deusto-B	4,488	2,500
Miranda de Ebro	2,810	1,200
Pamplona	2,800	1,200
Murgia-B	1,266	500

Basque prisoners found themselves detained in a number of prisons including Larrinaga in Santutxu (Bilbao), the University of Deusto (Bilbao), the Piarist School in Bilbao, the Convent of Mount Carmel in Begoña (Bilbao), the Convent of Adorers in Ondarreta (Donostia-San Sebastián), the seminary of Saturraran in Mutriku (Motrico), the Convent of Mount Carmel in Vitoria-Gasteiz, the Convent of Paul in Vitoria-Gasteiz, a requisition of young offenders reformatory in Amurrio, the Penitentiary of Dueso (Santoña), the Institute of Santoña, Ondarreta (Donostia-San Sebastián), and the prison ship *Upo-Mendi*. Others had already been moved

---

29. Ibid., 43, 92, 136.
30. Ibid., 59–60.
31. Rodrigo, *Cautivos*, p.118.

to Burgos and El Puerto. On visiting Nationalist Spain on November 23, 1938, a German journalist with the *Berliner Tageblatt*, Karlheinz Apking, was struck by the wide effect of war on Spanish life. He observed "One thing is not done in Nationalist Spain---study. The universities are closed . . . the great Christian gentleman is not above using religious houses as cages for his fellow creatures."[32] Basque captives, like other imprisoned Republicans, were often incarcerated in former religious institutions throughout Spain. These converted monasteries and convents were clearly unsuitable to house a large-scale influx of prisoners since they lacked space and the shortage of adequate sanitary accommodation gave rise to tuberculosis and other illnesses. In one case some 1,674 prisoners were crammed into a converted cloister with access to only thirteen toilets in El Puerto.[33] Even so it remained as a prison until its closure in 1981.

Molinero gives examples of the internment of around 33,000 prisoners in concentration camps in Santoña, Santander, Laredo, and Castro Urdiales in August 1937.[34] They were held there pending classification. (There were about 110 such camps between 1936 and 1940). The large numbers taken prisoner after the fall of Santander over a very short period presented the Nationalist authorities with accommodation problems that had been the case in other parts of Spain. Although it is likely that a large number of internees would have been Basque, there would also have been prisoners drawn from other northern areas. As far as deaths were concerned, Stanley G. Payne cites Astilarra *La Guerra en Euzkadi*, a work that mentions 15,500 *gudaris* and 10,550 civilians killed.[35] An extract from a diary of Basque prisoners between 1936 and 1943 shows that in El Dueso (Santoña) jail between October and November 1937, eighty prisoners were shot; while in Larrinaga (Bilbao) jail between December 1937 and July 1938 some 224 were executed.

What is most disturbing is to learn that of this number, some twenty-one were executed by means of the *garrotte vil*, which involved death by degrading and excessively painful strangulation.[36] This was clearly contrary to the Geneva Convention of 1929 concerning humanitarian protec-

32. Charles Duff, *The War in Spain* (London: United Editorial, 1938) is a weekly summary. Number 46, published by United Editorial Ltd on December 3, 1938. This is the front page and the sub title is <u>The Basque Country: Suppression and Exploitation</u> It is already included in my bibliography. Also see Pedro Barruso, "La represión en las zonas republicana y franquista del País Vasco durante la Guerra Civil," *Historia Contemporánea* 35 (2007), 669.
33. Martínez Cordero, *El Penal de El Puerto de Santa María 1886–1981*, 152.
34. Molinero, Sala, and Sobrequés, eds., *Una inmensa prisión*, 223.
35. Stanley G. Payne, *Basque Nationalism* (Reno: University of Nevada Press, 1975), 223.
36. Mendizabal, *Gudaris y rehenes de Franco (1936–1943)*, 272–73.

tion for prisoners of war.

The defeat of the Basque Country led to an increased interest in utilizing the industrial potential of the Bilbao area by Franco and his allies, with Germany exacting economic benefits and control over Basque industry. Such companies as the Spanish based Hispano- Marroqui de Transportes (HISMA) and the German based Rohstoff-Waren-Kompensation Handelsgesellschaft (ROWAK) worked to tap Basque raw materials for the German war effort. However Christian Leitz was to write about Goering's failure to mold the Basque/Spanish economy into a useful Nazi German dependent in the longer term.[37]

Within El Puerto the prisoner power groups lay between Basque nationalists and a left-wing base of Socialists, Communists, and the CNT in the early 1940s.[38] The majority of Basques sentenced were *gudaris* (soldiers) from the Basque militia and political activists, including those who had participated in such organizations as local Defense Committees. No Basque priests could be found among the prisoners' files of El Puerto. This was a result of the efforts of Cardinal Segura, bishop of Seville, who successfully pressurized the Ministry of Interior on behalf of the Basque priests in October and November 1939.[39] The matter is looked at again in more detail in Chapter 5. Although not directly connected with El Puerto, this provides an outstanding example of successful Catholic pressure on Basque prison conditions during the war.

The Basques had been described as "Soviet Separatists" by some; part of "*la horda roja*" by others. The Archbishop of Burgos called Basque priests "the dross of Spanish clergy, in the pay of the reds."[40] This approach was also pursued by other senior Spanish clergy who broadcast condemnations of all Basque Catholics who supported the Basque cause. This attitude was reinforced by the attitude of the Nationalists to Basque clergy. For example, an informative, but undated document simply headed *Sacerdotes Vascos Fusilados* (Executed Basque priests), which was obtained from the Basque Archive in Bergara, lists some sixteen named Basque priests, aged between twenty-four and sixty-four, shot by Nationalists,

37. Christian Leitz, "Hermann Goering and Nazi Germany's Economic Exploitation of Nationalist Spain, 1936–1939," *German History* 14, no. 1 (1996), 21. Also see Leitz, *Economic Relations between Nazi Germany and Franco's Spain, 1936–1945* (Oxford: Clarendon, 1996).

38. AHPC/PSM, Legajos 29258–29476. Four hundred left-wing and Basque nationalist prisoners were transferred on December 14, 1938 to Seville; Rubial, the PSOE organizer, was transferred sometime in late October 1940. Also see SAF/PSM/ANON/3/40.

39. See Santiago Martínez Sánchez, *Los papeles del Cardenal Segura, 1880–1957* (Barañáin: EUNSA, 2004).

40. Beevor, *The Battle for Spain*, 225.

almost all without trial.[41] This contrasts very markedly with the treatment afforded to priests elsewhere in Nationalist Spain. It should also be noted that the PNV assigned chaplains to Basque battalions.

Another reason why the majority of Basques in this prison attracted punitive penalties from the victorious Nationalists relates to Basque separatism and all that it involved. As has been indicated, almost 80 percent of Basques in the penitentiary of El Puerto had been charged with serious "crimes against Franco." Indeed some right-wing extremists had urged that the Spanish government should "actively repress Basque separatist agitation."[42]

Notwithstanding, on October 1, 1936, the Spanish Republican Parliament had approved the creation of a Basque Republic, followed by the formation of an autonomous Basque government under the PNV a week later. In reality, one could argue that Basque autonomy actually existed in Spain during the period from the outbreak of the Spanish Civil War to October 1937, or at least until the fall of Santander on August 26, 1937. In addition, an autonomy statute in 1936 had given the Basque provincial assemblies the authority to promote the use of Euskara as the co-official language with Spanish in any area in which they determined that it was a viable means of communication. Robert P. Clark maintains that by the outbreak of the Civil War, approximately half of the population of the Basque provinces spoke or understood Euskara, albeit in some form or another.[43]

All this was totally unacceptable to Franco, who was determined to reverse this state of affairs as rapidly and harshly as possible. Javier Rodrigo, in his study of incarceration between 1936 and 1947, observes the problems that the Nationalists perceived in converting Basque prisoners who had been allowed to become fervently nationalistic under "Red rule":

> one of the most well-known aspects of Francoist repression: its cruelty with peripheral nationalists, which in this case crystallized in the dispersion of Basque soldiers to different concentration camps. The enormous task of converting and "becoming Spanish" of a population supporting Bizkaia that during the Republic,

---

41. CPDE/PSM, Listado de Documentos Localizados, "Sacerdotes Fusilados,"undated. Also see Hilari Raguer, *Gunpowder and Incense: The Catholic Church and the Spanish Civil War* (London: Routledge, 2007).

42. See Aurelio Joaniquet, *Calvo Sotelo. Una vida fecunda, un ideario politico, una doctrina económica* (Madrid: Espasa-Calpe, 1939), 113–29.

43. Clark, *The Basques: The Franco Years and Beyond*, 136.

during the "red dominion," had enjoyed the unprecedented fervor of [Basque] nationalism, could not but be very difficult.[44]

Basque Experiences in El Puerto (April 1938– January 1943)

Nevertheless, accounts of life in El Puerto would suggest that a common Basque identity was maintained, helping these prisoners maintain a solidarity and united front. The Basque report of March 1940 confirms this.[45] It indicates that not all prisoners in this prison were united and that the mainly political prisoners from the Basque Country often had a different viewpoint from inmates from other parts of Spain. There was a very strong emphasis on maintaining a collective Basque spirit. One of the first Basque moves on entering the penitentiary of El Puerto was to set up a committee of the BBB in 1937–38. This undoubtedly made it easier for the Basque socialist, Ramón Rubial, to establish a large organization of inmates within the prison a few years later in 1940. An extract from the former prisoner's report provides a good example of the self-help that extended from the political area to that of welfare:

> Subscriptions were organized so that medicine and essential commodities could be purchased for prisoners . . . We mourn the death of Pedro de Uriate y Larrea de Yurre (Bizkaia) on May 10, 1939 at 12 pm. He died of pneumonia, contracted from the prison of El Dueso. We were denied permission to see the body and to extract his personal possessions in order to send to his family. A collection was made in order to purchase a gravestone in the nearby cemetery of San Fernando.[46]

Most Basque prisoners seemed to be prepared to try to help one another and some were able to raise material help from the prison and from outside. Another way was to solicit political help and the exiled Basque government made specific interventions at the international level in order to improve the lot of Basque prisoners. The prisoners often wrote home to solicit help, particularly with a view to obtaining medicine. One undated letter from a Basque prisoner, obtained from the archives in Bergara, illustrates this point well. Although no date is ascertainable, it is likely that it would have been between 1939 and 1940 and provides a good example of the way Basque prisoners set about organizing self-help in this prison.

44. Rodrigo, *Cautivos*, 42.
45. CPDE/PSM/ANON/3/40.
46. Ibid.

El penitenciario de El Puerto
Undated
Addressee:
Señorita Doña Elisa de Linazasoro
Zumarraga

> Please accept my sincere appreciation for remembering me. I should like to reciprocate, but strict prison regulations preclude it . . . I need your help . . . Recently our Basque comrades were buried in El Puerto, a prison in a deplorable state. Its deficiency is reflected in a diet of pumpkins twice a day, adversely affecting health . . . statistics reveal 90 tuberculosis patients and 300 more in a pre-tuberculosis state.
>
> . . . we ask for all possible help. Diet, medicine, clothes . . . acquisition of medicine is a priority. . . this month we have sent more than 282,000 pesetas . . . and I ask you from my heart for your contribution in the name of Christian charity . . . anti-tuberculosis sanatoriums and clinics sell medicines at a reasonable discount. More help is available there than pharmacies . . . we could more effectively help our poor brothers in pain.[47]

Tuberculosis was the largest killer in El Puerto and a permanent problem lay in the shortage of drugs. This letter suggests that this Basque prisoner had written similar letters before, and knew what the prisoners required and the value of bulk purchasing. He is apparently a Catholic and makes the appeal "in the name of Christian charity." He continues:

> Perhaps you are connected with the Mercedarian convent in Zumarraga. I know that you dealt with the Reverend Mother Superior Amparo of the Hospital –Sanitario of Eibar . . . Perhaps they could provide a solution by purchasing large quantities for the sanatoriums of Ondazarate, Eibar, etc. Please raise this matter with the Reverend Mother Superior Amparo soon . . . one has to proceed with tact, diplomacy, and knowledge of each person . . . If I write directly to Mother Amparo she could think that that it could lead to a request for another favor. [48]

---

47. Ibid.
48. Ibid.

The writer also demonstrates that he has prior knowledge of the names, contacts, and places likely to be useful. He was also sensible enough to use the recipient of this letter as an intermediary. The reference to Mother Superior Amparo "thinking that she might feel that it could result in my making a request leading to another favor" induces one to think that similar help has been sought in the past.

> All medicine helps these poor prisoners . . . our doctors could give injections of calcium and biocalcium . . . to treat pre-tuberculosis and also some orosanil. This will enable the doctors . . . including Guimón, to treat the tuberculosis of the prisoners. Another person could be contacted in my name, as a friend of your brother. She is a sister of a priest, Don Ignacio de Azpiazu, and belongs to the *Hermanas de la Caridad*. Before the war she had responsibility for pharmacy in the Hospital de San Antonio (Montes) in Donostia-San Sebastián. If she is still there, maybe she could do something. Try to discover prices of pharmacy medicine in order to help us with the purchase . . . Good luck. Now to work!
>
> Affectionate greetings to your family.
>
> Saturnino de Gantxegi.[49]

The reference is to the well-known Bilbao doctor, Dr. Guimón, who treated many Basque prisoners in El Puerto and a high degree of organization seems to have existed among Basque prisoners in medical areas. An interesting comment on Basque organization was offered by Juan López, CNT leader, following the movement of the Republican government to Barcelona in October 1937: "The Basques were perfectly organized in everything, but for the rest of the Spanish, everyone did as best he could."[50]

This 1940 prisoner's report also seems to emphasize the difference between the Basque prisoners and the others, which is perhaps unsurprising for a Basque source.[51] They appear to have questioned the conduct of the prison guards in their apparent tolerance of homosexuality among the prisoners, some of whom made no attempt to conceal their sexual proclivities, either by their behavior or bizarre dress. This led to very strong criticism of the prevailing prison culture from some Basque prisoners in

49. Ibid.
50. Juan López, *Una misión sin importancia* (Madrid: Editora Nacional, 1972), 123.
51. SAF/PSM/ ANON/3/40.

El Puerto. For example the report poses the question why such behavior is tolerated in such an institution operated by a Catholic state. Mirta Núñez Díaz-Balart has an interesting viewpoint on this theme: "The prison orders made constant use of the tricks of putting together a heterosexual and a homosexual in punishment cells in order to observe their reactions."[52]

This may well have been a device used by prison guards against heterosexual prisoners from all areas in El Puerto. It should also be remembered that some Basques came from small rural areas and might be insular and traditional, and conservative and religious. Payne goes further and states that "the Basque region stood out in 1931 as the major conservative region in Spain, vehemently denounced by Socialists and Republicans as the 'Vaticanist Gibraltar.'"[53] This does not take full cognizance of the strong right- and left-wing political presence in Gipuzkoa and Bizkaia in 1936. However it could explain the objections of some of the Basques to such activities within this prison.

Figure 2.3 gives an idea of the militarist control that prisoners were subjected to on a daily basis:

As with other prisoners in El Puerto, Basques experienced a penal system in which everything was set against the daily background of horrific overcrowding, humiliation, dehumanization, and an oppression in which prisoners did not know where they were from one day to the next. Above all, there was a climate of uncertainty and fear. Clearly some times were worse than others, but during the month when the prisoner's report was written, March 1940, there were no executions of Basque prisoners reported in El Puerto.[54] There were, however, at least thirteen recorded Basque deaths from other causes between 1939 and 1943 for those imprisoned for Civil War "crimes." [55]

It would appear that many Basque prisoners adopted a regime of personal survival and they undertook a variety of occupations within the institution. While these pursuits were invaluable for occupying time in a thoroughly repressive daily penal regime, I would suggest that they also acted as an antidote to an environment, whereas Preston observes "prisons [made] massive efforts to break not just the bodies of prisoners but also their minds."[56] These prison occupations included carpentry, in

---

52. Núñez Díaz-Balart, *Los años de terror*, 33.
53. Payne, *Basque Nationalism*, 122.
54. See SAF/PSM/ANON/3/40.
55. AHPC/PSM, Legajos 29258–29421.
56. Paul Preston lecture: "The Crimes of Franco," Study Day, BFI Southbank, London, January 19, 2008.

IRARGI. Fondo Blasco Olaetxea. Sig.: 2612/P3H19

IRARGI

Figure 2.3

which they made small chests and other domestic articles of use, as well as different kinds of art that included the production of paintings and the sketching of the prison inmates and buildings.

The drawing in figure 2.4 is particularly intricate and provides some idea of the background of Basque prisoners. In this case, the prisoner may well have had some kind of architectural training. This could be an indication of an education system in which literacy rates of the Basque Country were among the highest in Spain in in the early 1930s.[141]

The sketching of fellow inmates and the drawing of cartoons occupied the energies of some of the Basque prisoners. The cartoon in figure 2.5 entitled "El Abuelo" (the grandfather; figure 2.5) was drawn of a fellow prisoner by Pedro Berroga.[57]

The cartoon is accompanied by an ode to "El Abuelo" by the same prisoner, Pedro Berroga. This was discovered on the back of the sketch dedicated to the old prisoner.

"El Abuelo."
Instead of calling him Abrigueta
We call him "The Grandfather."

---

57. SAF/PSM/00565012.

Figure 2.4

Figure 2.5

He is a man of many friends.
Diminutive but resilient;
Although seventy-two years old
He scarcely notices his age.
"The Grandfather" rises at the sound of reveille
Albeit slowly from his bed.
He eats with a good appetite,
And usually adds an egg
And spoonfuls of milk
To the measly portions of food served
In the Prison.
When they leave him in peace
And he is not forced to speak
He indulges himself in the afternoon
With the pleasure of a siesta.
I am his honored guest
Who enjoys all the treats
Coffee in Fernando Pó
After succulent paella.
He has traveled the oceans
But has never seen the mermaids;
He says that the sharks
have migrated to the land,
He was surprised by the storm
In the town of Forlitz;
They condemned him to death,
And then commuted his sentence
Now he waits calmly
For the review of this sentence.[58]

—Pedro Berroga, prison of El Puerto Santa María, March 5, 1940

The name Berroga could well be fabricated to protect the identity of the prisoner. For example all diaries of prisoners had to be hidden from prison guards in fear of confiscation and further punishment. Unfortunately no records of Pedro Berroga [59]can be found in the prisoners' files in Cádiz, nor can the identity of *El Abuelo* (grandfather) be traced. The

---

58. SAF/PSM/CON/7/39, 00565/012, Pedro Berroga.
59. No evidence could be found concerning the surname in Basque prison lists. It almost certainly does not exist.

poem gives several clues. It refers to "coffee in Fernando Pó," a small is-
land off the west coast of Africa, and a Spanish colony until 1968. Spanish
vessels would certainly have called there before that date. It is now called
Bioko and is part of Equatorial Guinea. The poem then refers to the fact
that El Abuelo "has traveled the oceans and has not seen the mermaids . .
. [and] the sharks have migrated to the land."

The poem indicates that he was a sailor, along with other El Puerto
prisoners like Salvador Coll Broadvent from Valencia, Serafín Navarro
Oliver from Murcia, and Alvaro Pons from Barcelona. It is safe to assume
that "*El Abuelo*," at seventy-two, was among one of the older prisoners in
this prison, although another, Cirulo López López from Huelva, was seventy-one. This information confirms that old age was never a mitigating
factor for Franco when deciding on imprisonment and indeed execution.

Another prisoner in El Puerto was identified and he was Luis Rezola
Arana, a Basque *bertsolari*, an oral improvising poet and storyteller, who
is referred to again in Chapter 4.[60] The following extracts specifically relate
to El Puerto prison, written there in August 1938 by Rezola to his mother.

From Dueso to Cádiz by Luis Rezola

They have brought us here
Crammed into wagons,
Three days on the way,
On the brink of death.
Restroom visits denied
at all railroad stations.
To top it all, we are
nothing but skin and bones;
all the same we were relieved
to have arrived in good health.
Inside El Puerto prison. August 1938

(When prisoners were transferred from one prison to another,
they spent days locked up in punishment cells).

---

60. AHPC/PSM, Legajo 29299, Causa número 63 de 1938. Email from Joxemari Mendiz-
    abal Sarasua, February 23, 2015.

Listen to me, Madariaga,you know well that
you are a son of a Basque.
You have to learn Basque,
just like us, if you can;
don't you know that if we lose it
we are nothing at all?

(There were four of us in the punishment cell. Three spoke Basque,
the fourth one tried, but in vain. We were twenty-three-years-old, he was
twenty-one from Bilbao).

A dark day comes
And a hard night,
...a terrible sadness
Gets me in its grip!
The court sentenced me
To life imprisonment,
But I have done nothing.

(Other extracts from poem written to the mother of the prisoner).
Luis Rezola Arana.

Basque prisoners also played music and taught the skill to others. A
range of disciplines were studied. Above all, there was an overwhelming
desire to learn the Basque language. The day of Aberri Eguna (Day of the
Basque Homeland) was celebrated and the spirit of Basque nationalism
was kept alive. This was unusual, as although the first Aberri Eguna had
been held in 1932, it was banned after the defeat of the Republic. It is
difficult to ascertain the reason why this was allowed, but the recently accessed diaries of Basque prisoners may offer a clue. Although the records
on Sunday April 17, 1938 in Larrinaga prison indicate a day of *fiesta* or
holiday, the diary of José Manuel Mendizabal shows an abbreviated entry,
viz *A.Eguna* with a footnote that Aberri Eguna is purposely "entered in
a strange way in order to avoid problems in case of search."[61] If the same
practice had been followed in El Puerto it would indicate that an Aberri
Eguna had been celebrated, but not openly so.

One method of maintaining contact with families was sending Christmas cards. Such cards from prisoners were always particularly poignant
and specifically avoided reference to the horrors of death, starvation, over-

---

61. Mendizabal, *Gudaris y rehenes de Franco (1936–1943)*, 265.

crowding, illness, and ill treatment. The two cards drawn by prisoners and sent home in December of 1938 and December of 1939 say very little, but are a sad attempt at normality. They would also have had to be particularly bland to satisfy the prison censor, or they would not have been approved.

The first postcard indicates a gentleman of the road walking away from the year of sentence completed, 1939, toward a new year, 1940, with another year of his sentence to complete.[62] The card (figure 2.6) is a highly original design. He is heading for Oion in Araba, some 913 kilometers (567 miles) away from El Puerto de Santa María.[63] Certainly this conveyed a feeling of distance accentuated by the signpost to Oion, which would reinforce the length of time that the prisoner had to serve. As far as can be ascertained, the message on the card is unremarkable.

Figure 2.6

---

62. SAF/PSM/0167/003, Christmas greetings, Postcard, 1939–40. To María Luisa Quintana, sent by her brother Juan Quintana.
63. Both postcards translated by the author.

A Christmas message from a Basque prisoner to his sister:

El penal de El Puerto de Santa María

December 24, 1939

Dearest sister,

Two letters only to wish you one thousand Christmas greetings.

Please extend these to all my friends for me.

At the same time I wish you a happy and prosperous New Year.

With many hugs from your brother who loves you and does not forget you.

　　　Juan

The second postcard (figure 2.7) contains a bird feeding its young in a nest and the written message is harder to decipher.[64] It was written on December 17, 1938, once again by a prisoner to his sister.

A postcard message from another Basque prisoner to his sister

Figure 2.7

---

64. SAF/PSM/01067/003, Christmas greetings, December 17, 1938. To Eugeni sent by her bother Felix.

El Puerto de Santa María

December 17, 1938

To my dearest sister Eugeni and all the family,

You are increasing in my thoughts as the days go by --, receive this small but sincere testimony of affection toward you all, with the hope that everybody has a happy Christmas with a good end to this year and the next. In the hope that God gives us a long life.

In the hope that God gives us a good life.

I send a loving kiss. I will never forget you and hope to embrace you soon. .

A hug,

Felix

The design and the message of the two postcards merit further comment. Both are discernible from the available prison records, as is the case with Felix. There is no possibility of cross-referencing with the prisoners' personal documents. Unsurprisingly, the thoughts of both writers are with their families, and they are clearly missing them, especially at Christmas. Both are simply signed, one as "Juan" and the other as "Felix." The former is Juan Quintana, writing to his sister María Luisa Quintana. However, his messages are trying to convey a sense of optimism for the future. Oion (Araba) had a population of only 1,163 in 1940 and Juan may well have been the only imprisoned Republican supporter from that small village. Felix has possibly adapted an existing card, since part of the front heading is in English. There may be more of a concealed message in his card since it denotes a struggle with the provider of food and the chicks in the nest. As has been suggested earlier, the prisoners in El Puerto during the years 1936 to 1945 suffered permanently from hunger and some died.

The presence of so many Basques clearly had some influence within the penitentiary. The views of the Basque delegation report of July 1939 on conditions of prisoners were that "since the arrival of the Basque prisoners the treatment meted out to the prisoners in general has improved; until then, slaps and blows aplenty had been their lot. The disciplined level of behavior of the Basques had its effect on the prison staff, although some guards are still too ready to strike."[65] This may or may not be true since the two reports quoted are written by Basques (July 1939 and March

---

65. SAF/PSM/CON/7/39.

1940) and concentrate solely on prisoners from that area in El Puerto. On the other hand, the prison did contain a large number of prisoners from northern Spain, with a different language, a former separate Basque Republic, and strong support for the Catholic Church allied to quite a different approach to politics than the other prisoners. It could well be that this very large group of inmates did have some effect on the behavior of the prison authorities. Two good examples have been provided by the political organization of Ramón Rubial and the religious pressure exerted concerning the provision of Communion (see Chapter 1). Imprisoning so many Basques in a distant penal establishment, albeit far from home, offered a potential for political organization among the prisoners.

Basque Repression (During and After the War)

In some cases the military charges brought against the defeated were also accompanied by fines of 10,000 pesetas or more and confiscation of property, thereby making it extremely difficult for families of prisoners to live. Basque children were evacuated to a number of countries, with 4,000 to the United Kingdom alone.[66] Natalie Benjamin, secretary of the Basque children of the 37 Association considers that most of them went back in 1938 and in 1939 "in steady trickles"and by the the start of the Second World War in September 1939 there were only about 400 of them left in the UK. By the end of the war in May 1945 about 250 remained.[67]

On the other hand, the wide net of capture of Basques as a result of the Santander surrender resulted in a large number of their soldiers and civilians being deemed eligible for punishment by death. For example, it was reported in the Bilbao newspaper *Gaceta del Norte* that the following sentences by military tribunals, over sixteen days between July 18 and August 13, 1937, were carried out as follows:

In 29 percent of the 323 cases heard the defendants were condemned to death. They included:

> Don Ramón de Rugama, criminal lawyer; two women journalists who wrote for *La Tarde*; Padre Román de San José, rector of the Carmelite Convent in Amorebieta; Don Esteban de Urkiaga, a Basque poet; Don Justo de Lozano, owner of a tailor's shop and a well-known Christian; Don Alejandro de Mallona, mayor of

---

66. See Xabier Irujo, *Expelled from the Motherland: The Government of President Jose Antonio Agirre in Exile, 1937–1960*, trans. Cameron Watson and Jennifer Ottman (Reno: Center for Basque Studies, University of Nevada, Reno, 2012), 45–65.
67. Email from Natalia Benjamin, December 8, 2009.

Mundaka; Mateo de Agirregoitia, ex soccer player for Arenas FC; Don Juan de Zabala, industrial engineer.[68]

Another report headed *Euzkadi bajo el régimen de Franco: la represión en Guipúzcoa* (The Basque Country under the Franco regime: The repression in Gipuzkoa) and published in May 1939 gives an indication of how widely the vengeance of Franco extended as far as the Basque Country was concerned.[69] Some 340 people were executed in the towns where they lived (see table 2.4).

Table 2.4 Extract from report showing executions in different parts of Gipuzkoa by May 1939 Irargi-Centro de Patrimonio Documental de Euskadi/Euskadiko Dokumentu Ondarearen Zentroa

Place of origin	Number of prisoners shot in each town
Donostia-San Sebastián	66
Arrasate-Mondragón	39
Beasain	21
Errenteria	18
Pasaia	16
Hernani (14), Tolosa (14)	14
Oiartzun	12
Irun	11
Eibar (10), Loiola (10), Ordizia (10)	10
Oñati (9), Urnieta (9), Urretxu (9), Zarautz (9)	9
Deba (8), Bergara ((8)	8
Elgoibar	7
Altza	6
Lasarte (5), Leintz-Gatzaga (5), Usurbil (5)	5
Mutriku (3), Legazpi (3), Zamarraga (3),	3
Aretxabaleta (2), Azkoitia (2), Azpeitia (2), Soraluze (2)	2
Escoriaza (1), Lezo (1)	1
In total 340 were executed	

One of the arguments used by the Nationalists was that they were defending religion. In the case of Gipuzkoa, this was clearly not the case. In the example of the 340 executions reported there in May 1939, it may be deduced that Catholics, including priests, were involved. There is also an undated document in the Bergara archives that lists another sixteen Basque priests being shot in 1937, but the political and social grouping below refers only to those from Gipuzkoa. The situation here, as with all Basque matters, is rather more complicated. Although it is true that Basque priests were shot by Nationalists, Aguilar argues that "the Basque

---

68. CPDE /PSM, "Nombres de los fusilados entre el 15 de julio y el 13 de septiembre, 1937," *Gaceta del Norte*, November 27, 1937.
69. CPDE/PSM, *Euzkadi bajo el regimen de Franco: la repression en Guipúzcoa mayo 1939.*

Church . . . repeatedly intervened in favour of the Basque nationalists on account of their conservatism and exemplary Catholicism [and] helped to moderate the reprisals."[70]

Table 2.5. Extract from report showing affiliations of those executed in Gipuzkoa by May 1939.
Irargi: Centro de Patrimonio Documental de Euskadi/Euskadiko Dokumentu Ondarearen Zentroa, Bergara.

Sacerdotes	12
Nacionalistas y solidarios vascos católicos	130
Socialistas y U.G.T.	61
Republicanos	30
Comunistas	8
C.N.T.	4
Sin filiación o desconocida	95
Total	340

This retrospective punishment gives an indication of the remarkable thoroughness of the investigations of the Franco regime as it sought to identify every person in the Basque Country who had been involved, even at the lowest level, in any form of government or any kind of political activity (see table 2.5). It is notable that the regime was interested in the identity of persons previously making denunciations. Evidence of one of the relatives of the Basques in El Puerto confirms that he was denounced by one of his relatives for "sympathies contrary to the interests of the *Nuevo Estado*." Another relative in the women's prison of Durango was denounced by eleven people for having an "*ideología muy roja*." One of the denouncers was a *Margarita* (woman Carlist). The role of denouncers was encouraged and was fairly similar throughout Spain. Peter Anderson describes their contribution in north Córdoba:

> The Franco regime also went to great lengths to encourage denunciations. Following occupation of a village or town the new authorities set up special denunciation centres and placed announcements in newspapers and government publications exhorting people to denounce Republicans. Francoists even made it an offense not to register denunciations against Republicans known to have committed crimes . . . Denouncers simply had to report to a local official such as the mayor, Falange . . . or civil guard . . . it was because local officials and ordinary Francoist inhabitants worked in tandem that the repression became so

---

70. Aguilar, "The Memory of the Civil War in the Transition to Democracy," 10.

ferocious . . .The Falangist mayor of Villanueva, for example, had
no proof to offer against a day labourer from the town accused
of killing . . . he simply brushed aside this difficulty by asserting
that "to judge by his past [in a left-wing organization] it can be
assumed he took part in the killings."[71]

Indeed, until September 1941, military authorities could even accept
anonymous denunciations. This could be based on hearsay and was an
ideal opportunity to settle grudges, either with creditors or political enemies.

There is a good example of the use public denunciations used by the
Judge Advocate of the Sixth Military Region in the Basque Country in
his report of October 1939. This report extended to two periods.[72] The
first was related to the period from February 1936 to September 1936.
The second was from October 1, 1936, a date when the autonomous
Basque regime was approved by the Republican parliament, until August 26, 1937. Both sections of the report included the Civil Governor
and his staff, all local councils, local Defense Committees, and Popular
Front Committees. The Nationalist inquiry extended to the President and
Councils of the Basque Country, all civil servants, and all local councils
including town and village councils and central and provincial councils
of all Popular Front parties and "the separatists." All previous legislation,
methods of operation, and "abuses" were to be systematically exposed.
Fuller information was to be obtained by reference to the local Falange
and the Brotherhood of Ex-Prisoners (formed in 1939 by the Falange for
ex-prisoners who had been in Republican jails). Ruiz writes "Moreover,
the maintenance of 'Red Terror' memories was not solely the preserve of
the regime. It was also manifested by organizations representing ex-prisoners and victims' relatives . . . [such as] the Brotherhood of Ex-Prisoners
of Spain."[73] Another important victims' relatives' association was the Relatives' Association for the Martyrs of Paracuellos de Jarama y Torrejón de
Ardoz. Other statements were also sought from people who had suffered
because of support for the Glorious Movement.

One section of the report by the Judge Advocate specifically related
to prisons.[74] It recommended that a report on the history of each pris-

71. Anderson, "Singling Out Victims," 16, 18, 22–.
72. CPDE/ Judicial/PSM, Report by Judge Advocate of the Sixth Military Region urging a
    renewal of repression in the Basque Country, October 1939.
73. Ruiz, *Franco's Justice*, 38.
74. CPDE/Judicial/PSM, Report of Judge Advocate of Sixth Military Region urging new

on should include, where possible, the names of all prisoners held. The names and addresses of guards and other officials responsible for abuses should be sought. Once again, matters were to be reviewed in the closest detail in order that retribution could follow. These inquires were to extend to all prison staff appointed under "the Red Separatist rebellion," and included not only directors, inspectors, and administrators of prisons, but also guards and auxiliaries. All regimes of the prisons were to be examined. This included the food, prison cells, visits permitted, and events taking place within the prisons. It was suggested that the Brotherhood of Ex-Prisoners should again be involved, and could appoint a council of four or five ex-prisoners from each prison, in order to supply the prosecutors with a full knowledge of events.

The significance of these detailed measures, allied to the structure of public denunciation, would ensure that any prison staff suspected of Republican beliefs leading to sympathetic treatment of prisoners before the outbreak of the Civil War on July 18, 1936, would be exposed and almost certainly purged. The structure created another route whereby personal grudges could be settled by Nationalist prisoners and their families. The likelihood of a panel of inquiry containing the local Falange and the Brotherhood of Ex-Prisoners making dispassionate reports on prison guards, appointed by the Republic, must have been extremely remote.

Already mentioned but worth revisiting was the execution of sixteen non-combatant Basque priests between 1936 and 1937 by the Nationalists, the defenders of Catholicism. Irargi, the Centro de Patrimonio Documentalde Euskadi/Euskadiko Dokumentu Ondarearen Zentroa, Bergara, contains the following list of executed priests (undated information).[75] This is the spelling used by the archive at Bergara Later, the pressure of Cardinal Segura, then bishop of Seville, on the Ministry of the Interior in October and November 1939, helped secure the transfer of Catholic priests to Carmona. The Cardinal offered to supervise the priests in his capacity as bishop of Seville.[76]

Meanwhile, the Basque government had established an international presence before the Basque defeat in August 1937. For example, the Basque President, José Antonio de Aguirre, had condemned Germany and Italy

purge in the Basque Country, October 1939.

75. CPDE/PSM, Sacerdotes Fusilados: José de Ariztimuño; José Sagarna Uriarte; José Iturri Castillo; José Peñagaricano; Celestino de Onaindia; Martín Lecuona; José Joaquin Arin; Leonardo Guridi; José Marquiegui; Alejandro Mendicute; Gervasio de Albizu; José Otaño; José de Adarraga; Román de San José; Santiago Lucas Artamendía; Luis Alberdi Mendizabal.

76. See Martínez Sánchez, *Los papeles del Cardenal Segura, 1880–1957*.

for their failure to comply with the policy of nonintervention. Passports were issued by the Basque government, widely used by Basque refugees, and were accepted by some countries across the world. From October 1937 the new Basque government worked for separate Basque diplomatic relations with thirty-three countries, including the United States, France, Great Britain, Germany, Russia, Italy, and Mexico. Close relations were established with the US, who's Ambassador to Spain was Claude Bowers. He was to write "My sincere sympathies are with the Basques . . . when we visited Bilbao in order to evacuate our fellow countrymen, I was impressed with the honesty and intelligence of the Basque leaders."[77] Relations with the British consul in Bilbao, R.C. Stevenson, were also good (as indicated by the confidential report sent to him by the Basque delegation about conditions affecting Basque prisoners in El Puerto earlier). There were also cordial relations with the French Ambassador, Jean Herbette. The Basque President Aguirre also had direct contacts with President Roosevelt and Prime Ministers Chamberlain and Deladier.

An important pressure group in the Spanish Civil War was the International Red Cross. The Basque Red Cross also had direct contacts with the British, American, and the International Red Cross. Specific issues were raised concerning imprisonment of Basques; the London Basque delegation was very active, José Ignacio Lizaso particularly so.[78] The Basque delegation pressurized the British Red Cross to contact the American Red Cross concerning prison conditions; all of them would also use the International Red Cross to exert some kind of pressure on matters regarding prisoners. Interestingly in this context, Joxemari Mendizabal writes about his father, Joshe Mari, who was later to become a prisoner in the penitentiary of El Puerto. He cites a visit from the International Red Cross to Burgos prison on December 23, 1937.[79] This was a result of a complaint to the International Red Cross over the issue of overcrowding in the cells. The outcome of this visit is not known, but it is revealing to learn that the prisoners were "stupefied" to note that when the neutral Swiss representative visited them in the middle of the war, he gave a fascist salute, with his

77. Claude Bowers, *Misión en España: En el umbral de la Segunda Guerra Mundial, 1933–1939*, trans. Juan López S. (Barcelona: Grijalbo, 1977), 347–62. Also see Dante A. Puzzo, *Spain and the Great Powers, 1936–1941* (New York: Columbia University Press, 1962), 100; Irujo, *Expelled from the Motherland*, 35–36.

78. See letters from former Prime Minister David Lloyd George on November 13, 1937 and Robert Vansittart of the Foreign Office on March 25, 1938, CPDE/PSM: Executive Committe of the Council for Peace and Reconstruction. Also see Irujo, *Expelled from the Motherland*, 109–11,172–3.

79. Mendizabal, *Gudaris y rehenes de Franco (1936–1943)*, 234. Also see Marcel Junod, *El tercer combatiente, Comité Internacional de la Cruz Roja* (Geneva: CICR, 1985).

arm raised. However, there is no direct evidence that this kind of lobbying resulted in particularly successful outcomes for Basque prisoners in this prison, although its existence may have exercised some pressure on the way individual Nationalist prison governors related to prisoners. For example, it may explain their reaction to pleas for concessions for religious worship or the discovery of organized political Basque groups, as was the case in El Puerto. Perhaps one of the most successful outcomes of Basque pressure in their dealings with the United States, Great Britain, and France lay in the making of arrangements for Basque refugee children, some of whom may have had fathers in prisons in Andalusia.[80]

The situation concerning the evacuation of Basque children was not at all simple as Xabier Irujo points out.[81] The Church and the Nationalist government became involved in requesting the return of these children as their residence abroad constituted bad publicity for Franco, who sought their return. Despite this pressure, only 95 children were repatriated from France in 1937 with 265 children repatriated from Great Britain in 1937.[82] The Basque government had compiled 650 letters from Basque parents in France, Great Britain, and Belgium asking that their children be not repatriated.[83]

Nevertheless, the Basque delegation in London acted as a pressure point on British politicians concerning their imprisoned fellow countrymen. For example, Sir Archibald Sinclair, the leader of the Liberal Party, wrote to a number of parliamentarians, including Clement Attlee, the leader of the Labour Party, on October 29, 1937.[84] He stated that:

> The prisons are inadequate . . . All kinds of buildings are used as prisons. More than 35,000 souls are detained in them. Assassinations are perpetrated in thousands, including women. On October 18, 27 women were taken out of the Kursa[a] [palace, a casino, restaurant, and theater] at San Sebastián and were killed . . . these women formed part of an expedition of refugees, transferred to Basque territory by order of the French Government.

---

80. Alonso Carballés, "El Primer Exilio de los vascos 1936—1939," 691, writes that about 3,861 children were sent to the United Kingdom and 2,900 to France by June 1937.
81. Irujo, *Expelled from the Motherland*, 60–65.
82. Ibid., 65.
83. Ibid., 64–65.
84. Letter from Sir Archibald Sinclair to M.Ps C.R. Atlee, Noel Baker, Duchess of Atholl, October 29, 1937. See also letter from George Lansbury to Count Ciano, January 4, 1938; and Robert Vansittart to London Basque delegation, March 25, 1938, on matters dealing with Basque prisoners, CPDE/PSM.

Basque lobbying on prisons and other matters between 1938 and 1941 also had involved George Lansbury, the former leader of the Labour Party. Thus it may be seen that the activities of the Basque Republic were a contributory factor in ensuring that the Basque prisoners in El Puerto would be perceived as different, both by fellow prisoners and prison authorities. However, in view of the lengthy sentences received by Basque *gudaris*, it could be argued that this lobbying may have had a counterproductive effect on sentencing and release. Yet it could also be argued that this lobbying had an effect at a more local level, where perhaps it was able to restrain the response of the director of El Puerto, Ramón Caballero, in the matter of religious provision in his jail.

The extent of Basque lobbying is also well illustrated by the two reports that are quoted throughout this work.[85] The first report, which was compiled by a visiting Basque delegation in July 1939 to El Puerto, would have been seen by R.C. Stevenson, British consul in Bilbao. It may well also have been seen by the British Ambassador to Spain and the British Foreign Office. This pressure was not always successful, but it was an outlet that seems to have been denied to prisoners from other parts of Spain in El Puerto. The second report relating to prison life in El Puerto, by a former Basque inmate in March 1940, was deeply critical of the religious provision within the penitentiary. This provision subsequently improved and the report may well have been a contributory factor. The reports are invaluable for historians in providing detailed personal information about prison conditions and the response of those imprisoned, which archives do not contain.

Beyond the jails, the Basque families of the imprisoned suffered greatly as a result of Francoist purges, the full impact of which would be felt by the prisoners on their release. This included an estimated figure of at least 120,000 exiles, mainly to France and Catalonia; children were evacuated to many parts of the world and families separated; the civilian population of Durango, Gernika (Guernica), and Bilbao had been bombed; and the Basques had lost control of important parts of their industrial wealth. The Basque state that the prisoners had sought to defend was gradually dismembered a few days after the Pact of Santoña in August 1937. The first act of Franco after this was to formally declare that any speaking of Euskara was illegal. With an estimated figure of 86,500 civilian and military prisoners from the Basque Country (including over 2,000 in the penitentiary of El Puerto), outgoing contacts with the outside world were errat-

---

85. SAF/PSM/CON/7/39; SAF/PSM/ANON/3/40.

ic.[86] The prison censors ensured that the bland postcards said very little, and in some cases punishment could include a refusal to allow prisoners to write or receive letters from home. The full effects of imprisonment on the prisoners and their families did not always immediately emerge, although both struggled to survive.

The high level of Basque repression particularly applied to the confiscation of assets and fines. In the case of Julián de Abando y Oxinga, he was fined over 100 million pesetas and one of his sons, a distinguished doctor, had his clinic confiscated.[87] As Richards observes "Repression was also terrible in the north of Spain."[88] The withdrawal of foral (taxation) privileges in Bizkaia and Gipuzkoa was an indication that Francoist economic repression was most severe where national consciousness was strongest. At the same time in the Erribera (Ribera) area of Navarre, with the killing of over 2 percent of the population in Azkoien (Peralta) and nearly 7 percent in Sartaguda, the "town of widows," repression was some of the worst in northern Spain.[89]

Yet the Casado report in 1939 had urged further repression in the Basque Country. Examples of this personal repression are provided later, in which relatives of Basque prisoners in El Puerto have testified to its effects on individual families. While the vast majority of Basque prisoners in this penitentiary are no longer alive, fortunately some kind of collective memory of the descendants of these Basque prisoners between 1936 and 1949 still exists among a few.

---

86. CPDE/PSM, Summary of a report on the Rebel Persecution of the Basque People during and since the war. Undated.
87. Preston, *The Spanish Holocaust*, 439.
88. Richards, *A Time of Silence*, 41.
89. Preston, *The Spanish Holocaust*, 183.

3

Collective Memories of Basque Relatives of the Prisoners in the Penitentiary of El Puerto de Santa María between 1936 and 1949

"No nos lloréis, no nos olvidéis."

—a plea from imprisoned women of Saturraran, María González
Gorosarri-Eduardo Barinaga 2008

It was Franco himself who had written about memory in the context of the Spanish Civil War, which he considered to be the making "of a pact of the future with the past."[1] Notwithstanding, oral evidence in this war, as in other wars, is often one of the keys to historical memory of the protagonists. In the former, the victors had determined a culture wherein atrocities had been committed "only by Republicans, myths were perpetrated by Nationalists and "history was manipulated by the regime as it cultivated a particular memory."[2] This meant that the defeated were reluctant to talk about the war; even the new Spanish Constitution of 1978 was surrounded by a tacit understanding of silence and an agreement to forget past events.[3] However, we are reminded that "there are two sets of historical memory: the homogeneous Francoist one imposed on the country during four decades of dictatorship and the diverse Republican ones, repressed until recent years."[4]

---

1. Francisco Franco, *Palabras del Caudillo, 19 abril 1937–31 diciembre 1938* (Barcelona: Seix y Barral, 1939), 137.
2. Richards, *A Time of Silence*, 7.
3. Aguilar, *Memoria y olvido de la guerra civil española*, 34–5, 56–7.
4. Preston, *The Spanish Holocaust*, 519.

This chapter deals with one of the Republican memories, a Basque version afforded me by relatives of the prisoners in El Puerto.[5] It is based on the personal experiences of prisoners from the Basque Country, mainly drawn from Durango and Bilbao and surrounding areas in Bizkaia and, to a lesser extent, Donostia-San Sebastián and surrounding areas in Gipuzkoa. All witnesses were asked similar questions concerning life before detention, imprisonment conditions, and reception by their communities on release. Some relatives were able to offer more than others but they maintained that this was the first time that they had discussed the matter outside their families.

Almost all stressed the theme of hunger. Gómez Bravo writes "the months of February and March 1941 were particularly terrible. In the penitentiary of El Puerto de Santa María the diet was restricted to low grade vegetation with vinegar, because the price of spinach was between four and six pesetas per kilo."[6] In El Puerto uncertainty was always prevalent as constant movement took place, often at the whim of the penal authorities. On the other hand movement outside prison was not easy as "travel and search for jobs were controlled by a system of safe conducts and certificates of political and religious reliability."[7]

Perhaps one of the most difficult obstacles confronting Basque prisoners in this jail involved almost insurmountable problems brought about by the location of the prison itself. Joxemari Mendizabal Sarasua, a Basque local historian (who insists that he is an intermediary passing on prisoners' testimonies, notes and diary extracts) had a close relative Joshemari Mendizabal, who was a prisoner in El Puerto between August 1938 and August 1940. Mendizabal Sarasua again stressed problems arising from the remoteness of Andalusia and any further transfer: "Anyway, from the testimony gathered, there were very few prisoners in El Puerto de Santa María who had a family visit during the two years of imprisonment there; it was not necessary to send them to the Canary Islands in order to avoid contact with their families and friends."[8] This then was the demoralizing background to the experiences of the prisoners and their families; the former were either soldiers or civilians with some kind of political affiliation.

---

5.   As a result of initial contacts made in the Basque Country between May, June September 2009, 2010 in each month of each of the two years during residence in Spain. For other oral testimonies see also Fraser, *Blood of Spain;* Cuevas, *Mujeres en las cárceles franquistas.*
6.   Gómez Bravo, *El exilio interior,* 97.
7.   Preston, *The Politics of Revenge,* 46.
8.   Letter from Joxemari Mendizabal Sarasua, Donostia, May 1, 2010. The intimation here is that El Puerto was far enough.

That these stories could be told was the outcome of moderate success in actually locating relatives of Basques who were imprisoned in El Puerto between 1936 and 1949. Unusually, these families were prepared to talk about both the experiences of these relatives during and immediately after the Spanish Civil War and the long term effects of imprisonment. Paul Thompson quotes George Ewart Evans when the latter writes, "although the old survivors were walking books . . . they were [also] persons."[9] In the case of the Basque prisoners, the information obtained from their relatives complemented data obtained mainly from the prisoners' files located in the Provincial Historical Archive in Cádiz. This chapter has thus involved an amalgam of intelligence obtained from archival, written, and oral sources. All have been invaluable and I am grateful that relatives of deceased prisoners were prepared to share their personal reminiscences. Thompson considers that "oral history is a history built around people. It thrusts life into history itself and widens its scope."[10] It is to be hoped that the reports of the in-depth interviews, allied to communications with different relatives of Basque prisoners, have enabled the experiences of ordinary people to be heard above the formal prison records of the archives.

Mary Vincent writes that "the effects of the blanket repression in the Basque Country were such as to rewrite historical memory."[11] The Basque repression took different forms that included not only executions, but also an embargo on pursuing previous occupations (doctors, teachers, lawyers, engineers) that was allied to "a significant amount of fines and confiscations."[12] This chapter seeks to give an insight into how prisoners and their families existed in this hostile climate; it also seeks to ensure that the forgotten voices of Basque prisoners are heard in the cause of historical memory. It examines the experiences of some of the Basque prisoners (now deceased) as recounted by their relatives and is clearly reliant on their own memories.[13] The telling of their stories could be seen as part of the rejection of the *pacto de olvido* and an endorsement of the countrywide creation of associations in Spain dedicated to the recovery of historical memory (see the Introduction). This general wave of interest may have encouraged some of these relatives to relate their family experi-

---

9. Paul Thompson, *The Voice of the Past: Oral History* (Oxford: Oxford University Press, 1988), 57.
10. Paul Thompson, "The Voice of the Past: Oral History," in *The Oral History Reader*, ed. Robert Perks and Alistair Thomson (London: Routledge, 1998), 28.
11. Vincent, *Spain 1833–2002*, 218.
12. Preston, *The Spanish Holocaust*, 439.
13. See Mikel Urquijo "La memoria negada: la encrucijada de la vía institucional en el caso del Gobierno Vasco y las víctimas del franquismo," *Hispania Nova. Revista Contemporánea*, 6 (2006).

ences. Some of the testimonies have been made available for the first time; in other cases relatives had previously kept this information (including a prison diary) concealed within the family for seventy years. Not only was the diary of great sentimental value, but there had been a feeling that this information might be of little worth. This chapter seeks to redress that balance using testimony from Durango, Abadiño (Abadiano), Loiu, Mungia, Bakio, Amorebieta, Urduña, Zarautz, Erandio, Bilbao and Greater Bilbao, and Donostia-San Sebastián; a great deal of evidence is from the Durango area in particular.

A brief survey of Durango at that time provides a background for the testimonies. It was a town of mixed political views, with a substantial right-wing majority in 1931 when the local council was dominated by thirteen Monarchists, two Basque nationalists (PNV), and one Republican.[14] The national coalition government of Radicals led by Alejandro Lerroux, with the CEDA (Confederación Española de Derechas Autónomas, Spanish Confederation of Autonomous Right-wing Groups) as junior partners, proceeded to close down local left-wing headquarters after October 1934 throughout Spain. Earlier, on January 2, 1934, Ignacio Rojo Ugarte, chief of local police was shot; this was followed by an incident in the town between security forces and railroad workers who belonged to the CNT, the UGT, or the PNV. There were three deaths: José María Galíndez (aged nineteen), Gregorio Larrea (aged thirty), and Pedro Miota (aged sixteen). All three were shot by the Civil Guard.[15] Some nine workers were convicted, and the majority was sentenced to death.[16]

The situation in Durango was like that of many other Spanish towns as there were very clear divisions between the left and right. Identifiable support for the left included the labor unions and Basque nationalists while the right had the backing of sixty-three *Requetés* (with military training from Cantabria).[17] In early 1936 the town council had nine Traditionalists, two Republicans, and three Basque nationalists (PNV). The mayor, Adolfo Uribasterra Ibarrondo, was a Carlist. In July 1936 he issued arms to the local Carlists, who were convinced that the Civil Guard would rise in support. However, the response from their Goienkale Barracks was that all fourteen would follow the lead of Bilbao and remain loyal to the

---

14. Jon Irazabal Agirre, *1937 martxoak 31 Durango 31 marzo de 1937* (Abadiño: Gerediaga Elkartea, 2001), 14.
15. *Euzkadi* October 26, 1934. See also Vicente Talón, *Memoria de la guerra en Euskadi*, vol. 1, *De la paz a la guerra* (Barcelona: Plaza & Janés, 1989), 89.
16. Irazabal Agirre, *1937 martxoak 31 Durango 31 de marzo de 1937*, 18.
17. Ibid.

Republic.[18] On August 8, 1936, the town hall removed all Traditionalists, including the mayor.[19] The new council initially consisted of six, then sixteen members. This was followed by the addition of the remaining PNV and Republican Group (Agrupación República) members, leading to a majority of PNV members, with six from the Popular Front (a Spain-wide electoral coalition in 1936 made up of center, left, and nationalist parties).[20] In August and September the Durango Defense Committee (one of whose members was Ángel Gorosarri Gojenola sent to El Puerto on July 17, 1938) and some one hundred supporters of the rising were detained. It was the testimony of some of these supporters that was to condemn members of the local Defense Committee to death or long sentences of imprisonment.

On September 25, 1936 Durango had been bombed, leaving twelve dead. In reprisal, twenty-two Nationalist supporters were executed, with Gorosarri allegedly involved. On March 31 and April 2, 1937, General Mola ordered the Condor Legion to bomb Durango again. This time some 337 people were killed, 71 buildings were destroyed, and some 234 other buildings were partly destroyed.[21] We also learn that Durango "from 1937 . . . enjoyed the . . . cruel renown of being the first defenceless town in Europe to be mercilessly bombed."[22] In this instance Durango was bombed in relays by Ju 52 Junkers and Italian 5-81s that had flown from Soria in Castile and León and was the most terrible bombardment of a civil population in the history of the world up to that time.[23] A Basque newspaper reported the condemnation by the Dean of Canterbury of the fascist outrage on a civilian population.[24] Another atrocity followed against the Basques at the end of April: the much better known bombing of Gernika. This time the story was covered by several important western journalists, including George Steer.[25]

---

18. CPDE/PSM, Sesión del ayuntamiento de Durango, August 8, 1936.
19. CPDE/PSM, Dirección General de la Administración Local del Gobierno Vasco, 18, November 22, 1936.
20. Irazabal Agirre, *1937 martxoak 31 Durango 31 marzo de 1937*, 22 As stated above the Popular Front was a coalition mainly of the political left, led by Manuel Azaña.which was established on 15 January 1936 to fight the general election in Spain the next month.
21. Ibid., 96–108.
22. Thomas, *The Spanish Civil War,* 617.
23. See "Poem X111 Redoble funebre a los escombros de Durango" (Funeral drum roll for the debris of Durango) in R.K. Britton in *César Vallejo* (Eastbourne, 2016) 208-209.
24. See *Euzkadi,* April 11, 1937.
25. George Steer described the bombing in *The Times* and the *New York Times* on April 28, 1937. Christopher Holmes also covered the incident on April 27 in the *Glasgow Herald* and the *Manchester Guardian.*

By the end of April 1937 Durango was in Nationalist hands and Republican supporters of both sexes were imprisoned; some males would eventually find their way to El Puerto sixteen months later. These included Serapio Echeandia Apriz, Ángel Gorosarri, and Isidro Echaburu Irastorza. All were to emphasize the very considerable problems arising out of their imprisonment, both for their families and themselves. As Mirta Núñez Díaz-Balart writes "Thousands of families were left without work, with the head of the family in prison or executed . . . official sources estimated that more than a million and a half persons, were more or less directly affected in some way, for what they called the Spanish prison problem."[26]

The years from 1937 to 1949 brought together political and other types of prisoners from different parts of Spain in El Puerto; a large Basque contingent arrived there in the summer of 1938.[27] (Other Basque prisoners, mainly sent from El Dueso, went to different parts of Andalusia, including Seville, Huelva, Granada, Osuna, and Cazalla de la Sierra).[28] Inmates from different strata and occupations of Basque society found themselves thrown together in El Puerto. This proved to be a highly significant factor in forging the Basque element into a cohesive unit. There was a varying mixture of cellmates. For example, Jabier in his testimony cites the experience of his father Ángel, who was a carpenter, imprisoned with Julián Guimón, who was a prominent doctor from Bilbao.[29]

The testimonies included here also give an indication how the relatives of Basque prisoners managed, in a very hostile climate, with the family breadwinner absent. The account begins with the experiences of a prisoner from near Durango: Serapio Echeandia Apriz was a member of the PNV and the mayor of Zaldibar (Zaldivar) in the 1930s.[30] Zaldibar is a very small town some seven kilometer (four miles) from Durango. Originally an agricultural worker, Serapio also worked as a cabinet maker, and was married with seven children. Although he had a large family, only the eldest son and his wife seemed interested in talking about this

26. Mirta Núñez Díaz-Balart, Manuel Álvaro Dueñas, Francisco Espinosa Maestre, and José María García Márquez, *La gran represión: Los años de plomo del franquismo (1939-1948)* (Barcelona: Flor del Viento, 2009), 177.
27. The largest Basque intakes were between June and August 1938, although there were intakes before and after this date. See SAF/PSM/, Legajos 29268–29341.
28. See the report of the Basque delegation in July 1939 regarding the distribution of Basque captives to Andalusian jails, SAF/PSM/CON/7/39.
29. Interview in Berriz, September 9, 2009.
30. AHPC/PSM Legajo 29277, Causa número 853 de 1937. Emails from María González Gorosarri, November 7 and December 14, 2008. Interview with Asunción Gerediaga Garamendi in Durango, September 8, 2009.
   One footnote disappeared as a result of elimiation of repitition.

aspect of their father's life. Like some other Basque prisoners in El Puerto, Serapio had never participated in the Civil War as a soldier. Captured by the Nationalists in Zaldibar, he was allegedly denounced by relatives who had Nationalist sympathies. Others in Serapio's family shared a similar allegiance and one of his uncles was held in the nearby prison of Urduña. Serapio was arrested twice and on the first occasion was set free, after being initially sent to the prison at Elorrio, a neighboring town. On the second occasion he was sent to Larrinaga prison in Bilbao after his sentence for *"rebelión"* on September 17, 1937.[31] He was moved to the penitentiary of El Puerto on July 1, 1938 at the age of fifty-two. At the time, his prison documents indicated that his date of release was to be July 31, 1967.

His eldest son, Juan María, felt that the treatment received by his father during his internment "was very bad," but that "he did not want to talk much about it." His daughter-in-law, Asunción, substantiated this and stated that Serapio told the family that "the prison of El Puerto was grossly overcrowded where prisoners were treated like animals."[32] Both Juan María and Asunción confirmed the loyalty and solidity of fellow Basques in El Puerto, where many close and lifelong friendships were developed. These comments reinforced the view that there was a Basque cohesiveness in this prison. Serapio developed appendicitis during imprisonment and was operated on not by the prison doctor, but by the Basque doctor, Julián Guimón (who is also mentioned in the letter by Saturnino de Gantxegi in his request for medical supplies to be sent to El Puerto). An interesting point relates to religion in the prison, where there existed *deberes cívicos religiosos* (religious civic duties). This implied not only attending Mass, but attending religious meetings at which the prisoners were compelled to give the fascist salute. There appears to have been some disagreement about the willingness of Serapio to attend these meetings. It is alleged by María González that prison officials claimed to have a signed copy by Serapio indicating he wished to attend this kind of religious meeting. However, according to María, he strongly maintained that he did not sign anything volunteering for *deberes cívicos religiosos* and was not interested in religious provision as offered by the prison authorities.[33] This is an interesting aspect that directly contradicts earlier examples in which devout Catholic Basque prisoners in El Puerto had criticized the penal authorities for insufficient pastoral care.

31. Email from María González, December 14, 2008.
32. Interview with Asunción Gerediaga Garamendi in Durango, September 8, 2009.
33. As former mayor of Zaldibar and an active member of the PNV, this stance is quite feasible.

Serapio's son was of the view that his family thought visits were out of the question. "We never even considered it since it was too far away and too expensive." There was no communication with his family and, sadly, when he returned, Serapio had even forgotten the name of his youngest son, since he had never seen him. This provides a poignant example of the disruption and alienation families suffered as a result of the imprisonment of the family breadwinners. During his imprisonment the whole weight of supporting the family was borne by his wife, supported by the children where possible. Survival was made a little easier by the family having access to a few chickens, potatoes, milk, and corn. According to the family, the local Nationalists took the harvests as of right, but family members were allowed to remain where they were. Juan María maintains: "life was very harsh during the time of the imprisonment of our father. It was also very sad." Corruption and black market dealings were widespread. Asunción stated that "the children had to work on the smallholding and as a result they often could not take advantage of the limited schooling opportunities available to them. There was a tightly knit supportive small community as there were no *Falangistas* among them, but things were very different in the town of Durango."[34]

Although some form of Auxilio Social (state welfare) was available in Durango, there also seems to have been a reluctance to pay out to families of known political opponents of the Nationalists. Smaller areas like Zaldibar fared worse. The Auxilio Social was a Falange institution, originally named Auxilio de Invierno (winter welfare), which was founded by Mercedes Sanz Bachiller, the widow of Onésimo Redondo, the cofounder of JONS (Juntas de Ofensiva Nacionalista Sindicalista, Unions of the National-Syndicalist Offensive) in Valladolid.[35]

On his death, his wife became a bitter rival of Pilar Primo de Rivera for prominence in the Falange Party. Changing its name to Auxilio Social in order not to confuse it with a similar body in Nazi Germany, it served in theory as the state social welfare service. Richards considers that this "this corrupt Falange-inspired charity was a very poor substitute for real state provision. In rural Murcia, during the late spring of 1942, Auxilio's supplies were virtually exhausted."[36] Dishonesty, political antipathy, lack of supplies, and poor organization would explain the difference in treat-

34.
35. See José Juis Rodríguez Jiménez, *Historia de Falange Española de las JONS* (Madrid: Alianza Editorial, 2000).
36. Richards, *A Time of Silence*, 164. See also Ángela Cenarro, *La sonrisa de la Falange: Auxilio Social en la Guerra Civil y en la posguerra* (Barcelona: Crítica, 2005).

ment experienced by families of prisoners in Durango and Berriz: several relatives of prisoners made this point very forcibly.

Asunción thought that at that time mobility was greatly restricted and it was impossible to leave their area without prior permission. In the case of the church, their local priest "neither helped nor hindered the family." The necessity of obtaining a safe conduct pass regulated all movement and ensured that the authorities knew the whereabouts of all released prisoners. It was clearly a very restricted society controlled by fear and uncertainty.

In Serapio's absence, several of his possessions had been confiscated under the Political Responsibilities legislation of 1939, which allowed economic penalties to be exacted by fines and expropriations on prisoners and their families. Before his release from prison on *libertad condicional* on July 23, 1941, his family had to pay a final instalment on fines of about 3,000 pesetas. According to Asunción, Serapio had considerable trouble in retrieving his possessions before leaving prison.

The first observation that he made on returning home was to comment on the thinness of his cows. Neighbors in Zaldibar treated him well, but the situation continued to be quite different in Durango, where "there was a great hostility that lasted forty years." Serapio found great difficulty in obtaining employment although his situation was partly mitigated as he had a smallholding. Finances were extremely difficult as Republican money was unusable and some people simply burned it. This total devaluation of Republican currency deprived many of spending power, reducing them to near penury. Black market dealings continued to be rife; where possible, people took to growing tobacco to raise income for their families.

The second testimony of prisoners' relatives from the Durango area was that of Jabier Gorosarri, son of Ángel Gorosarri Gojenola originally a carpenter, he was also a prominent member of the local Defense Committee.[37] This was controlled by the PNV on the outbreak of war; one of his colleagues on the Committee, Juan Mari Eskubi, was executed by the Nationalists in October 1938. As noted above, after the first bombing of Durango on September 25, 1936, some twenty-two supporters of the uprising were executed in the local cemetery in reprisal.[38] It appears that not all of them were Nationalist sympathizers: according to María González, one was reputedly a drunk who had been locked up for making a nuisance

---

37. AHPC/PSM, Legajo 29273, Causa número 111523.
38. Irazabal Agirre, *1937 martxoak 31 Durango 31 marzo de 1937*, 28.

of himself the previous night.[39] The story was that the perpetrators were some passing militiamen from Asturias, although allegedly both Eskubi and Gorosarri tried to dissuade them.

There indeed seems to have been a problem with some militia from Asturias. José Manuel Martínez Bande wrote that "The number of Asturian battalions in Bizkaia is now more than ten, and they are continually involved in pillage. When they passed through Abadiño [also in the Durango area] they shot the parish priest, one municipal councilman of the PNV, and two more of the ANV [Acción Nacionalista Vasca, Basque Nationalist Action, another Basque nationalist party]. They stole cattle from the farms as they passed."[40] Clearly the coordination of the northern Republican army was not as effective as that of their Nationalist opponents. Beevor writes about the lack of centralization in the north:

> The councils of Asturias and Santander still reflected the union-based organization which followed the rising, while the Basques regarded themselves as autonomous allies of the Republic. Although Basque volunteer units had fought at Oviedo, and Asturian and Santanderino militia helped in Vizcaya, the northern regions were not united, except in their objection to a centralized Republican command.[41]

The story in Durango was that militia from another part of Spain were guilty of certain actions that would not have been perpetrated by local people. This does appear to have been a very common experience during the Spanish Civil War. Allegedly, some of the executed Nationalist supporters in Durango on the night of September 25, 1936 were *Requetés* and Carlists who supposedly had undergone some training in Altsasu, Navarre, in 1934, in which Count Ciano (son-in-law of Mussolini) participated.

Jabier Gorosarri displayed quite a large scar on his shoulder on meeting him in Berriz.[42] A casualty of the Spanish Civil War at the age of seven, he maintained that he had been accidentally shot by *milicianos*. This was an indication of how dangerous life was at that time for young children. Arrested after the fall of Santander in September 1937, his father Ángel was sentenced on April 23, 1938, and convicted of *rebelión* at the age of

39. Email from María González, August 15, 2008.
40. José Manuel Martínez Bande, *El final del frente norte* (Madrid: San Martín, 1972), 135.
41. Beevor, *The Battle for Spain*, 223.
42. Interview in Berriz with Jabier Gorosarri, reported in *Deia*, September 9, 2009.

twenty-three with thirty years servitude.[43] He was admitted to El Puerto on July 17, 1938, with a projected date of release of February 3, 1968.

Until Ángel wrote to his family from the El Puerto penitentiary, they had no idea where he was or whether he was still alive and had not known for nine months. His trial notes stated that, as a member of the PNV, he played a prominent role in public order as a secretary of the local Defense Committee; that he denied safe conduct and access to Nationalist prisoners by their families; that he detained a priest from a nearby locality; and that he was involved in the seizure of goods belonging to Don Felipe Aguirre, who was shot by "reds" in a local cemetery.[44]

Ángel was released from prison early on November 16, 1940 on *libertad condicional*. His son, Jabier, says that Ángel would not say much about his experiences, although he did talk about his cellmates, especially Dr. Julián Guimón and another prisoner named Ortiz from Zarautz (although he was unsure of his second surname). Ángel told his son a certain amount about other inmates and his surprise at the composition of the intake from different parts of Spain, with a wide diversity of levels of education. This confirms the views expressed earlier by the two reports in 1939 and 1940 concerning Basque prisoners.[45] There were six prisoners to a cell that had accommodated two around 1935. Surprisingly, he also alleged that there were Russian inmates in El Puerto between 1940 and 1943. This is confirmed by the prisoner document from the Cádiz archives (figure 3.1) that reveals the presence of at least eleven Russians.

Communications within the prison were not always easy for prisoners and Jabier remembers that his father told him that "one particular Basque commander was renowned for using pigeons to carry cigarettes and messages to cells on different floors."

During the war, Ángel's wife and children moved to France (with a safe conduct certificate), where they remained until 1938. During the stay in France the evacuees tried to live a normal life. For example, Jabier displayed an impressive certificate of his first Communion in 1938, which he has kept to this day. However, exiles from the Basque Country (and later Catalonia) faced a dilemma whenever the French border was opened and then closed. Closed on August 8, 1937, the French opened the border on March 17, 1938, which was then closed on June 13, 1938. Alicia Alted writes "On January 15, 1939 after the fall of Tarragona, there began a massive exile whose heartrending march all took place on the road to

43. AHPC/PSM, Legajo 29273, Expediente 34.
44. AHPC/PSM, Legajo 29276.
45. See SAF/PSM/CON/7/39, SAF/PSM/ANON/3/40.

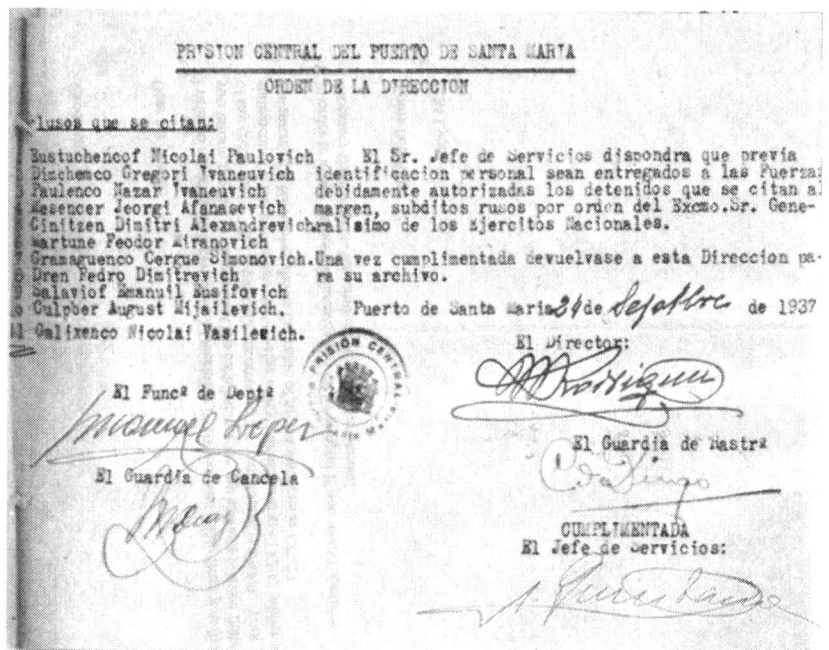

Figure 3.1

France."[46] During late spring of 1938, Ángel's family had to decide whether to return home to Durango, already in Nationalist hands, or go to Catalonia, still controlled by the Republic. They returned to Durango, where
they were mortified to find that their house was occupied and that their
furniture had been either sold or stolen. This dilemma faced other Basque
families in which the breadwinner was imprisoned. Ángel's family went
to live with his parents in their smallholding. On release on November 16,
1940 with a *certificado de libertad* from El Puerto, Ángel returned home
with quite severe lung-related problems.

This kind of illness was an unfortunate legacy that afflicted prisoners
released from El Puerto, affected their later quality of life, and often made
employment more difficult. Work in Durango was impossible to obtain
and Ángel went to Bilbao to work as an orderly in the private hospital of
Dr. Guimón, his El Puerto cellmate. He remained there for fifteen months.
He never again obtained employment in the railroad company where he
had worked before the war. An unforeseen benefit for Ángel and his fam-

---

46. Alicia Alted, *La voz de los vencidos: el exilio republicano de 1939* (Madrid: Aguilar,
    2005), 42. Note: MUME, the Museu Memorial d'Exili-Museo Memorial del Exilio
    established at La Jonquera, Catalonia, in 2007 contains many photographs and details
    of Spanish refugees marching to France.

ily was that before the war he had been a carpentry teacher with pupils whose parents were Falangists. As a result, Ángel's children received free training classes at a time when education was made difficult for the children of defeated Republicans. The children also had friends who were Falange supporters, but their parents were hostile to Ángel and his wife. The subject of problems of everyday subsistence for released prisoners was discussed and once again the role of the Auxilio Social emerged. Jabier confirmed its existence in Durango at this time, and he also thought that it operated in the town, but not in the small villages around. Eventually Ángel obtained employment at a firm in Abadiño, Puska Pneumatic, not an exclusive local organization, but one with international contacts. This made previous political dealings not quite as important as they might have been where a sole Durango employer was concerned. He also secretly resumed work as a carpenter nearby.His son also remembers Ángel reporting to the Civil Guard every Sunday for some time.

The third testimony of relatives of prisoners from Durango and the surrounding district was obtained as result of an interview that took place in Berriz with Yolanda Echaburu Alzaa, daughter of Isidro Echaburu.[47] Yolanda said that her father had been sentenced to death twice: once after an alleged involvement in an explosives case in 1933 and again during the Spanish Civil War. Some prison records showed that Isidro was aged twenty-four, but Yolanda argued that he was twelve years older and single at the outbreak of the war. (This was not the first time that relatives have argued that details in the prison files were incorrect). Before the war Isidro used to work in an industrial factory as a machine operator.

On the outbreak of hostilities, Isidro joined the Sukarrieta Battalion, a Basque nationalist unit, in which he became a lieutenant and after seeing action, was subsequently captured at Santoña. Initially imprisoned for thirty years for *adhesión a la rebelión* in El Dueso, Santoña on September 17, 1937, he was transferred to El Puerto penitentiary on August 6, 1938 with a projected date of release on August 24, 1967.[48]

His daughter Yolanda confirms that Isidro found conditions in El Puerto "horrific, full of insects (including a large number of mosquitoes), where prisoners were hungry all the time." Initially, Isidro was imprisoned in a large room with no facilities. This could well have been one of the converted chapels not unlike the drawing by an anonymous Basque prisoner showing the conversion of the chapel of *Nuestra Señora* to prison

---

47. AHPC/PSM, Legajo 29273, Causa número 89. Interview in Berriz, September 9, 2009 with Yolanda Echaburu Alzaa.
48. AHPC/PSM, Legajo 29273.

cell Brigada VI (see chapter 2). He was then moved to a cell that housed six prisoners. Isidro received no visits.[49] Here again, prisoners had to sing *Cara al Sol*. Isidro told his daughter that, in his view, Basque prisoners tended on the whole to be better treated than many of the other prisoners because "Basques were men of their word and gained more respect from the guards. " This is clearly a value judgment, but reports and comments from other Basque prisoners tend to reinforce the notion that their sense of Basque unity was certainly a factor when dealing with the prison authorities. Yolanda remembers that her father believed that prisoners were treated worse at Burgos, where some of them had come "from Larrinaga prison in Bilbao before arriving at El Puerto."

Larrinaga was part of the prison chain leading to El Puerto, serving as a transit prison for Basque prisoners such as Serapio Echeandi Artiz and Pablo Gamboa Larrondo, who were to end up in El Puerto. It had a bad reputation for executions; Clark writes that "In the middle of November [1937], many of the *gudari* officers were moved to Larrinaga . . . in June 1938 . . . 1,014 of [its] 2,437 prisoners were condemned to death."[50] Joxemari Mendizabal considers that "while the majority of the 224 executions were by shooting between December 1937 and July 1938, 21 were by *garrote vi*".[51]

Isidro did not arrive at El Puerto until August 1938, by which time some 60 percent of executions had already taken place; the identities of those shot in this prison between 1936 and 1940 have not revealed any Basques to date. That is not to say that the Franco regime was any more merciful to Basque prisoners than captives from other parts of Spain; it might simply mean that the majority of executions were carried out at the initial feeder prisons like El Dueso, Santoña (Cantabria) and Larrinaga (Bilbao) before Basque prisoners were moved to prisons in Andalusia.

Isidro was allowed one letter home a year, which was heavily censored as "bits were crossed out." This is not surprising: the two postcards shown in Chapter 2 indicate the typical messages that were allowed to be sent. During the imprisonment of Isidro once again the wife had to support the family. There were five brothers and sisters and his mother worked in a hotel. Hunger was widespread and life was very hard. However, it appears that in a small town like Berriz, the majority of neighbors were helpful to his family, regardless of their political persuasion. There were Carlist and Fascist families involved; Yolanda made the observation that her father

---

49. Ibid.
50. Clark, *The Basques: The Franco Years and Beyond*, 84.
51. Mendizabal, *Gudaris y rehenes de Franco (1936–1943)*, 273.

intimated that the size of the neighborhood had been the crucial factor. Other testimonies of relatives of prisoners appear to confirm that this indeed was the experience of other prisoners.

Yolanda reiterated the fears expressed earlier by the relatives of Serapio concerning the restrictions on speaking Euskara outside the family. In the matter of fines levied in her area, Yolanda remembers that the local practice was a fine of around 100 pesetas (or more) or even imprisonment. She maintained that, as some former Republican prisoners in Berriz received about 11.75 pesetas a week at this time, this was an impossible penalty to meet. This clearly placed greatly increased pressures on Basque families and was part of the climate of alienation encouraged by Franco.

Isidro was released from the penitentiary of El Puerto on August 28, 1940 on *libertad condicional* (after the usual clearance from the Mayor, Falange head, and the Civil Guard commander of Durango). On his release Isidro married a much younger woman. His daughter Yolanda says that "at this time there was a local scarcity of unmarried men and a large number of unmarried women." After a while her father worked in a number of agricultural factories, for derisory payment. There was much exploitation of released prisoners, and dealings in the black market were rife. Yolanda considers that many people were *"franquistas falsas"* (false Francoists) in order to survive; here again, the Civil Guard and Francoists helped themselves to goods without payment. For example, they did not pay for jewelry. This practice seems to have been the experience of other Basque families whose relatives had been Republican prisoners. Richards confirms this situation: "In practice, Falangists were *given carte* blanche to go to family dwellings and make off with whatever they pleased. Cruelty was at once institutional and capricious." [52]

At school after the cessation of hostilities, Yolanda recalls that "while the nuns simply regarded the children of released Republican prisoners as *rojos* [reds], the attitude of the children was totally different." Around the period of 1945–55 Yolanda remembers the boys at school exchanging the usual name-calling and insults that included "Reds" and "Francoists." She felt that this had no real meaning in that it was simply boys behaving as normal, reflecting the group dynamics of young people in that area at that particular time. In my view, the reception of released ex-Republican prisoners during and after 1942 into the Basque communities was extremely variable in that there seems to have been a direct correlation with the size

---

52. Richards, *A Time of Silence*, 52.

of the neighborhood, the attitude of the grandparents and parents, and the political complexion of the town. For example, Durango had a large Nationalist/Traditionalist element and an unrelenting hostility to those who had supported the Republic. Yolanda also remembers her father being involved in some kind of demonstrations in Durango after the Civil Guard had killed three people in the early 1950s. Isidro received *libertad definitiva* on October 2, 1945.

The fourth testimony of relatives from Durango and the nearby area concerned Vicente Pujana Galíndez from Otxandio; his story was provided by Miren Pujana Bolibar, his daughter.[53] Vicente was a member of the UGT labor union, which he joined in Eibar in 1918. As a socialist, he experienced problems from nearby Durango where there was a strong Carlist presence at this time. Unrest had caused the deaths of three railroad workers and the Durango authorities suspended the local fiestas of San Fausto.[54] Jon Irazabal Agirre, a local historian of Durango, contends that as a result of the involvement of Vicente in the railroad union, he did not work for the local town hall until later.[55]

In 1936 Vicente subsequently obtained another job with the town hall in Durango; in 1937 he volunteered to serve in the Rusia Battalion, affiliated to the JSU, in which he served as a private soldier. Like so many other Basque prisoners in El Puerto, Vicente was captured after the fall of Santander on September 1, 1937. His daughter Miren strongly felt that the *gudaris* were betrayed by Franco, given his non-observance of the conditions of the Pact of Santoña made by the Italians. This obviously continues to be a great source of bitterness among some Basques.

Condemned for *rebelión militar* and sentenced to thirty years' imprisonment, Vicente started prison life at El Dueso and was transferred to El Puerto on August 11, 1938. His daughter Miren remembers that her father told her that "Life was very hard for me. I was so far from my family, without the possibility of receiving clothes or food, always very hungry, and in a constant state of fear. The other prisoners helped one another in order to survive." One of the most poignant memories of prison life specifically related to her father's recollection concerning the hours of daybreak each day. This was filled with suspense, since all prisoners knew that guards would come to the cells at that hour, sometimes to collect individual prisoners for execution. The prisoners would also know how

53. AHPC/PSM, Legajo 29359, Expediente 28. Emails from Miren Pujana Bolibar, July 10, 2009, March 3, 2010, April 1, 2010, and April 7, 2010.
54. *Euzkadi*, October 26, 1934.
55. Irazabal Agirre, *1937 martxoak 31 Durango 31 de marzo*, 16.

many steps had to be taken to reach their individual cells, and they used to make a practice of counting the number of steps of the guards as they walked along the corridors. An extract from the diary of a Basque inmate, Ramón de Galarza, in Larrinaga prison, follows a similar theme. In this case the steps of the guards along the corridors ended at the cell of one prisoner who never made the transfer to El Puerto:

¡Señor! ¡Señor!
¿Por qué me das esa dicha de ser de los elegidos?
¡Podría haber muerto como he vivido!
¡Así morimos los llamados rojos!
¡Fui leal a la República y al juramento que hice a ella,
a mis ideales, a mi honor!

Lord! Lor!
Why give me that good fortune to be one of the chosen?
I could have died as I had lived!
This way, we'll die as reds!
I was loyal to the Republic and to the oath I swore to it,
to my ideals, to my honor!.[56]

According to Miren, her father Vicente told her that "some support came from the nuns in the infirmary and the kitchen, and the Mother Superior complained to the director of the prison that inmates were dying of hunger."[57] One of Vicente's companions did die of hunger around this time. His daughter remembers being told that, "fortunately I was in a cell with several important members of the PNV who had access to money and food; I was thus able to improve my diet." Vicente was not particularly keen to go to Mass, which was obligatory; he was one who preferred to stay where he was and clean his cell.

Miren recalls that during the imprisonment of her father, the care of his family was shared by his relatives: his son lived with an aunt and the rest lived with a grandmother. Unfortunately, the bureaucracy of Franco's prisons added to the stress of the prisoners. For example, in the case of Vicente, there appeared to be some confusion relating to his eventual release; his daughter particularly remembers that her father told her that the prison secretariat continually returned his release papers to the bottom of

---

56. Mendizabal, *Gudaris y rehenes de Franco (1936–1943)*, 232. Extract from Ramón de Galarza, *Diario de un gudari condenado a muerte* (San Sebastián, 1977).
57. Email from Miren Pujana Bolibar, March 3, 2010.

the pile. Eventually Vicente was released from El Puerto on November 26, 1942, based on *libertad condicional provisional sin destierro* (provisional conditional release without leaving the country) although Vicente was not able to remain in Durango. He went to live in Bilbao, with permission from the authorities. For the first few years he had to report to the police every day and then weekly on Sundays. He knew at all times that if he transgressed, he would be sent back to prison. If he wished to leave the town for any reason, he had first to seek the permission of the authorities. Failure to do so would involve a loss of liberty. Miren mentions that her father married her mother in 1947and she was born in 1949.

Vicente had great difficulty in obtaining a job on his release, eventually having to work long hours for little pay. His daughter remembers that a climate of great exploitation of prisoners existed and she maintains that in some jobs her father was only paid "a miserly amount." When Vicente eventually retired, he did so in greatly reduced economic circumstances. This applied to many other released Republican prisoners: in many cases these former prisoners were to remain in penury for the rest of their lives.

As was the case with other Basque ex-prisoners, their reception on release differed and Miren remembers that her father told her he faced a mixed reaction. Some neighbors were quite reasonable but others who went regularly to church and supported the Nationalists were unremittingly hostile. "We were Reds and it would have been better if we had all been killed." Miren concludes her testimony rather sadly by adding that "she would have liked to have contacted an old former Basque soldier aged ninety regarding these matters, as he knew much of the history and background. But sadly he died in the previous March." This was the case with two other families, thereby losing invaluable primary sources.

The fifth testimony of relatives from Durango and the nearby area concerned Santiago Arrondo Elgea from Abadiño. This was provided by his son, José Luis Arrondo Uriarte.[58] His father's story is of particular interest in that Santiago seems to have been able to survive in a variety of changed circumstances. Originally sentenced to death, his sentence was commuted to thirty years for *rebelión militar*. He survived the prison regime of Larrinaga and was then transferred to El Dueso, where many of his companions were shot; José Luis later spent over four years in El Puerto, where he was admitted on August 11, 1938 and freed on October 7, 1942. Here he managed to survive better than most by helping the priest, thereby greatly enhancing his food supply.

---

58. AHPC/PSM, Legajo 29357; Letters from José Luis Arrondo Uriate, August 18, 2009 and March 15, 2010.

Before the war he was a mechanic in the Durango firm of Hijos de Mendizabal; this previous occupation proved to be of invaluable help after the war. Santiago was also implicated in some form in local Basque politics and during the war he served as a sergeant in the supply section of the Kirikiño Battalion. His son José Luis remembers that "my mother worked hard to raise the question of mediation on behalf of my father in connection with his death penalty with the lawyer Carmelo Bengoa [from Durango], who was a relative of Esteban Bilbao, then president of the Cortes [the Spanish parliament]." Following this intervention he was transferred to El Puerto.

Santiago found the conditions in El Dueso from 1938 and 1940 terrible, and the inmates could not leave their cells. Again, the most frequent time that they heard the doors open was early in the morning when prisoners were taken out to be shot. While in El Puerto, Santiago counted many people who collapsed with hunger in the prison courtyard since their food consisted of "boiled cabbage stalks." In his case, there could be at least four prisoners to a cell during this period, all of whom were Basques. Apart from Santiago, there was José Tirado from Barakaldo and Lucio Antxia from Etxano, who died in the arms of Santiago in the cell. As mentioned earlier, his son recalls that "after some time my father discovered a way to survive in El Puerto: he became an altar server for the priest. He helped the priest to celebrate Mass and thereby increased his survival status in the prison. This resulted in him becoming well regarded by the nuns of the convent. They used to give him some tobacco and food that he took to the cell to share with his fellow prisoners."

During the absence of his father, the only person who sustained the family was his mother. In order to do this she was compelled to do a variety of jobs. For example she used to work in a shoe factory, was also a daytime agricultural worker, and on Sundays and festivals she used to serve in a cafeteria. Moreover, in order that the family could eat, she had to buy other cooking utensils and crockery as they had all been stolen during the war.

Santiago was released from El Puerto on December 4, 1942 and returned to his home. He was then visited by the manager of the factory of the Hijos de Mendizabal who offered him the same job as he had before the war. This was quite unusual as many ex-prisoners were not able to return to their previous place of work in Durango due to the considerable hostility that existed there. José Luis observes that, "my father was a good person and well liked in the neighborhood where we lived." He concludes his testimony with one other anecdote from the factory: "When he had been working about a month in the factory, on his return, the firm's doctor visited him and asked who had given him permission to work at the factory again. You can imagine the response. My father would have been aware that the doctor was a Francoist." The inference here was that, as a former prisoner who fought against Franco, he should not have been offered work. José Luis concludes with the statement that, "the authorities continued to watch my father and made life difficult for him. He had to present himself every Sunday at the barracks of the Civil Guard and this lasted for several more years."

The first testimony from Bilbao and the surrounding area was Martín Aurrekoetxea Unzueta from Loiu, who was the eldest of nine children, with five boys and four girls in the family.[59] His nephew Martín wrote about the impact of the war on his extended family that also included his father Roke, who volunteered to serve in the Sabino Arana Battalion. As in many Basque families at that time there were strong religious elements and one of the daughters of the family was to become a nun in the Madres Irlandesas Order (Congregation of Jesus). In July 1936 Martín, the uncle, was married and lived in his smallholding with his wife, two daughters, and mother. Apart from his farming, he also worked as a longshoreman on a part-time basis at the port of Bilbao. He belonged to the PNV and represented this party as a councilman in Loiu, but did not enroll in the Basque Army.

The Nationalists took Loiu on June 16, 1937 and Martín was arrested on June 31. He was found guilty of *rebelión*, and condemned to serve twelve years and one day as opposed to the usual thirty years for Basque soldiers. His history of incarceration was somewhat different from the majority of Basque prisoners since he reached El Puerto via a prison ship. Initially imprisoned in the Larrinaga, he was transferred to the *Upo Mendi*, a grossly overcrowded prison ship that then left Bilbao with the intention of integrating prisoners in the notorious concentration camp of the Isla de San Simón (Pontevedra, Galicia). It eventually anchored off Vigo, from where Martín was transferred, via the notorious cattle wagons, to El Puerto via Seville. Several other witnesses have complained about the transportation that their imprisoned relatives had to suffer, stating that they were transported in cattle trucks and treated as livestock.

Martín did not survive incarceration. His nephew says that the family always believed that his uncle died in El Puerto, but further investigation

---

59. Emails from Martín Aurrekoetxea, October 4, 16, and 18, 2009.

indicates that he died on August 8, 1939 in Huelva prison.[60] The unhappiness caused by this confusion was further compounded by "an unsolicited visit of several cousins, dressed in Carlist uniforms. The visit was ostensibly to express condolences and assure the family that Mass had been said for his uncle." This was considered to be a provocative and humiliating act by the family. Martín, his nephew, gives this as an example of the way he felt that families of Basque prisoners were treated and writes that, "the graves of the defeated have left a living testimony of that barbarity."

During the imprisonment of Martín Aurrekoetxea Unzueta, his family lacked the presence of an adult male on the smallholding. Life was austere and the death of the head of the family marked an irreplaceable gap in the Basque agricultural network. Consequently, one of his married brothers moved in with his family until the younger brother Roke returned in 1943. Roke was a *gudari* in the PNV's Sabino Arana Battalion and had been captured and was compelled to fight on the Nationalist side; it was not uncommon for Republican prisoners to be conscripted from the concentration camps. (It should be mentioned that both sides widely used this form of boosting recruitment). There they were subject to special supervision and Martín says that he knew of cases in which "several Basque forcible conscripts were shot for not performing with sufficient courage."[61] He remarks somewhat bitterly that, "Those fallen for God and Spain were honored with plaques and monuments in the church and yearly funeral thanksgiving ceremonies. As a child, I remember, very well, how they took us from school to the Town Hall where they heard Mass and then bestowed the fallen Francoist Nationalist soldiers with crowns of laurels."[62] I am unsure whether this would have included the names of captured/pressed men from the Basque Country who supported the Republic..

The second testimony from this area concerned León Arruza Bilbao from Mungia, provided by his son Joseba Arruza Goitia.[63] León worked in a bank, the Banco de Crédito de la Unión Minera. Unusually, León was neither a soldier in the Basque army nor was he involved in local politics. He was, however, a sympathizer of Basque nationalism and played for a soccer team known as Irrintzi, based in la Plaza Barria in Bilbao. Before the Civil War León he lived in Bilbao and studied in the School of Business, located in the present-day Plaza de Unamuno.

---

60. AHPC/PPH, Signatura 07510/062. Emails from the director of the Provincial Historical Archive of Huelva, October 16 and 18, 2009, and April 5, 2010.
61. Email from Martín Aurroetxea, October 16, 2009.
62. Email from Martín Aurrekoetxea, October 18, 2009.
63. Emails from Joseba Arruza Goitia, October 5 and 8, 2009.

His son Joseba argues that León was a genuine liberal, but neverthe-less found himself as yet another Basque prisoner in El Puerto. Joseba remembers that his father "never communicated to his family his resent-ment or the hardships of imprisonment." However, among friends it was known that in the prison of El Puerto the inmates suffered from subhu-man overcrowded conditions, with the constant fear of execution hang-ing over them. His son alleges that his father told him that many of the prisoners suffered psychological damage as a result of the uncertainties facing them, with sometimes four or five prisoners executed at regular intervals. In addition, León suffered severe stomach problems as a result of imprisonment, which made it impossible for him to undertake regular employment on his release.

During León's imprisonment his family managed with great difficulty. Under the Law of Political Responsibilities their house in Bilbao was con-fiscated as was their property in Mungia. Joseba spent a year living with his brothers in exile and then another year living with his grandmother, where he slept in a barn. Economic conditions were dire. Joseba says: "If it had not been for my grandmother we might not have survived." This provides yet another example of the key role grandparents often played in supporting the family when the father was imprisoned.

After two years of protesting and complaining, his mother was finally allowed to open a small store in her house in Mungia, but life was still made very difficult for them by the authorities. Joseba remembers there were various occasions when the sale of specific items was prohibited. Various fines were imposed on the family that they could not afford. The net result was that their store simply had to close on several occasions. This is yet another indication of what Richards describes as "the day-to-day economic violence which was inflicted upon the defeated in the 1940s."[64] He cites as an example the action of the Nationalist authorities who confiscated a sewing machine, thereby depriving a household of the main way of providing basic economic sustenance.

After León was released, his neighbors proved not to be hostile and treated him correctly. He continued to live in Mungia. Unfortunately, his medical condition had deteriorated and he had to follow a rigorous health regime. Sadly, León was not the same man as he had been before impris-onment. This was not uncommon with released prisoners.

---

64. Richards, *A Time of Silence*, 52.

A third testimony from the Bilbao area concerned Diego Pablo Gamboa Larrondo from Loiu;[65] this was provided by a relative of his daughter María Angeles, Joseba Andoni Bikandi Arana. This case was rather different from others cited as he underwent forced labor in Dos Hermanos (Seville). A PNV councilman in Loiu, he was denounced by a neighbor, Modesto Asla, and then imprisoned at Larrinaga aged forty-six. Transferred to the *Upo Mendi* prison ship and originally bound for the camp on the Isla de San Simón, he was then moved to the prison of Dos Hermanas, finally arriving at El Puerto. Two other Basque prisoners were released at the same time: Juan Cruz Orozco from the Berreteaga district of the Larrondo neighborhood in Loiu and an unnamed prisoner from the Fartuntenes . Both these prisoners died after a short while as a result of the injuries that they had on leaving El Puerto.

During the imprisonment of Diego, as was usual, the weight of maintaining the family fell on Alejandra, his wife. Misfortune not only befell inside the prison but often on their families outside. Antonio, the oldest son unfortunately died in a traffic accident at the age of fifteen, while his second son, Benito, was conscripted at the age of eighteen and had to serve for six years. This meant that five children had to be maintained, once again with help of relatives.

After his release, Diego had to work the smallholding. As with all released prisoners he had to report to Civil Guard, which he did at 12:00 noon every Sunday, presenting himself for six months at the Civil Guard barracks in neighboring Asua, Erandio. His full integration into society by 1979 appears to have been somewhat easier than some other Basque prisoners; the PNV local authority in Loiu recognized his service shortly before his death at the age of eighty-nine on June 11 of the same year.

The fourth testimony of relatives in the Bilbao area concerned Jesús Mendibil Manrique from Urduña—an enclave of Bizkaia within Araba—and was provided by his son Rafa Mendibil Sobrón.[66] Jesús worked on the railroads, Vías y Obras de los Ferrocariles del Norte (which later became RENFE). On the outbreak of war in 1936 he joined the PNV's Araba Battalion, Second Company Aiala, in which he served as a lieutenant (this battalion was mainly formed by people from Aiara (Ayala), Laudio (Llodio), Orozko, Amurrio, and Urduña). On his capture in September 1937, he was charged with *adhesión a la rebelión* and sentenced to twenty years and one day. Initially incarcerated in El Dueso (Santoña), Jesús was released from El Puerto in July 1940.

---

65. Email from Joseba Andoni Bikandi Arana, October 5, 2009.
66. Emails from Rafa Mendibil Sobrón, October 3 and 30, 2009.

During the imprisonment of his father, his son Rafa says that, "life was extremely difficult . . . a wife without work and two children, the oldest was three-years-old and the second born at the start of the war. The family had to split up in order to survive." The mother and the youngest daughter went to live with the maternal grandparents while the oldest went to live with the paternal grandparents. This action, allied to the fact that the families had agricultural connections, made life possible.

On release from prison, Jesús was unable to obtain his former post with the railroad and could only obtain temporary jobs such as work in a gypsum plant, a stone quarry, and in construction. Several years passed before he was able to obtain a permanent post as a security guard in a company. He was able to remain in his home town of Urduña, where the majority of his neighbors were Basque nationalists. There were, however, two hostile incidents that Rafa can still remember. One involved his father, Jesús, walking out with his wife and two daughters and being approached by several men. The threats were of such a magnitude that he had to return home with his family. On another occasion he had to make a rapid exit from the back door of a bar owing to the entrance of several men who had arrived with the sole intention of attacking him. These are examples that indicate that, after the war, former Republican prisoners were not necessarily completely safe in their own smaller towns.

The case of Jenaro Ruiz de Aguirre is very different from any of the others in that not only have I been able to obtain far more information about him, but also he came from Vitoria-Gasteiz in Araba.[67] However, at the time of his involvement in the war he was living in Amorebieta on the outskirts of Bilbao. The considerable information provided by his granddaughter, Irantzu Bustinza, and his daughter Carmen Ruiz de Aguirre Mintegui, illustrates very clearly the life of a Basque prisoner in the penitentiary of El Puerto before, during, and after his imprisonment.[68]

Jenaro had a background as a typographer. He started work with the printer Domingo Sar at the age of twelve, eventually moving to Amorebieta when he was over thirty-years-old and did not speak a word of Basque; he started to learn the language before the war (his first wife had unfortunately died in 1932). During this time, Jenaro was affiliated to the PNV and volunteered for the Basque Army, after having lost two months of sal-

---

67. AHPC/PSM, Legajo 29298. Emails from Irantzu Bustinza, October 4 and 21; November 8, 15, and 29, 2009; January 24, March 5, and April 1, 2010. Copy of El Puerto prison diary by Jenaro Ruiz de Aguirre Ariz, November 24, 2009, from Irantzu Bustinza, his granddaughter.
68. Email from Irantzu Bustinza, November 8, 2009.

ary with his printing firm beforehand as a result of the advance of Franco's forces. On joining the army, he became a second lieutenant in the Quartermaster Corps and later became a full lieutenant in the Alkartzeak Battalion, affiliated to the PNV, commanded by Alfredo Irazabal and based in Amorebieta. On surrendering to the Italians on the beach of Santoña, he was transferred to El Dueso on September 10, 1937. On December 4, 1937 he was found guilty of *rebelión militar* and sentenced to thirty years' imprisonment, but he was then released on *libertad condicional* from El Puerto on August 17, 1940.

Jenaro kept a diary while in the prisons of El Dueso and El Puerto, which was concealed for over seventy years.[69] The cover is dated 1938 and the diary, which was used for both prisons, carries the slogans "*Arriba España*" and "*Viva Franco.*" It is dedicated to "The soldier heroes of Spain . . . martyrs of this crusade giving their hearts to God." This was clearly a diary meant for a Nationalist soldier, and might explain its non-confiscation by prison guards. The question of how Jenaro was successfully able to maintain and conceal such a diary from the attentions of the prison guards in El Dueso and El Puerto is answered by his granddaughter Irantzu. She explains that, "the first page of that diary carried the words that looked like '*Deut*' . . . there was a first page, largely damaged, which appeared to be written in German . . . This language was purposely used because the learning of German was particularly valued at this time." Germany was a major ally of Franco and Jenaro was also aware of the limited education of the prison guards, who were easily persuaded by this ruse.

The first note in the diary dates from September 10, 1937, the day Jenaro arrived in the prison of El Dueso. He stayed there for eleven months, moved to El Puerto on August 11, 1938, and was released on August 19, 1940. Jenaro did not devote much diary space to the treatment of prisoners. There are, however, regular entries that give an insight into prison life and matters that affected basic survival. Diary entries from February 12, 1938 to August 19, 1940 from both prisons give a good indication of subjects that were important to a prisoner at this time:

---

69. Highlighted extracts from prison diary of Jenaro Ruiz de Aguirre 1937–40 from Irantzu: 1937: December 1, 24. 1938: January 2, 20, 24; March 19; April 26; May 4; June 6, 8, 14; July 10, 11, 18, 30; August 1, 5, 18, 19, 22; September 12, 14, 21, 25; October 5, 20, 23, 28; November 19; December 1, 4, 11, 24, 27; 1939: March 14, 24; April 15, 28; May 9, 18; June 12, 16; July 13, 16, 19, 27, 28; August 21, 22; September 3, 5, 7, 8, 9, 20, 23, 25; October 20; November 6, 19, 27; December 11, 27; 1940: February 7; March 19; April 26; May 4, 6, 8, 14; June 1; July 10, 11, 16, 18, 30; August 3, 5, 18, 19; on August 22 he arrived home.

Receipt of money (where identified) from former father-in-law, former mother-in-law, and a friend ranging from 10 pesetas to 55 pesetas.

Receipt of food parcels from home (former mother-in-law, others not identified) including: chocolate, fish, canned peas, cookies, sausage, cheese, ham, bread, apples, milk, coffee, meat, a dessert made with almonds, tuna, cookies, butter, tomatoes, lettuces.

Receipt of other parcels from similar sources including parcels other than food including: matches, tobacco, stamps, a pen, toothpaste, soap for himself, laundry detergent, a pair of pants, a shirt, shoes, disinfectant, a cream that dealt with skin complaints, insecticide (mosquitoes in El Puerto abounded), and a wooden spoon.

On November 10, 1937, Jenaro wrote that he received 30 pesetas from home. Whenever he received monies from home, a record was kept of everything received. Jenaro mentions his health in his diaries, but solely confined to El Puerto. On September 27, 1938 the prisoners received their first typhus injection, followed by a second injection on October 5, 1938. Only on July 27, 1939 did the prisoners receive a medical examination for the first time since their admittance to prison. However, this does not appear have done much to redress the major cause of death, tuberculosis. On September 3, 1939 he records anthrax symptoms that necessitated later surgery, without anesthetic, on September 7; he left the medical section on September 17, after a fourteen-day stay in the medical center. Another illness is recorded between December 1 and December 5, 1938, when he was sick in bed as a result of "falling when getting into bed as a result of fever." This was followed by another period in bed between March 20 and 25, 1939.

The scarcity of food was obviously an important issue with prisoners. Clearly, food parcels from home were fundamental to survival. Although the prison guards threatened to confiscate parcels and sometimes did so, it appears that the prison authorities at El Puerto do not seem to have permanently adopted a policy of prohibiting these parcels. It appeared to have been at the discretion of individual guards. At the same time, the authorities would also be aware that seventy-eight prisoners in El Puerto died of hunger in March 1941. Perhaps somewhat surprisingly, Jenaro does not mention food very often, although he does refer to a banquet of "fish, meat, butter, and coffee at El Dueso on May 5, 1938 in connection with something religious." In El Puerto he mentions that, on June 16,

1939, after "forty-nine days of eating lentils at lunch and dinnertime every day, on this date they had potatoes with clams for lunch."[70]

Living conditions were certainly affected by the weather. Jenaro mentions the temperature on September 7 to 9, 1939 as being 35° C (95° F) in the shade. The cells with up to six prisoners would have been insufferably hot because of the narrow corridors and extremely limited ventilation. He was also in Brigada 8, a converted chapel with 343 prisoners and only six toilets, again tremendously overcrowded; these close living conditions would have exacerbated the high temperatures. To mark the time, Jenaro also entered the saints' days of all his and his previous wife's relatives and recorded his visits from the outside world. He received a visit from Father José León on May 14, 1938 in El Dueso prison, who returned to visit him at El Puerto on October 28, 1938. His granddaughter Irantzu thinks it likely that that this could have been the Father José León de la Inmaculada who was the Provincial Priest of the Carmelites in Amorebieta the 1940s. In this context, it is interesting to note that the Father Superior of the Carmelite monastery in Amorebieta was shot by the Nationalists on May 16, 1937 as a Basque nationalist sympathizer.[71] Irantzu's grandparents had a great deal to do with the Carmelites of Amorebieta and had worked with the church and local people. The other visitor was Juan José Labarga from Bilbao on September 25, 1939, but the family remembers nothing about him.

The tenor of the diaries is basically descriptive and non-judgmental, possibly as a safeguard against confiscation by the guards. There was, however, a serious incident concerning an event that took place in El Puerto on March 19, 1940 on St Joseph's Day. Jenaro simply records that "140 cellmates were punished as a result of an incident"; this appeared to be a demonstration against the way Mass was being conducted.

> 140 of the prisoners were punished because of some incidents during Mass. The prisoners were called to make individual declarations in front of the director of the prison . . . during this time some ten prisoners were held for three hours in cell number 36 . . . grandfather was able to convince the prison authorities that he was not a guilty party.[72]

---

70. Email from Irantzu Bustinza, November 8, 2009.

71. Preston, *The Spanish Holocaust*, 435.

72. Diary of Jenaro Ruiz de Aguirre, March 19, 1940.

This may well be related to one of the episodes referred to in Chapter 2 in which the Mass conducted by Don Laureano or the Dominican priest later led to prisoner unrest.

Basque prisoners had also been involved in similar incidents elsewhere. For example, in El Dueso in the summer of 1940 they sang in Basque in the prison chapel and narrowly escaped transportation to the Canary Islands.[73] In Burgos there were also problems with a consecration service by a Father Bolinaga on Maundy Thursday 1939 with some 120 members of a Basque choral society. Here the priest asked for prayers for "violated nuns and martyred and shot bishops," which induced a response of "My Jesus, why can you not tell the truth?" As a result the director of the prison authorized that the offenders be lashed.[74]

Jenaro was released from the penitentiary of El Puerto on August 19, 1940. Soon afterward he married Ruperta Mintegui Uriguen from Amorebieta, who was a member of the PNV and treasurer of its women's organization, the Emakume Abertzale Batza. Irantzu writes of the help given to her grandparents by the Carmelites, who encouraged them to leave Amorebieta as the police would go to the town looking for them. The priest had given them correct information, because the police did visit her house, following a visit to other houses of her relatives in Bilbao. There was almost certainly a connection with Father José León, as noted the Provincial Priest of the Carmelites, who had visited Jenaro in prison on October 28, 1938. The continued house visits of the police also provide an example in which ex-prisoners (and their wives) of the prison of El Puerto were kept under increased surveillance on their release.

Jenaro was able to find work soon after his release in 1940 as a printer in Eibar, Gipuzkoa, at the firm of D. Cruz Irasuegui, where he remained for seven years. Initially he lived in Vitoria-Gasteiz, then moved to Deba in Gipuzkoa before returning to Amorebieta. He cofounded a printing firm in 1948 in Amorebieta, but owing to his fear of confiscation of assets by the Franco authorities, it was not registered in his name. This provides an excellent example of the constant harassment exerted on former prisoners. While Jenaro was well received by his neighbors in Amorebieta, a town with a strong tradition of Basque nationalism, life continued to be difficult. It seems apposite to end this testimony on Jenaro with an account by his daughter (and mother of Irantzu), Carmen Ruiz, of the kind of constant pressure experienced by children of the families of former Basque prisoners

---

73. Mendizabal, *Gudaris y rehenes de Franco (1936–1943)*, 208.
74. Ibid., 286–87.

The only thing that I remember, as if it were today, is the many times that the Civil Guard came to our house, in order to make us display the Spanish flag in the window on the days that the Civil Governor passed by on a visit to Durango. I also remember the general strike of May 1, 1947. I was only four years old . . . they called at the door of the house and I ran to open the door where I met two Civil Guards and they asked for my father . . . not content with the reply of my mother, they hid themselves in a part of the house in order to check on the authenticity of the reply or whether my father had hidden himself there . . . We used to live near the barracks of the Civil Guard. I imagine that it was very hard on my father to live for all that time in front of their headquarters.[75]

The impact of constant surveillance of her father by the Civil Guard on a four-year-old child is clear. A general strike on May 1, 1947, some eight years after the cessation of the Civil War, meant the police searched her house again. Her father, like so many supporters of the Republic, had been criminalized by an illegal sentence and was an automatic suspect in the event of any future disturbances.

The third region from which testimony of relatives was obtained relates to Donostia-San Sebastián and the surrounding area. The first of these concerns Joshemari Mendizabal, a native of the city. He was employed as an accountant by a nearby firm in Pasaia (Pasajes) and at the outbreak of war joined the PNV's Saseta Battalion with his brother José Manuel.[76] Charged with *adhesión a la rebelión*, he was sentenced to thirty years' imprisonment in Santander on July 2, 1938, initially held in El Dueso, and admitted to El Puerto aged twenty-five on September 11, 1938. His nephew Joxemari states that his uncle did not receive any visitors during his incarceration there.

During the imprisonment of his uncle, his family fell on very hard times. One of his sons was condemned to death and the other condemned to thirty years' imprisonment. The family was supported by one of the grandfathers who sold cider; one of his younger daughters, Maripi, kept a small grocery store, but was sentenced to eight months imprisonment in Ondarreta jail (Donostia-San Sebastián) for organizing collections for

---

75. Letter from Carmen Ruiz de Aguirre Mintegui(mother of Irantzu), November 11, 2009.
76. AHPC/PSM, Legajo 29303. Also letter from Joxemari Mendizabal Sarasua, May 1, 2010.

prisoners in her store. After the fall of Teruel in February 1938, the local mayor ordered that monarchist and Francoist flags be displayed; his grandmother refused and was fined 100 pesetas. On his release on August 19, 1940, Joshe unsuccessfully attempted to get his old job back. Thereafter, he made a living with his father by selling cider.

The second testimony of relatives from Donostia-San Sebastián and the surrounding area concerns Fernando Aguirre Lertxundi, originally from Ibarra, but who spent almost all his life in Donostia-San Sebastián.[77] There he studied accountancy and obtained employment in the offices of a cement factory, Rezola, on the outskirts of the city. He served in the Saseta Battalion and was later promoted to lieutenant. On being captured he was convicted of *auxilio a la rebelión* and was sentenced to imprisonment of twelve years and one day in Santander on July 3, 1938. Initially sent to El Dueso, he was admitted to El Puerto on August 24, 1938.

The major caption on the card in figure 3.2 is headed Aberri Eguna, the Day of the Basque Homeland. The card is quasi-religious and shows a rising sun with a Christlike figure standing over a kneeling person. One of the other captions is *Askatasun Eguzkia* meaning "the sun of freedom." Prison authorities would not know that this was the first sentence of a poem, "Itxarkundia" (Awakening), by Sabino Arana, the founder of Basque nationalism. This card is signed by Fernando and some of his fellow prisoners and is a good example of the use of Euskara to boost Basque morale by sending out a message that excluded all others in El Puerto. It appears that this was not censored. Figure 3.3 is a humorous birthday card drawn by fellow prisoners (signed by "his admirers") and sent to Fernando on his birthday on May 30 in either 1939 or 1940. Arguably, this provides an outstanding example of the comradeship that used to exist among Basque prisoners in El Puerto. This is included because not only is it an excellent example of espirit de corps amongst a section of the prison population but is the only one in the prison files that I have found.

Families of Basque prisoners in El Puerto and elsewhere met periodically at their houses in order to contribute money and food for prisoners' parcels. Fernando Aguirre, a prisoner in El Puerto, writes in his diary "The prisoners in Puerto were saved from hunger by bread brushed with tomato and oil."[78] This provides a further illustration of the organized self-help that was offered to Basque prisoners in El Puerto by their community at home.

---

77. AHPC/PSM, Legajo 29269.
78. Extract from diary of Fernando Agirre in Mendizabal, *Gudaris y rehenes de Franco (1936–1943)*, 209. It could be argued that it was like Catalan "pan amb tomàquet" although there were not many Catalan prisoners in El Puerto.

Figure 3.2

On the release of Fernando on August 19, 1940, he had to go to live at the house of a fellow released prisoner, "Txartxa," for a while, as the parents of Fernando had left for Bilbao and then France. Fernando was unable to obtain employment for around eight months. In 1947 he was detained for around ten months in the prison of Ondarreta, where his family alleges that he was tortured by Melitón Manzanas, the chief of Franco's secret police.[79] This is the first instance I have come across of allegations of further detention and torture after leaving El Puerto.[80]

---

79. Melitón Manzanas was commander of the Political Social Brigade (Brigada Políti-co-Social), Franco's political police in Donostia-San Sebastián in 1941.

80. Letter from Joxemari Mendizabal Sarasua, May 1, 2010.

My information suggests that, contrary to what might be expected, prisoners from the Basque Country and other parts of Spain were aware of domestic and international news during their incarceration. Joxemari Mendizabal Sarasua has written about the *gudaris* in the prisons of Burgos, Larrinaga, El Dueso, and El Puerto; he raises the general question of prisoners obtaining and concealing illicit information and smuggling out letters from Franco's jails. Reference has already been made to the way Jenaro Ruiz de Aguirre evaded the attentions of jailers in concealing his diaries while in El Puerto. Fernando de Aguirre mainly wrote his diary in El Dueso, but also in El Puerto, hiding it from guards by writing in a small diary. The contents were kept secret by using forms of words that concealed the true meaning and making the entries in English. Like Jenaro, his diary was kept hidden after his release; in the case of Fernando, it was not found until three years after his death. Joshe Manuel Mendizabal also kept a record of events and remembers that, while in the prison of Burgos he heard that on January 19, 1942, "Churchill had arrived by airplane in the USA."[81] He used a concealed radio and the magazine *Espetxean*, edited by the Sabino Arana Foundation. As this took place before his transfer to El Puerto on September 11, 1938, it follows that this kind of would find its way to the next prison.

Some of my other Basque contacts have not provided so much information, or have included accounts of very similar experiences. In these cases, I have decided to group them together, and have related their accounts to themes dealing with confirmation of a high level of tuberculosis, further evidence of destruction of families, the reaction of local communities on release, and employment by the church.

The next three testimonies are from Bizkaia. Peli Garay Hormaza, from Bakio, was away for almost five years. His daughter Arantzazu Garay criticizes the placing of her father in such a distant jail that made it almost impossible to visit him. She too points out the fearful transport conditions for prisoners to arrive at these locations, traveling without food or water for the whole duration of the journey. Arantzazu relates her father's account of the major cause of mortality, the widespread tuberculosis that existed in El Puerto.[82]

Gregorio Arieta-Araunabeña Velar from Mungia was a PNV councilman in Erandio, imprisoned in El Puerto for his Basque nationalist

---

81. Diary of José Manuel Mendizabal while in Burgos prison, January 1942, in Mendizabal, *Gudaris y rehenes de Franco (1936–1943)*, 302.
82. Email from Arantzazu Garay. October 6, 2009. Chapter 2 mentions that 37 percent of the deaths between 1939 and 1940 in El Puerto de Santa María were due to tuberculosis.

Figure 3.4

sympathies.[83] His experience illustrated another aspect of the destruction of families since his son tells us that his father was forced to flee to France and later went into exile in Venezuela. Once again, the grandmother was left with sole responsibilities of looking after children and managing the smallholding.

Antonio Torrontegui Elguezabal was born in Maruri and was also a PNV councilman, but in Mungia, during the Republic. He appears to have been imprisoned between 1937 and 1940. Like many other Basque prisoners, he was first imprisoned in El Dueso and then transferred to El

---

83. Email from Mikel Arieta-Araunabeña, October 22, 2009.

Puerto. His granddaughter Begoña Torrontegui only knows that he found confinements in both prisons very hard and that his absence made social and economic difficulties for the family. Torrontegui Elguezabal was released on July 18, 1940 and returned to the same district where he was self-employed and had a small workshop; this was allied to agricultural work in which he worked as a carpenter in a saw mill. Begoña confirms that, after the war, "people of the district of Mungia treated Antonio with respect."[84] His experience indicated that where an ex-prisoner returned to a Basque nationalist area, had a trade, and was self-employed, there was a reasonable chance of work and acceptance.

Jesús Etxabe Aldai from Zarautz, Gipuzkoa, studied chemistry and worked as a health officer and then served in the San Andrés Battalion affiliated with the Basque nationalist STV (Solidaridad de Trabajadores Vascos, Basque Workers' Solidarity) labor union.[85] He was the public health officer. Formerly, Etxabe Aldai had established contact with a group of Basque nationalist students in Zaragoza. His grandson, Galder Unzalu Etxabe, writes that he cannot recall the name well but it could have been called something like Ikasle Abertzaleen Batza (Basque Nationalist Students' Association). Taken prisoner after the surrender at Santoña on August 26, 1937, he took the usual path of Basque prisoners from El Dueso to El Puerto.

During the war the family of six dispersed, mainly in service for the Basque cause. A remaining sister looked after their parents and ran a small store in Zarautz where they were denounced for selling a liberal paper in the store. Many of the possessions of some of the family were confiscated and they were fined 100,000 pesetas. Jesús was an unusual case in that he was the only prisoner contacted whose details were known to me that was actually involved in a prisoner exchange. In his case, it was for a journalist from Aragon. It appears from his prison records that Etxabe Aldai was transferred to the provincial prison in Donostia-San Sebastián on September 2, 1938, before ending up in free France. Between 1939 and 1940 he moved to Bilbao, where he married a local girl who had a sister who was imprisoned in the Gurs concentration camp in southwest France, one of the largest centers of Basque imprisonment.[86] Coincidentally, her brother, Agustín Aidatz Alberdi, was imprisoned in El Puerto as

---

84. Emails from Begoña Torrontegui, October 14 and November 13.
85. Emails from Galder Unzalu Etxabe, October 3 and 5, 2009.
86. See Josu Chueca, *Gurs: el campo vasco* (Tafalla: Txalaparta, 2007). One of the largest Basque camps, with 60,000 internees having passed through its gates by 1945; today the local cemetery only records some 2,745 Basques buried there.

well. Etxabe Aldai returned to Zarautz in 1945 and his grandson says that he eventually obtained a post teaching mathematics and sciences to high school level. This was then followed by other teaching appointments with the Escolapians and Jesuits; on retirement, he dedicated himself to further teaching, not sciences but the Basque language.

In a recent evaluation, Ricard Vinyes considered that there were some 50,400 women political prisoners in 1940.[87] In the context of a Basque perspective, there are two women prisoners from Durango whose experiences may be considered relevant to this chapter, as they were relatives of the men imprisoned in El Puerto. One was politically involved, the other was not.

Vicenta Garnica Lasera had four daughters and was the sister-in-law of Ángel Gorosarri, a prisoner in El Puerto.[88] Before the war she was a factory worker at the Hijos de Mendizabal firm. Vicenta became a member of the UGT, participated in demonstrations, and took part in the 1936 Parliamentary elections as a campaigner for the Popular Front coalition. After the second bombing of Durango, Vicenta went with her family to Santander, and then to France. Deported in 1938, she returned to Durango when she was arrested.

Reported to the Nationalists for "*una ideología muy roja*" (a very red ideology) she was tried for the crime of *auxilio a la rebelión*. Some twelve Carlists and a Margarita who had formerly been imprisoned gave almost exactly similar statements against Vicenta, accusing her of constantly threatening and insulting them. She was sentenced to twelve years and one day on June 4, 1938 in the Provincial Prison of Bilbao.[89] During her stay, other prisoners taught her to read at the age of forty. Never one to talk about her prison experiences, she once commented that, "the worst thing about prison was that they would come and take someone away, we never saw them again."[90] She thought that her husband had died, as he had disappeared without trace. He later appeared, though, having been held in a concentration camp and did not visit his wife in prison. As was customary in these cases, the children were looked after by relatives. Vicenta received *libertad condicional* on June 16, 1941.

---

87. Vinyes, *Irredentas*, 13. Also see Cuevas, *Presas en las mujeres franquistas* for a detailed account of treatment of women prisoners.
88. Email from María González Gorosarri, December 17, 2008.
89. Prisión Provincial de Bilbao June 4, 1938, Causa número 13.629.
90. Many of the nuns appear to have been held in low esteem by the women prisoners who viewed them with the same suspicion as the male prisoners viewed the priests/chaplains in El Puerto.

María E. was the wife of a prisoner in El Puerto who had been admitted on November 28, 1938.[91] She was sent to Saturraran prison in Mutriku, Gipuzkoa, which was located on a beach and had the reputation of being a particularly bad female penitentiary. It housed women between the ages of sixteen and sixty and there were daily stories of humiliation, punishments, and constant hunger. Allegedly, between the years 1938 and 1944, there were 1,571 prisoners in Saturraran, where 116 prisoners died, of whom 61 were children. In this prison the youngest child remained with María E. until he was three and then was taken by relatives. On the release of her mother, the child did not recognize her. The family lost all its possessions while the parents were in jail and went to live in Amorebieta where their children had been cared for while the parents were imprisoned. This case provides yet another example of the devastation imposed on a family in which both parents were imprisoned at the same time.

A summary of the information imparted by relatives of prisoners in El Puerto in this chapter confirms the impact of a harsh and punitive penal regime both on the prisoners and their families. Undoubtedly some fared a great deal better than others, depending on their health and local connections. Some of those who survived were often so incapacitated that they were unable to work; if they obtained employment, it was often for a pittance. The Law of Political Responsibilities hit some harder than others, as did a purge of the professions and the civil service. Many prisoners were economically ruined and had no immediate pension unlike the former Nationalist soldiers;[92] they were bitter that any monetary savings that they had were no longer legal tender. The Nationalists had declared all banknotes issued since 1936 to be illegal, the only legal tender acceptable was that issued by the Fascist Bank of Spain and, by July 1937, three times as many government pesetas as the Nationalist peseta were needed to buy a similar number of French francs.[93]

The quality of the lives of former prisoners depended on the locality

---

91. Email from María González Gorosarri, December 17, 2008. See María González Gorosarri and Eduardo Barinaga, *No lloréis, lo que tenéis que hacer es no olvidarnos. La cárcel de Saturraran y la represión franquista contra las mujeres, a partir de testimonios de supervivientes* (Donostia: Ttarttalo, 2008). Also see Fernando Hernández Holgado, *Mujeres encarceladas. La prisión de Ventas: de la República al franquismo, 1931–1941* (Madrid: Marcial Pons Historia, 2003).

92. Serapio Echeandia Apriz from Zaldibar, near Durango, admits to receiving a pension in 1996; but many of the ex-prisoners of El Puerto who were released in the period 1941–42 in severe ill-heath may well have died by then after suffering years of poverty.

93. Tereixa Constenla, "How Franco Banked on Victory," *El País* (English edition), June 13, 2012.

and political allegiances that determined the response of neighbors. In other areas like Loiu, Amorebieta, and Mungia, with a sympathetic PNV presence, former prisoners may be well have been regarded in a more favorable light. But even in Amorebieta their businesses were at risk of confiscation and were registered under false names. Security and even personal safety could never be taken for granted. In Mungia, stores were compulsorily closed on several occasions and sewing machines could be seized on a whim.

The difficulty in finding work after release from prison was part of Franco's policy of the vengeance. Illegally criminalized, former Republican prisoners often faced another sentence outside prison. In cases in which an ex-prisoner had a trade or a special skill (like teaching science) it could prove to be a saving asset. Where large cities had diverse political allegiances like Bilbao or Donostia-San Sebastián, it was easier to conceal individual past history and find employment. But in the case of smaller town like Zarautz, near to Donostia-San Sebastián, Jesús Etxabe had to move to Bilbao to find a job. In places like Durango, meanwhile, hostility could be enduring and according to Serapio Echeandia Apriz lasted "up to forty years." However in other smaller nearby places like Berriz and Zaldibar, it was easier to live, where even Franco supporters proved not to be hostile. In Otxandio and Abadiño the experiences in finding work differed; in the former, Vicente Pujana Galíndez had to go to Bilbao while in the latter Santiago Arrondo found work in his original job, but met with some hostility. In Urduña, Jesús Mendibil Manrique was unable to regain his former job. In areas with a significant Basque nationalist following, integration into the community was much easier. Yet the economic, social, and political climate for all released Basque prisoners was that of permanent uncertainty, accompanied by a fear that there would be further confiscations of their property or revocations of their freedom on the slightest pretext.

Above all, this testimony of relatives of prisoners by mostly older people was formed against a background in which casualties approximated to between 450,000 and 650,000.[94] [95] Another approximately 450,000 people fled or were exiled during the Civil War and its near aftermath.[96] The pressure on the defeated to keep silent at the time is depicted well by Richards,

94. Paul Preston, *The Spanish Civil War: Reaction, Revolution and Revenge* (London: Harper Perennial, 2006), 302.
95. Victor Alba, *Transition in Spain: From Franco to Democracy*, trans. Barbara Lolito (New Brunswick, NJ: Transaction Books, 1978), 172.
96. Filipe Ribeiro de Meneses, *Franco and the Spanish Civil War* (New York: Routledge, 2005), 119.

who observes:

> The monopolisation of public memory and the public voice
> by the victors occupied the space within [the economic and
> cultural] barriers . . . After 1939 . . . half of Spain was denied any
> collective identity beyond the state's own construction of Family
> and Fatherland. Individual identity was inevitably severely
> circumscribed in the process.[97]

The witness statements contained in this chapter serve to revisit what
were traumatic memories, in order that the events of the war can be heard
from the perspective of Basque prisoners. Although "more than 70 percent of the Spanish population has not lived through the Civil War, the
trauma still remains."[98]

There was also a feeling among the witnesses that Basque prisoners
had been detained for longer than others, with more restrictive release
conditions. These comments, allied to a further reading of the Cádiz
sentence and release situation, caused me to examine the possibility of
Basque discrimination. Later chapters investigate these allegations in
the light of a comparative experience of those inmates in El Puerto from
Cádiz province.

---

97. Richards, *A Time of Silence*, 4, 25.
98. Paloma Aguilar, *Memory and Amnesia: The Role of the Spanish Civil War in the Transition to Democracy* (New York: Berghahn Books, 2002), 268.

4

Case Studies of Prisoners in the Penitentiary of El Puerto de Santa María

> ...En descanso tu paz. En paz tu guerra.
> Herido mortalmente de vida, camarada
> —César Vallejo, *Cortejo tras la toma de Bilbao* (1937)

It has been suggested that there may have been three types of Republican activist, an industrial worker, a rural labourer and a thinker[1]. In my experience all these types of Republicans fought for the legitimate government, many died and many were convicted for lengthy periods, often on spurious charges. The long arm of Franco reached into every nook and cranny of Spanish society.

This chapter contains an analysis of a cross section of the convictions on the many charges and the erratic sentences, often differing for the same "offenses."

The information extracted has been somewhat tortuously obtained by what Frances Espinosa refers to as "the hundreds of hours [spent] in the solitude of archives."[2] Examples of the large number of different charges under which prisoners were convicted and then incarcerated in El Puerto are examined. These, allied to an extremely wide range of backgrounds of the prisoners, illustrate the enormous number of Spaniards from all walks of life who fell prey to the "creative and purifying regeneration of Fran-

---

1. See R. K. Brittain,*The Poetic and Real Worlds of César Vallejo* (Eastbourne: Sussex Academic Press, 2016) 206.
2. Espinosa, *La Justicia de Queipo*, 4.

co."[3] In total, around one hundred individual sentences have been chosen from different tribunals. They have been selected for different reasons; the main one was that prison files contained sufficient legible information and illustrated something different either in relation to sentences or the range of occupations previously held. Not all files of prisoners contained the same amount of information and it could be that in some cases the prison authorities' versions do not accord with those of the families of the prisoners.

This chapter falls into four sections: (1) an evaluation of the prison files as primary sources and the interpretation of documents; (2) cases that include a diverse variety of charges; (3) cases that highlight a wide range of different categories of "offender"; and (4) cases that relate to Nationalist prisoners.

An Evaluation of Prison Files as Primary Sources and Interpretation of Documents

The problem of destroyed documents relating to Republican prisoners in the Spanish Civil War has already been referred to in the Introduction. As Preston comments, "many police and Falange [Civil War] records have simply disappeared."[4]

However, the difficulties of interpreting the prison documents did not cease, once they had been located. All individual files of prisoners in El Puerto were divided into two sections. The first part related to specific individual and personal details, including date of birth, place of origin, family details, and profession. It also sometimes contained physical details relating to nose, mouth, face, eyes, beard, hair and height. Almost all had a date of admittance to El Puerto. The second part of the report was always typed, with single-line spacing, usually in one paragraph per page, and sometimes faded. This contained details of the "crime" but sometimes could list up to forty other prisoners in what was clearly a collective trial.[5] I have mainly avoided minor sentences and have mostly concentrated on the treatment of political prisoners.

In the case of captured soldiers, especially those from the Basque Country, the prison documents contain extremely similar information.

---

3. See Rafael del Águila Tejerina, *Ideologia y fascismo* (Madrid: Centro de Estudios Constitucionales, 1982), 212–31.
4. Paul Preston, "An Awareness of Guilt," *Times Literary Supplement*, June 29, 2001.
5. Where I have taken details of other prisoners charged under the same indictment number (*causa número*), they are included to illustrate the scope of action of the prisoner mentioned in the first part of the file.

As with prisoners' files from other areas, some data was almost illegible, while other prison files contained scarcely any information and some nothing at all. Other reports were simply repetitive and full of Spanish legalese that, more often than not, ends in an almost automatic award of a thirty-year sentence to Basque prisoners.[6]

The prison files of El Puerto provide information from all parts of Spain, but mainly relate to the large prison intake in El Puerto from Andalusia and the Basque Country. Many sentenced from the former were either laborers or agricultural workers;[7] while those from the latter included a much wider spread of occupations. In the case of some of the agricultural laborers, individual files sometimes included a reference to "*sin instrucción*" (uneducated).

Nevertheless, my research proved profitable in that there was a sufficient number of individual prison reports that contained different details of the alleged "crimes" and sentences deemed worthy of imprisonment. The captive net of Franco was all-embracing and involved a wide range of occupations and sentences for different "crimes." These cases also provide a fascinating insight into the psyche of the *Nuevo Estado* in its desire to punish the defeated, sometimes for trivial actions. For example, military tribunals would sentence someone to six years and one day imprisonment in a major prison for the wrong use of a greeting or an alleged verbal insult to the Francoist state. In other instances, the case studies give an idea of the involvement of some of the prisoners in El Puerto in events of national importance during the Spanish Civil War. These included the interception of the *Mar Cantábrico* by the *Canarias*, the major outbreak of naval violence in Cartagena, and an unsuccessful Falange challenge to Franco.

Cases have also been selected where they provide examples of different tribunals' treatment of prisoners who had pursued different occupations before the war. Examples of other cases of interest include a wide range of different categories of "offender," including a Republican soldier who served in the Spanish Foreign Legion, members of the *Soccoro Rojo Internacional* (International Red Aid, commonly known by its Russian acronym MOPR), a merchant navy captain, doctors, Assault Guards (a Spanish police force created during the Second Republic), a primary

---

6. It is worth emphasizing that most of the trial examples cited deal with collective trials.
7. While this is true, it is not the whole story. For example, the vast majority of Freemasons imprisoned in El Puerto came from Andalusia. Their previous, occupations included electricians, managers, lawyers, bakers, employers, industrial workers, carpenters, pharmacists, and agricultural laborers. AHPC/PSM, Legajos 29347, 29349, 29351, 29352, 29353, 29354, 29355, 29357.

school inspector, freemasons, and a diverse variety of charges. These include desertion, sedition, criticism of the Franco regime, the giving of a Republican salute, destruction of church images and artifacts, treason, and censorship. Several also provide an illustration of the attitude of the military tribunals toward the aged. Most surprisingly, the files of prisoners indicated that not all the inmates were Republican supporters. For example, on the Nationalist side they provide an example of the imprisonment of one commander for negligence, a case of cowardice, and, perhaps surprisingly, a case of an important Falange territorial head caught up in a power struggle between Franco and himself. Further examples have been provided that illustrate evidence of intervention by the Falange or the Church, pending release of prisoners or employers supporting the prisoners pending some form of *libertad condicional.*

Nevertheless, a strong word of caution should be inserted before reading these cases because decisions on sentences were scarcely reached by impartial judgments and neutral witnesses. Two of the Basque testimonies of relatives of the prisoners in the previous chapter give examples in which there were denunciations. To recap, Serapio Echeandia, mayor of Zaldibar, was denounced by relatives;[8] whereas Diego Pablo Gamboa Larrondo was denounced by neighbors.[9] Evidence given to the military tribunals could be extremely hostile, sometimes with aggrieved Nationalist relatives, especially where widows were the preferred witnesses. The large number of collective trials gave little or no time to hear individual cases; assumed guilt by association was one of the driving forces surrounding the harsh sentences handed down to highly vulnerable and mostly undefended prisoners, some of whom were illiterate; mass repression was the order of the day before, during, and after *el primer franquismo,* early Francoism. Cases heard by different military tribunals have been presented as an indication of the kind of evidence presented to the tribunals and their varying responses. I have taken names, places, and alleged "offenses" directly from prison files in order to demonstrate the exact grounds on which people were imprisoned.

Despite the above, it would not be true to say that these prison reports serve little purpose since they provide an indication of the scope of military tribunals and the "rationale" of their punitive sentences. One could argue that the documents represent a kind of explanation as to why the prisoners were convicted, thereby ending up in the penitentiary of El

---

8.   See chapter 4 regarding statement of relatives of Serapio Echeandia.
9.   See chapter 4 regarding statement of relatives of Diego Pablo Gamboa Larrondo.

Puerto between 1936 and 1949. The prison reports also give some idea of the way in which prisoners were moved from one institution to another at the caprice of the Nationalist authorities. Above all, they illustrate the totally disruptive effect of the Spanish Civil War on the everyday lives of the defeated.

In all cases, the indictment number or *número de causa* is the key.[10] Where prisoners are grouped together under the same number, it indicates that they will have been investigated together leading to a collective trial.[11] This number will have been allocated by the military judge (*Auditor de Guerra*) when the original *denuncia* or police classification report was passed on to the investigating judge (*juez instructor*). This does not always mean that the number investigated or then tried would remain the same. Some could have other cases brought against them whereas some will simply have died. In other cases, the military authorities may have decided to drop the accusations at the prosecutor stage. There could even be instances in which military tribunals processed different cases at the same time. Multiple denunciations could lead to repeated appearances in court.

In other instances, individual prison files unusually include Nationalist documents that illustrate the difficulty in securing release from prison or being able to work without military, Civil Guard, or Falange clearance. One such document from the local Falange of Candás, Asturias, objecting to the release of a prisoner from El Puerto is shown in figure 4.1

Claudia Verhoeven, an American historian, has written on "Court Files" in the context of interpreting sources of information. Much is relevant to the prison files of El Puerto in that they reflect the philosophy and creed of the early Franco era, bent on a policy of vengeance. They also give an insight into the prevailing Francoist perspective and culture, during and after the Spanish Civil War. Verhoeven writes:

> Skimpy as sometimes they may be, court files can be among the few primary sources that actually grant access to the world of popular culture, which is precisely why twentieth-century historians turned to them in the first place . . . The testimony of someone falsely accused has a radically different aim from the speeches of the prosecution . . . Second, court files can be riddled by deliberate distortion.[12]

---

10. I am most grateful to Julius Ruiz for his helpful explanation that clarified some of these issues.

11. In some cases in which the indictment number was not easily available, I have provided the prisoner file number (*número de legajo*). In most cases, I have cited both.

12. Claudia Verhoeven, "Law and History," in *Reading Primary Sources: The Interpretation*

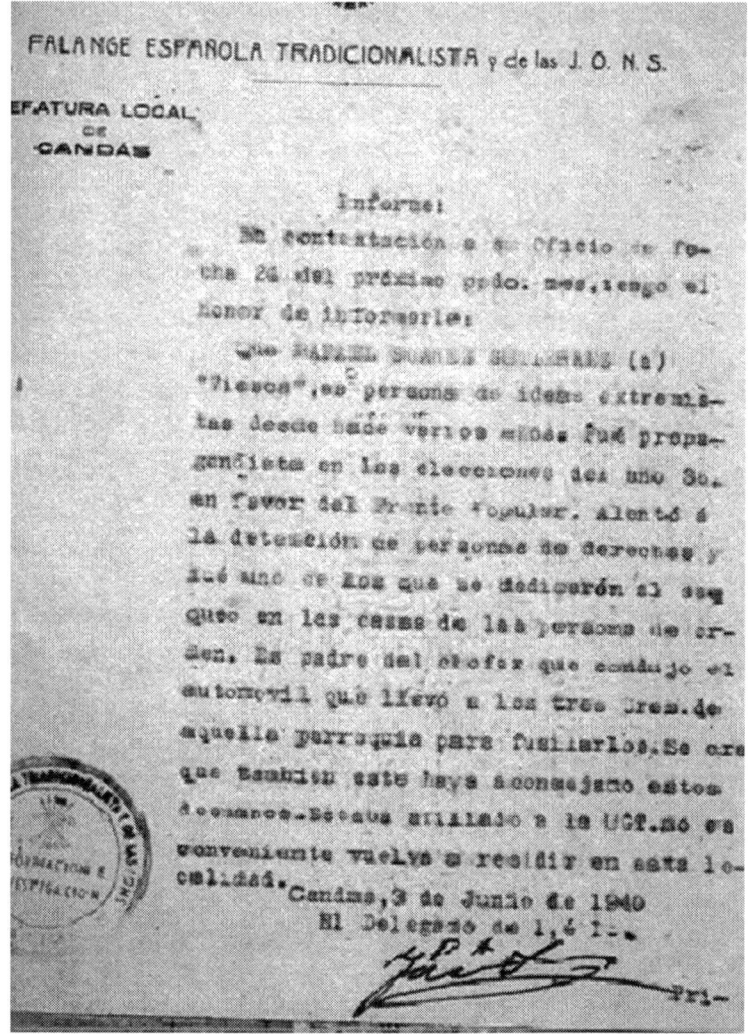

Figure 4.1

Verhoeven's reference to the testimony of someone falsely accused has direct application to the military tribunals of Franco in which testimony could be extremely limited: collective trials left no time for individual testimony. Furthermore, the reference to deliberate distortion was not unlikely in the face of hostile testimony for the prosecution. While this chapter does not seek to wander into the labyrinth of Nationalist military tribunal procedure, a very brief mention illustrates the climate that prisoners of El Puerto had faced on trial. The defending lawyer (where there

of Texts from Nineteenth- and Twentieth-century History, ed. Miriam Dobson and Benjamin Ziemann (Abingdon: Routledge, 2009), 91–92.

was one) was always a military officer, junior in military rank to the officer presiding over the tribunal.[13] Preston cites an interview with Franco by Randolph Churchill for the *Daily Mail* on March 1, 1937 and observes that "he [Franco] omitted to mention that the defence counsel would be named by the court and would often outdo the prosecutors in demanding fierce sentences."[14] Often, defense counsel would only see the charges on the same day with no more than three hours to examine the charges. Sometimes the president of the tribunal would be someone like the Duke of Seville. All persons connected with the tribunal would be Francoists. Few trials lasted as long as that of Julián Besteiro, former President of the Cortes. His trial lasted nearly five hours.[15] Eduardo Guzmán, tried with the poet Miguel Hernández (on trial with twenty-eight others in January 1940), writes that his trial lasted twenty minutes.[16] On the other hand, Arthur Koestler reported that trials in Seville in March and July 1937 lasted three minutes.[17]

Prison files relating to El Puerto have covered sentences from a wider number of military tribunals than those mentioned in this chapter. However, in order to avoid repetition, it has been decided to utilize cases that I believe enable some kind of comparison to be made. The examples that have been cited were cases heard by military tribunals in the following areas: Bilbao (by far the most), Logroño, Seville, Valladolid, Cartagena, Valverde, Valencia, Cádiz, Ceuta, León, Cáceres, Talavera de la Reina, Algodonales, Ubrique, Badajoz, Huelva, Vitoria-Gasteiz, and Las Palmas. Evidence has been mostly taken from the trials held in 1937 closely followed by 1938 (and occasionally later); there are also some taken from 1936. During these years military tribunals in Spain were in a powerful position to formulate their own interpretation of what exactly constituted the different kinds of legal rebellion, only subject to a review by the Judge Advocate on technicalities. This largely explains the discrepancies of charges and indeed sentences that are included in this chapter. Once the State Security Law was introduced on March 29, 1941, the military tribunals lost their autonomy and had to follow state guidelines, which required more evidence for convictions.

---

13. While this is true of courts martial procedure in the United Kingdom, the point here is that military justice entirely subsumed civilian justice.
14. Preston, *Franco*, 226.
15. Ignacio Arenillas de Chaves., *El proceso de Besteiro* (Madrid: Revista de Occidente, 1976), 23.
16. Eduardo de Guzmán, "1940: Juicio y condena de Miguel Hernández," *Nueva Historia* 15 (1980), 82.
17. Arthur Koestler, *Spanish Testament* (London: Victor Gollancz, 1937), 336.

A Diverse Variety of Charges

When it came to the charges brought, the Francoist authorities had several different options from which to choose.

Adhesión a la rebelión/ rebelión militar

Adhesión a la rebelión/ rebelión militar (support for the rebellion/ military rebellion) was the most common charge for political prisoners as is indicated in chapter 5.[18] As this was the usual charge for prisoners in this category, more often than not it carried a thirty-year sentence. I have selected a few examples from Andalusia and the Basque Country.

Andalusia (Huelva and Jerez de la Frontera)

The first Andalusian case selected is that of Juan Diaz Estevez, aged thirty-five, an agricultural laborer from the Huelva district who was charged with *rebelión militar* alongside fifty-five other defendants.[19] Allegedly Marxist elements in the town patrolled the streets, arresting certain people and killing fifteen of them. In this case, there were varying degrees of culpability ranging from responsibility to active violence against Nationalist supporters to membership of the UGT, CNT, or the JSU to spreading propaganda and desecration and setting fire to the chapel of the Virgen del Valle and local churches. Even though Diaz Estevez was not a major offender, he was sentenced for *rebelión militar* in Huelva alongside sixteen others to thirty years' imprisonment on October 11, 1937. He was admitted to El Puerto on November 28, 1938.

In the second Andalusian case, José Aquilera Jaén, an agricultural laborer aged forty-seven from Jerez de la Frontera, was charged with *adhesión a la rebelión* alongside six others.[20] They were also agricultural laborers and were neighbors from San José de la Valle. Here again, there were degrees of anti-Nationalist opposition involved, including membership of the Communist Party, the CNT, and the Izquierda Republicana (Republican Left) party. The tribunal regarded most of the group as "extremists," "bad workers," "dangerous characters," "admirers of the revo-

---

18. In the case of Basques, political charges far outweighed those of nonpolitical charges; in the case of Andalusian prisoners, political and nonpolitical charges were almost equal. See chapter 5.
19. AHPC/PSM, Legajo 29357, Causa número 701 de 1937.
20. AHPC/PSM, Legajo 29308, Causa número 153 de 1937.

lution," and people who had acted as propagandists and "inciters for the Marxist cause." José Aquilera Jaén was sentenced to thirty years' imprisonment in Arcos de la Frontera on May 10, 1937, alongside three others. However, one of the neighbors, Miguel Pérez Benítez, was executed. The additional "evidence" against him was that he had also served in the La Sauceda district of Cortes de la Frontera (Málaga), an area in which he had led a group with shotguns, was a former member of the Vicente Ballester Battalion (affiliated with the CNT) and had operated previously in the Tolox area before returning to San José del Valle. He was considered to be a person of "extreme ideas," whereas his neighbors were classified as "dangerous characters," "bad workers," and "admirers of the revolution." This case is interesting in that it illustrates that an identical charge could often lead to drastically different outcomes, depending on previous background. It also raises the question of whether this military tribunal was capable of any kind of impartiality when the term "bad worker" could appear on a criminal charge sheet and undoubtedly adversely affected the tribunal ahead of the trial.

The Basque Country and Cantabria (Oñati, Bilbao, Barakaldo, Sestao, and Santander)

The Basque example in this category is illustrated by the collective trial of Marcelino Astizaran Leturia and three other Basque soldiers.[21] I have used three of the cases as I have been able to extract (and decipher) much more personal information than is usual, although even here there is a disparity of data in relation to each soldier. Most of their fighting took place between July 1936 and the fall of Santander in August 1937. Five out of the six were charged with *rebelión* and sentenced in Bilbao on April 20, 1938 to thirty years' imprisonment.

Marcelino Astizaran Leturia came from Oñati, Gipuzkoa, and was a member of the Izquierda Republicana.[22] Aged twenty-four and described as a trader/dealer, he was regarded as a propagandist for the Republic. After the outbreak of hostilities he joined security patrols to ensure law and order for the Republic. In the following August he joined a section that organized young socialists who fought Nationalist troops in Lasarte, Gipuzkoa. In November he joined the UHP Battalion (a Basque leftist battalion that took its name from the slogan "Uníos Hermanos Proletari-

---

21. AHPC/PSM, Legajo 29308, Causa número 1575 de 1938.
22. Astizaran Leturia was the lead prisoner in a collective trial. It follows that his file contains more personal details than the others tried with him.

os," "Unite, Proletarian Brothers!").[23] Astizaran Leturia then fought on the Elorrio front and in the ill-fated Vitoria-Gasteiz offensive in November 1936. He was promoted to sergeant and saw further action in Santo Domingo de la Cazada, La Rioja, where he was promoted to lieutenant. He withdrew to Santander, where he fled in a boat and was apprehended on the high seas by the Nationalist vessel *Virgen de Begoña*. Sentenced for *rebelión* with seven others in Bilbao on April 20, 1938, Astizaran Leturia was committed to thirty years' imprisonment, as were the others mentioned in this extract. Transfer to El Puerto followed on July 17, 1938.

Jesús Agustín Anapistate from Bilbao was a member of the Izquierda Republicana. He undertook accountancy duties until October 1936, when he joined the Capitán Casero Battalion number 7, affiliated with the Izquierda Republicana as a driver. He had the rank of corporal. Soon afterward, he joined the Capitán Casero Battalion number 1, being promoted to lieutenant and then captain with command of a company. His prison file suggests that he was engaged in enemy encounters at Mounts Bizkargi and Santo Domingo, just outside Bilbao, prior to the capture of the so-called Ring of Iron (Cinturón de Hierro) defensive system around the city[24] and the fall of Bilbao itself on June 19, 1937. If this was so, Agustín Anapistate was one of the few identifiable Basque prisoners in El Puerto who defended the Ring of Iron. He withdrew to Santander and was intercepted by Nationalist naval forces while trying to escape in the Bay of Biscay.

Florencio Martínez came from Barakaldo and had been an important member of the UGT since 1932 as well as being a member of the PSOE since February 1936. On September 19, 1936 he enlisted in either the Meabe Battalion number 1, Largo Caballero, or Meabe Battalion number 2, Stalin (affiliated with the JSU).[25] He fought on a variety of fronts including Eibar and Elgeta, both in Gipuzkoa, where he was wounded. Florencio Martínez joined the Zapadores Battalion as a lieutenant. He left for Erandio, where he had to withdraw to Santander. His escape by sea was thwarted by an interception of the Nationalist naval forces.

Emilio Carrera García came from Sestao and was a member of the PNV. In his case, there is slightly more information available than for his

---

23. Formed in February 1934 to support the rising in Asturias, it consisted of an alliance of socialists, the UGT, and the CNT of Asturias, León, and Palencia.
24. This was a vast labyrinthine fortification of bunkers, trenches, and tunnels built around Bilbao as defense against the Nationalist army by the Basque government. This was not, though, a sufficient defense against modern aircraft.
25. AHPC/PSM, Legajo 29308, Causa número 1575 de 1938. The prison file does not make clear the Meabe number.

colleagues. He joined as a militiaman on October 10, 1936 and served in an armory workshop.[26] In early December he joined the PNV's Gordexola Battalion, in which he served in Legutio (Villareal in Spanish), Araba. He was forced to withdraw to Bilbao, where he obtained a position with the Basque military police. Carrera García held this post until the end of February 1937. The varied military career of Emilio developed when he joined the Military Academy of Artillery that he left in the following May with the rank of lieutenant. Further withdrawals saw him arrive at Santander. On August 26, 1937, he fled in a boat but was captured. (Other prisoners convicted at this collective trial fled by boat, but the prison files do not make it clear whether it was the same boat).

Rafael Ramos from Santander acted as inspector of refugees for the local authority. In February 1937, at the request of the Commander of Engineers, he worked on fortifications in the Puerto de La Sía, a mountain pass between Burgos and Cantabria, with the grade of sergeant. He then became a lieutenant, working at an air force camp at Liendo, Cantabria, followed by further promotion as a captain working in the defense of Cicero, also in Cantabria. Republican propaganda was found in his home. His prison file also contains an unusual reference relating to "*mala conducta*," which stands out because the usual comment was "*buena conducta*." Although his details are relatively brief, he received the maximum custodial sentence as the Nationalist authorities clearly felt that his war effort on the part of the Republic was substantial.

Although most of the Basque prisoners (and the one Cantabrian inmate) were sentenced following a *rebelión militar* charge, it is worth examining the more minor charges such as *auxilio a la rebelión, excitación a la rebellion*, and *injuria al ejército*, because they illustrated inconsistencies of sentence.

Auxilio a la rebelión (Cádiz, Ceuta, Seville and Granada)

The charge of *auxilio a la rebelión*, aiding the rebellion, carried less weight than *adhesión a la rebelión/ rebelión militar*, but it remained a serious offense.

The first of these cases is that of Manuel López Sierra, which illustrates the reaction of the Franco regime to those not paying due obeisance. López Sierra, aged forty-nine, a porter from Cádiz, was charged with *auxilio a la rebelión* in la Plaza de Ceuta for using improper forms

---

26. AHPC/PSM, Legajo 29308, Causa número 1575 de 1938.

of address.[27] The changed form of address had been remarked upon by George Orwell when visiting anarchist-controlled Barcelona in December 1936.[28] He writes: "Servile and even ceremonial forms of address temporarily disappeared. Nobody said '*Señor*' or '*Don*' or even '*Usted*'; everybody called everyone 'Comrade' and 'Thou' and said '*Salud*' instead of '*Buenos dias*.'"

The prison report stated that "López Sierra had entered a taxi, number 1243, on the taxi rank of the Plaza de Ceuta on August 3, 1938. On hearing one of the women who had accompanied him saying goodbye with the words '*Arriba España*', he vigorously corrected her. "One does not say that, one says '*Salud*'. His friends taking the same taxi heard this clearly. They remonstrated with him and one said 'man, what are you doing? 'The other said 'For God's sake Manolo what are you saying?" He denied that he had said '*Salud*', but was found guilty. My view is that the tribunal would have reached this decision on the grounds that not only had López Sierra used an improper form of address, but by doing so he had demonstrated a clear attitude of resistance in using a popular form of Republican address. Both aspects were doubtless taken into consideration by the military tribunal when awarding him a sentence well above the usual tariff for the charge of *auxilio a la rebelión*."

Part of his guilt was assumed to be evidenced by the fact that he used to be an employee of the Post Office, where he had already been punished by suspension of his salary and employment. He had also been present at a demonstration by the Popular Front on May 1, 1936, had voted for the left wing candidate Manuel Pedroso in the Spanish general election in 1936 in Ceuta and was a proven supporter of the Popular Front, having taken part in in a demonstration on May 1, 1936. Another matter that was drawn to the attention of the tribunal was that one of his friends, Ruiz Pujol, had supported a strike and had been dismissed from the electricity and water company in which he worked. Further evidence of guilt by association was that the company had been forced to reemploy him and pay him some six months back pay as a result of the victory of the Popular Front in February 1936.

The case of López Sierra was heard by the investigating judge, Deputy Infantry Lieutenant Don Fernando García Braojos in Ceuta on August 24, 1938.[29] Initially imprisoned for a very short while in the Hacho Fort prison in Ceuta, he was admitted to the penitentiary of El Puerto on October 24,

27. AHPC/PSM, Legajo 29288, Causa número 366 de 1938.
28. George Orwell, *Homage to Catalonia* (London: Penguin, 2000), 3–5.
29. AHPC/PSM, Legajo 29288, Causa números 366 y 198 de 1938.

1939. The prison file confirms that Sierra was charged with *auxilio a la rebelión* and sentenced to thirty years' imprisonment, which was far longer than the recommended sentence. This is surprising on two counts. First, the usual maximum sentence for this charge was twenty years, although other prisoners were also given thirty years under this same charge. The usual charge for this length of sentence was *adhesión a la rebelión* or *rebelión militar*. Second, this seems an inordinately severe sentence for this "crime" which was clearly influenced by guilt by association.

Another example of a case involving the charge of *auxilio a la rebelión* was that of Francisco Serrano Perula, a delegate of waiters in the CNT and Fernando Fernando Lopéz, a labor union activist and member of the Casa del Pueblo, a branch office and meeting place affiliated to the PSOE and the UGT, in Madrid, as part of a collective trial.[30] Both were known for "their extremist views" and were sentenced to imprisonment of twelve years and one day on March 31, 1937 in Seville. Serrano Perula was considered to be an extreme propagandist. On July 21, 1936 he was heard telephoning from the establishment of José Parcal Fernández, asking whether it was true that General Franco had surrendered to Azaña, adding that there would be no more talk of the Glorious Movement in his house. Fernando López had belonged to the Casa del Pueblo in Madrid and had expressed joy at the activities of the Republican army in Toledo and the siege of Alcázar in July 1936. He had been heard expressing hostility to the Glorious Movement.

Excitación a la rebelión (Granada and Ceuta)

An additional lesser charge was *excitación a la rebelión* or incitement to rebellion.

This next example indicates a very considerable inconsistency in sentencing for what appears to be a not dissimilar "crime" to that of López Sierra mentioned above. This time the same investigating judge in the same place sentenced the culprit to imprisonment of only six years and one day, not thirty years. In this case, Lorenzo González Vilches was charged with a "lesser crime," *excitación a la rebelión*, which attracted a lower sentence ranging between six months and one day to twelve years.

González Vilches, an agricultural worker aged thirty-six from Granada, was arrested for insulting Franco and the *Nuevo Estado* and was

---

30. AHPC/PSM, Legajo 29357, Causa número 54 de 1937. A collective case heard under the lead charge of Luis Fernández Pérez (the same *causa número* and *legajo* number). The others do not have personal details.

charged with *excitación a la rebelión* and sentenced on March 31, 1938.[31] His conviction was based on the five witness statements of José Rojas, Julián Borrego Runiera, Pedro de Mantras, Andrés Pardesa Pulido, and Luis Salazar. They all confirmed that he was an extreme red supporter and had sung insulting songs in two bars mentioned in the statements.

The prison report states that, "González Vilches was heard by five witnesses on two separate occasions in 1937, viz December 18 in a bar called La Campaña and December 21 in a bar called La Valencia in the area of Bab-Tazza. On the first occasion he was singing songs referring to Marxists that intimated that they were worth more than the Nationalists. On the second occasion he directed his comments to Sgt Ernesto Rodriguez when Vilches claimed to be the most ardent Red supporter in the area of Bab-Tazza." The tribunal considered that he was a person of extreme ideas and of obvious dubious conduct. González Vilches was charged with *excitación a la rebelión* and was sentenced to imprisonment for six years and one day on March 31, 1938 and was admitted to the penitentiary of El Puerto on June 7, 1938.

Another variation in the same military tribunal for the same charge involved the case of Bartolomé Morejón Pizarro, who was sentenced to eight years' imprisonment on July 10, 1937 in Ceuta.[32] In this case, Morejón Pizarro, aged thirty-seven from Benarrabá, Málaga, and a security guard, was charged with seventeen others. Some defendants were members of cell number five of the local Communist Party, had formed a guard for the mayor Sanchéz Prado (executed on July 10, 1937), and had prepared to defend Ceuta against the second *bandera* of the Spanish Legion, led by Juan Yagüe. It was alleged that Morejón Pizarro was a propagandist and helped to organize order after the Nationalist attack. In view of his rather active background, including membership of the Communist Party, it was perhaps surprising that he was only imprisoned for eight years. Morejón Pizarro moved to El Puerto in June 1938 from the military prison on Mount Hacho, Ceuta.

Injuria al ejército (Salamanca and Cuidad Real)

The charge of *injuria al ejército* related to slander of the military. There are further incidents of apparently similar offenses not always attracting the same charges at different military tribunal hearings. For example, some

---

31. AHPC/PSM, Legajo 29319, Causa número 1131 de 1937.
32. AHPC/PSM, Legajo 29294, Causa número 518 de 1937.

prison files listed charges under *injuria al ejército*. Agustín Mata Ratón, aged forty-four and a storekeeper from the Salamanca area, wrote to the Communist newspaper *Mundo Obrero* about the Spanish Foreign Legion in disparaging terms in early September 1936.[33] He was charged with *injuria al ejército* and was sentenced to six years and one day on September 26, 1936 in Ceuta. In this case, it should also be noted that the Law of Jurisdiction of 1906 had already established the ethos of punishing civilians for "crimes" against the nation and had extended military jurisdiction over civilians. Francisco Nieto Álvarez, aged forty and an agricultural laborer from Jerez de la Frontera, was sentenced in Ceuta for a similar period on July 23, 1936 for having said that the Nationalists were criminals and cowards for having bombed Ceuta.[34] On the other hand, Antonio Traverso González, aged forty-three and a fisherman from Chiclana, was charged with a different offense, *auxilio a rebelión*, but sentenced to the same period of imprisonment in Cádiz.[35] He was charged as a result of comments he made in the Venancio bar in Cádiz. On seeing photos of Nationalist Generals he said that "they were shameless '*hijos de puta y mierdas de generales* [sons of bitches and absolutely useless generals]'". He was sentenced on December 24, 1936 and the military tribunal considered that that "these comments could have led to a state of depression among those that heard them." Despite the fact that this charge carried a maximum sentence of twenty years, he was sentenced to serve the same time for a similar offense as those charged with *injuria al ejército*, six years and one day.

Another variation in sentencing is provided by the case of Zacarías Mora Rodríguez of Puertollano, Ciudad Real, who was convicted of *injuria al ejército* on October 28, 1936 in Tetouán (the capital of Spanish Protectorate of Morocco between 1913 and 1956) and sentenced to twelve years' imprisonment.[36] He had made two adverse comments about the Civil Guard and the Army. The first comment referred "disrespectfully" to the Civil Guard and the second referred to the Nationalist Army when he was heard to say "the Army *was* destroying the country." The following witnesses signed statements to this effect: Antonio Villaba Rubio, as per file Antonio Moreno, Francisco Girón, Joaquim as per file Porres, José Heredia, and Esteban Collado. The military tribunal decided to sentence him to six years' imprisonment for each offense.

33. AHPC/PSM, Causa número 209 de 1936.
34. AHPC/PSM, Legajo 29266, Causa número 371 de 1936.
35. AHPC/PSM, Legajo 29266, Causa número 610 de 1936.
36. AHPC/PSM, Legajo 29294, Causa número 840 de 1936.

This sentence was double that of González Vilches, who was sentenced some seven months earlier in Ceuta for two similar statements, made at different times, for a not dissimilar offense when he was heard insulting the Nationalists. I would suggest that these examples relating to the less serious charges provide a good indication of the fickleness and the arbitrariness of military tribunals, which often convicted people on extremely flimsy evidence. The intervention of higher military authorities reduced the power of local tribunals in 1940.

Sedition (Granada)

Sedition is generally understood as some form of overt conduct, such as speech and organization that tends toward insurrection or subversion against the established order.

A further example not unconnected with the spreading of doubt and dissent was that of José Villanueva Moreno, whose behavior led to a charge of sedition. He was aged twenty-five and a mechanical fitter from Granada.[37] Villanueva Moreno was sentenced to thirty years' imprisonment in Talavera de la Reina, Toledo, on September 29, 1937 for this "crime" and sentenced for *rebelión militar*. He was a soldier in the Nationalist Battalion of the Infantry Regiment, Argel, number 27, in Seville.

The military tribunal was told that during the previous April, on the Ciempozuelos front in Madrid, he expressed comments to his fellow soldiers that showed disaffection and induced civil order. The particulars of the case were unusually complete in that there were full details of what he said. Allegedly, he said that "General Franco directed and maintained this war with the object of completely annihilating the working class. Our [Republican] troops suffered reverses reported by a hostile press."

The Nationalist authorities were clearly quick to respond to anything that cast doubts on the mission of the Great Movement or could lead to a loss of morale, whether made by soldiers of Franco or civilians. It could also be that the charge of sedition was brought against a Nationalist soldier at this time because the Battle of the Ebro was reaching a crucial point, as well as the continuing fighting in nearby Madrid. Notwithstanding, Villanueva Moreno was released on *libertad condicional* in September 1942.

---

37. AHPC/PSM, Causa número 643 de 1937.

*Robbery and Black market dealings (*El Puerto de Santa María, Seville and Zufre*)*

Other kinds of charges with less overtly political dimensions were also brought against inmates in El Puerto.

A study of the prison records of El Puerto during the Spanish Civil War indicates that there were relatively few prisoners in the penitentiary who had been convicted solely under the charge of robbery. There were some 125 prisoners from the province of Cádiz convicted solely under the charge of robbery, but only seven during the period 1936 to 1939.[38] The rest fell into the time frame between 1940 and 1950. In the case of the Basque Country, some twenty-three were held who had been imprisoned under the charge of robbery (two from Araba, three from Navarre, four from Gipuzkoa, and fourteen from Bizkaia) but none during the 1936–1939 period.[39] This is further confirmation that where the Nationalists used El Puerto as a detention establishment for Basques, its punitive isolation made it more attractive for political prisoners. Richards tends to support this view that Franco adopted a more vindicatory policy toward them and is of the opinion that "crimes" were considered "political"for the purposes of allowing a military tribunal to be held in each case"[40] Official records show at the end of 1942, 80 percent of the prison population were detained for crimes of rebellion while only 20,137 were imprisoned for common crimes."[41],

This point is well illustrated by the case of Antonio García, who was given an extremely light sentence of two years and four months for robbery in 1940.[42] This compares incredibly favorably to the normal sentence of thirty years for *rebelión militar.* Aged thirty-three, a laborer and a native of El Puerto de Santa María, he was insolvent, *sin educación* (illiterate), and the possessor of a previous bad record for a similar crime.[43] This was due to his previous imprisonment on September 27, 1931, when he had been imprisoned for robbery for one year and one day. On October 23, 1939 he offered to sell some boxes of sugar and 125 kilograms (275 pounds) of coffee to Clemente Parejo Arrecha in Sanlúcar de Barrameda.

---

38. AHPC/PSM, Legajos 29246–29474.
39. AHPC/PSM, Legajos 29257–29357. Also see Eiroa San Francisco, *Viva Franco*, 263.
40. Richards, *A Time of Silence*, 78.
41. Eiroa San Francisco, *Viva Franco*, 263.
42. AHPC/PSM, Legajo 29347, Causa número 92 de 1940.
43. AHPC/PSM, Legajo 29466, Expediente número 3. These files show that a prisoner of the same name and same place of origin was imprisoned in El Puerto for robbery on March 5, 1946. In this case, release was not until January 2, 1951.

Coffee was particularly scarce at this time and was regarded as a luxury. A sum of money was paid to him and Antonio García Benítez disappeared. However, he was arrested by the Civil Guard the following day and detained in the penitentiary of El Puerto. This sentence of two years and four months for robbery (in Cádiz on June 24, 1940) also partly reflected a period when prison sentences were less harsh and when prisons were less overcrowded than they had been a year earlier.

It was highly likely that García Benítez was involved in the black market that was rife in Spain at this time. "Scarcity was used to control the population. At least twice the quantity of essential food was sold on the black market as was issued officially. Significantly, this black market . . . was popularly considered as a central part of the Francoist terror."[44] Hunger, unemployment, and deliberate discrimination contributed to the terror of the defeated. The fact that a possible small-time racketeer was imprisoned in El Puerto with people serving thirty years' imprisonment would have been small consolation to them or their families.

While accepting that this case is somewhat different from the next two examples, it compares very favorably with the examples that involved participating in a robbery, quite probably as accessories to looting that the tribunal could link with Nationalist property and membership of a political party. The two cases involved Eduardo Cánovas Martín from Seville[45] and Germán Caballero Hato from Zufre, near Huelva.[46]

Both were charged with *rebelión militar* at a collective trial involving thirty-six others and both were accused of being members of the UGT, with connections to the Izquierda Republicana, and with the objective of helping "the Marxist cause." Both were agricultural laborers and had stood guard while robbery had taken place, in some cases allegedly from the property of Nationalist sympathizers. Both ended up with sentences of thirty years' imprisonment on September 13, 1937. Any kind of political connection would seem to have attracted a heavy sentence, even if the person himself had no previous criminal record but appeared to be on the outside of the political group under trial and was involved as an accessory to a robbery.

44. Richards, *A Time of Silence*, 135.
45. AHPC/PSM, Legajo 29357, Causa número 526 de 1937.
46. AHPC/PSM, Legajo 29357, Causa número 518 de 1937.

Freemasons (Mainly from Andalusia and one from Bilbao)

Together with the threats of Marxism and separatism, Franco considered Freemasonry a particularly spectral presence and a dangerous challenge to the regime.

There was a small Freemasonry presence in El Puerto and the prison reports examined show that fifteen Freemasons were imprisoned there, incarcerated as a result of the Law for Repression of Freemasonry and Communism of 1940. They were admitted to this prison in either March or August, 1942.[47] Some of the prison documents contain very brief reports of *El Tribunal Especial para la Represión de la Masonería y del Comunismo*, the special tribunal set up to deal with the aforementioned law. None of them contains much information about the conviction and they compare extremely badly with the rest of the prison files. All bar one of the prisoners came from one of the heartlands of Spanish Freemasonry at that time, Andalusia. Indeed, between late 1941 and early 1942, investigative judges visited Andalusia and the vast majority of the 1,305 sentences awarded by the special tribunal applied to this area. [48]

In El Puerto the ages of people convicted for this "offense" ranged from twenty-one to seventy-one and their occupations included agricultural laborer, electrician, head of telephones, lawyer, baker, employer, salesman, carpenter, and shoemaker. Where prisoners had also been members of a society like the Freemasons the sentence could be thirty years.[49] Although in El Puerto the maximum sentence for membership of the Freemasons was twelve years and one day, in El Puerto there were greatly reduced sentences and actual time served at this penitentiary for this "crime" in 1942 was seven months maximum and one month minimum.[50] It may be that those imprisoned belonged to the lowest Masonic grade and that this was taken into consideration. In Madrid, for example, the relevant tribunal discovered that over 70 percent of those charged belonged to the lowest Masonic grades (1 to 3).[51] On the other hand, it was probably more likely this was part of early release brought about by enormous overcrowding in Spanish jails that led to early release for the vast majority of offenses.

One example of imprisoned masons in El Puerto is that of Antonio Ruescas Pérez.[52] Aged forty-one, he was an urban postman from Almería.

---

47. AHPC/PSM, Legajos 29298, 29347, 29349, 29352, 29353, 29354, 29355, 29357.
48. Archivo General de la Administración, Presidencia 4026 and 4027.
49. Ruiz, *Franco's Justice*, 214–17.
50. AHPC/PSM, Legajos 29298, 29347, 349, 351–55, 357.
51. Archivo General de la Administración, Presidencia, 4026–4034.
52. AHPC/PSM, Legajo 29347, Causa número 29512 de 1939.

He supported the Izquierda Republicana Party and was a Freemason from 1932 to 1938. According to his prison file, Ruescas Pérez was a member of the Evolución lodge number 403, and was of the lowest masonic grade, somewhere between 1 and 3; he was also the lodge treasurer and president of the local postal workers' union that was affiliated to the CNT.[53] The tribunal considered that he had been an active political propagandist on behalf of the Republic. In view of his additional political involvement, he attracted a sentence of twelve years and one day by the Almería military tribunal on December 1, 1939, later being transferred to El Puerto on June 10, 1940.

The only Basque prisoner detectable in El Puerto for Freemasonry was Abel Fiat Paul, head of a government telephone department, aged fifty, from Bilbao.[54] He was sentenced to twelve years and one day on October 21, 1941 in Bilbao for the "crime" of Freemasonry. He reached El Puerto on December 17, 1941, apparently via the Porlier prison number I, Conde de Peñalver Street, Madrid.

Freemasons were required to provide a retraction of their membership of a "criminal organization" and a repudiation of their mistakes in becoming a Freemason. Perhaps the most interesting document (figure 4.2) concerning those incarcerated for Freemasonry at this prison relating to retraction is that provided by the Vicar General of the Diocese of Andalusia. The document concerns a confession by José Medina Flores to membership of the Freemasonry movement in Estepona, Málaga, and accepts that this has been followed by his reintegration into the Catholic Church.[55]

While the fate of Freemasonry under Franco is not within the remit of this work, there are two points worthy of note. The first is to note that members of the armed forces who were also masons were not considered by the special tribunals set up by the 1940 Act. Specific "honor tribunals" dealt with them and the only apparent sanction, which was not always applied, was dismissal from the forces.[56] This meant that all of the Freemasons imprisoned in El Puerto were civilians. Second, the law against Freemasonry was not abrogated until 1963, but real progress in this regard had to await the death of Franco in 1975.

53. Of all the prisoners sentenced for membership of Freemasonry, this particular prisoner has most detail about his membership in the El Puerto file.
54. AHPC/PSM, Legajo 29354, Causa número 248 de 1941.
55. AHPC/PSM, Document of retraction to the Church.
56. There is an interesting reference to membership of the Freemasons on the part of senior Francoist generals in Thomas, *The Spanish Civil War*, 43, in which he cites Manuel Goded, Gonzalo Queipo de Llano, and Miguel Cabanellas as belonging to the military Masonic lodge.

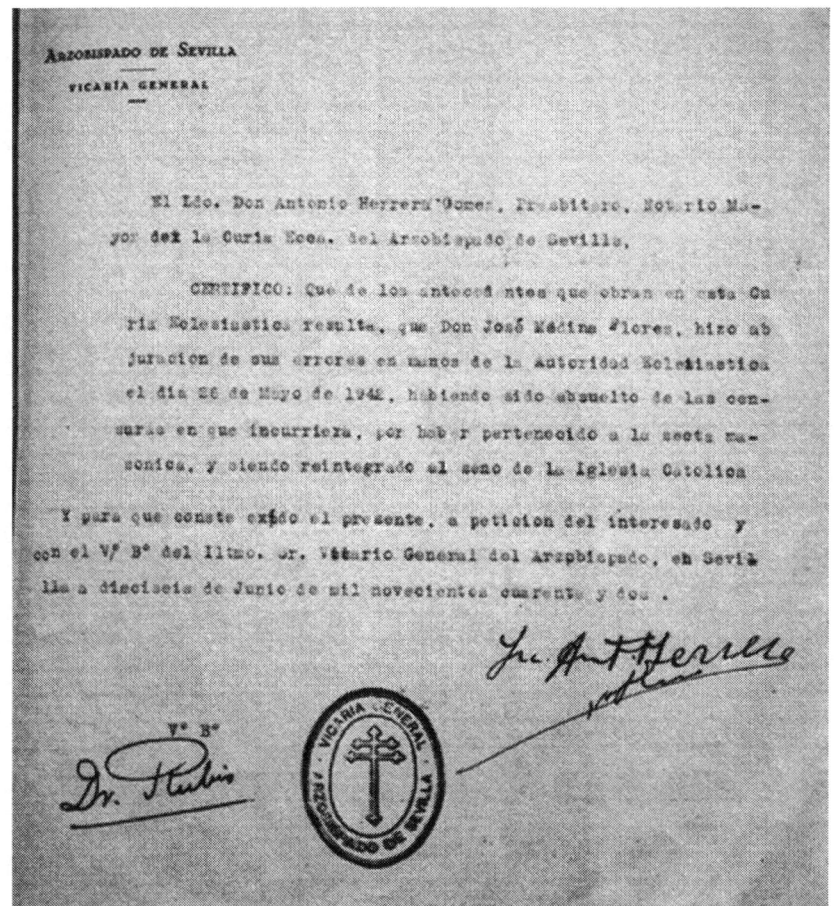

Figure 4.2

Destruction of Church Images (Villaluenga del Rosario, Grazelema)

The charge of destroying church images fitted in with the religious dimension of Franco's "crusade" for Spain"

The destruction of church images, and indeed churches as a whole, varied considerably in different parts of Republican-controlled Spain. For example, in Barcelona, out of fifty-eight churches, only the cathedral was spared.[57] At the beginning of August 1936 militiamen destroyed the Sacred Heart of Jesus church located in Getafe.[58] Two weeks later, in Almería, once again militiamen reduced their Sacred Heart church to rubble.[59] The resulting executions by firing squad were "a famous example

---

57. David J. Mitchell, *The Spanish Civil War* (New York: F. Watts, 1983), 46.
58. Archivo Militar de Madrid, Consejo de Guerra 52600/47667.
59. Archivo Histórico Nacional, Causa General Legajo 1164–70, Almería pieza no.10,

of an assault on the public presence of Catholicism."[60] Desecrations of religious symbols in different parts of the country were widespread and the militia often used vestments for uniforms and burned wooden images of saints for fuel.

My research into prisoners' files relating to charges of destruction of church images of unearthed one such case. Dionisio Ruiz Valle, aged forty-three and from Villaluenga del Rosario, was a supervisor for the Popular Front in Grazalema in the February election of 1936. He was also a member of the CNT and later the UGT as well as serving asa councilman in Villaluenga. Ruiz Valle was sentenced to thirty years for *rebelión* for destroying and burning images of the parish church of Villaluenga del Rosario.[61] The date of sentence was August 24, 1939, and he arrived at El Puerto on August 11, 1941, via Jerez de la Frontera prison. It is noteworthy that substantial sentences could be handed down for this type of "offense" as late as August 1939.

On the other hand, in the Basque Country the situation regarding destruction of church images tended to be different in view of Catholic support there. In the case of Eibar, Gipuzkoa, on August 15, 1936, steps were taken to protect church images. Their Defense Committee transferred certain articles from the Arrate Shrine that were of interest to the Church. The priest, Saturnino Gantxegi, chaplain of the old folks' home and hospital, obtained safe conduct to organize this transfer, which he did by means of a van. These articles involved an image of the Blessed Virgin, four paintings by Ignacio Zuloga, ceiling chandeliers, all religious ornaments, and miniature flutes and drums used by the Basques for religious purposes. All moved articles were transferred to the hospital.[62] On February 25, 1937 the Director General of Arts, Archives, and Libraries of the Basque Government authorized the transfer from Eibar to Bilbao of a stained glass window containing a cross inlaid with mother-of-pearl and an ivory figure.[63]

---

expediente 2/90.

60. Chris Ealham and Michael Richards, eds., *The Splintering of Spain: Cultural History and the Spanish Civil War, 1936–1939* (Cambridge: Cambridge University Press, 2005), 80, 168.

61. AHPC/PSM, Legajo 29335 de 1939.

62. Jesús Gutiérrez Arosa, *La Guerra Civil en Eibar y Elgeta* (Eibar: Eibarko Udala/Ayuntamiento de Eibar, 2007), 109.

63. Archivo Histórico Nacional, Guerra Civil, sección Político Social, Bilbao, Gobierno de Euskadi, Justicia y Cultura, Dirección General de Bellas Artes, carta al delegado de plaza de Eibar, 335. See also Paul Preston on censorship in in the rebel zone in *We Saw Spain Die: Foreign Correspondents in the Spanish Civil War* (London: Constable & Robinson, 2008), 144–154.

Sabotage (Bergara, Gipuzkoa, and Various Places in Bizkaia)

The Cádiz prison archives which include individual prison files of El Puerto show that extremely few prisioners were convicted under this charge between 1936 and 1944. (The situation completely changed between 1945 to 1947 where there were many acts of sabotage conducted by guerrillas).[64]

While acts of sabotage were obviously regularly carried out by retreating Republican soldiers, relatively few prisoners' files specifically made mention of such acts. However, the case of José Altura Garitano was an exception. Altura Garitano, aged twenty-eight and a soldier from Bergara, had previously had a background of support for the Popular Front.[65] He became a captain in the San Andrés Battalion (affiliated with the STV) and was involved in the counterattack at Bermeo and the Battle of Sollube between May 6 and 14, 1937. Details of his charge involved the destruction of Bilbao's bridges, but also including the bridge at Ormaiztegi (Gipuzkoa), an iron bridge over a railroad line linking Irun to Madrid.[66] Altura Garitano surrendered in Barakaldo and was eventually sentenced to thirty years' imprisonment on the charge of *rebelión* on March 9, 1938. Initially held at Logroño, like so many Basque prisoners, he arrived at El Puerto in June 1939.

Censorship (Tétouan)

An abiding obsession of the Franco regime was control of information and, to this end, censorship was one of its key strategies.

(Tetouán) Preston, Graham and Thomas spell it as Tétouan and the army unit in question is shown on Spanish Google as Regulares no.1 de Tétouan.

This was an issue taken very seriously by Franco, who operated a strict press censorship.[67] Although this policy particularly applied to Nationalist soldiers (and Republican prisoners), it was also applied rigorously to the many journalists who supported the Republican cause.[68] The example

---

64. Andrew Cowan,"*The Guerilla War against Franco*", European History Quarterly vol 20 1990, 227.
65. AHPC/ PSM, Legajo 29308, Causa número 17508 de 1938.
66. See Francisco Manuel Vargas Alonso, *Bermeo y La Guerra Civil. La Batalla de Sollube* (Donostia: Eusko Ikaskuntza, 2007).
67. Archivo General Militar, Zona Roja, Caja 3037, c.44/1. Franco issued norms for censorship in view of complaints about uncensored correspondence.
68. See Preston, *We Saw Spain Die*.

quoted here is one detected by the military censor who acted against a Nationalist soldier.

José Cañadas Penas, twenty-three, was a soldier from Tetouán.[69] He was serving in the Tetouán Regular Forces number 1, which had participated in the major engagements of the Spanish Civil War. He wrote a letter to one Sixta Saldana in Alcalá del Río, a small town in Seville province. In the letter he referred to his officers in a derogatory manner and indicated that he was reluctant to fire on his own countrymen. The letter of Cañadas Penas never arrived as it was intercepted by the military censor. He was sentenced to imprisonment for one year by the military tribunal on August 25, 1936.

Cases highlighting a Wide Range of Different Categories of "Offenders"

Sailors (Valladolid, Barcelona, and Murcia*)*

Surprisingly, there are several interesting naval cases that resulted in the conviction of sailors who had been engaged in action in the Cantabrian Sea, only to be incarcerated in a distant Andalusian prison. One of these was Salvador Coll Broadvent, a merchant navy officer aged thirty-eight from Valencia, who was tried in Valladolid on May 8, 1937 for *rebelión*.[70] As he was in the navy, his case was tried in front of the investigating judge, Navy Commandant Don Antonio Barreiro López. Coll Broadvent was the First Officer on the *Mar Cantábrico*, a Republican merchant ship. This case was quite well-known at the time because the *Mar Cantábrico* was the last Republican ship to escape before the United States introduced a ban on shipment of arms to Spain.

The prison report stated that the Nationalist cruiser *Canarias*, responsible for sinking the Basque ship *Navarra*, was acting under instructions with the object of a blockade against the "red ports" of the north of Spain. One of the vessels involved was the *Mar Cantábrico*, which had left from New York and was due to call at Veracruz in Mexico. The merchant ship was suspected of gunrunning and the Spanish naval historian, Juan Pardo San Gil, writes that it had "left Mexico with a cargo that included 27 cannons, 31,800 grenades, 2,000 rifles, 47 machine guns, 12 million cartridges, and other materials."[71] Prior to the interception at sea of the *Mar*

---

69. AHPC/PSM, Causa número 468 de 1936.
70. AHPC/PSM, Legajo 29352, Causa número 50 de 1937.
71. Juan Pardo San Gil, *Crónica de la Guerra en el Cantábrico: Las Fuerzas Navales Republicanas 1936–1939* (San Sebastián: Txertoa, 2004), 130.

Cantábrico, she was flying a British fllag with the name of "Adda Newcastle" painted on the stern. On being apprehended, she answered the *Canarias* in English. The sea was very rough and after skirmishing fire, the *Mar Cantábrico* surrendered and was escorted back to El Ferrol, Galicia, on March 8, 1937. The prison report is unusually informative about the crew of the captured ship. A surprising detail is that one of them was a Mexican woman, Socorro Barberena, who, contrary to the ship's rules, had married one of the waiters, Eugenio Elorena.

A subsequent trial resulted in the execution of the captain, Serafín Santa María Ruiz, and twenty-five crew of the *Mar Cantábrico*; the rest were sentenced to imprisonment.[72] Interestingly, two English historians were of the view that all Spanish seamen on the *Mar Cantábrico* were executed.[73] Documents in the Provincial Historical Archive in Cádiz appear to tell a different story in that the first officer of that ship, a Spaniard, Coll Broadvent, was not executed. He was condemned to thirty years' imprisonment in Valladolid May 8, 1937, arriving at the penitentiary of El Puerto on October 5, 1938. Unusually for a transfer to Andalusia, Coll Broadvent had been first a prisoner in another Andalusian jail, Casería de Ossio, San Fernando (Cádiz), before his transfer to El Puerto.

This case also provides an indication of the power of the local Falange, which was usually able to influence suitability for employment following release from prison. In his case, this power is well illustrated by a certificate from the Valencia party, issued on May 4, 1943 (figure 4.3). This authorized him to continue his previous occupation as a navigating officer; without such clearance, he would not have been authorized to resume work on Spanish vessels. He was fortunate, as difficulty in obtaining work on release was one of the major problems faced by prisoners.

Another naval case with some similarities to the *Mar Cantábrico* was that of the *Isla de Tenerife* and Captain Álvaro Pons Abelló.[74] Aged forty-eight, he was a married man from Barcelona. Here again, his personal file also contains a fair amount of detail about his crew. It is probably true to say that his case is perhaps more typical of a master of a merchant ship serving the Republic who was captured by the Nationalists.

Prior to his service on the *Isla de Tenerife*, Pons Abelló was first mate of the *Ciudad de Cádiz*, which was a Republican merchant vessel concerned with transporting gasoline from Marseilles to Barcelona. Argu-

---

72. *La Voz de Galicia*, December 30, 2006. See also Xosé Manuel Suárez, *Armas para la República. La Aventura del 'Mar Cantábrico'* (El Ferrol: Embora, 2006).
73. Beevor, *The Battle for Spain*, 288; Thomas, *The Spanish Civil War*, 575.
74. AHPC/PSM, Legajo número 29351, Causa número 488 de 1938.

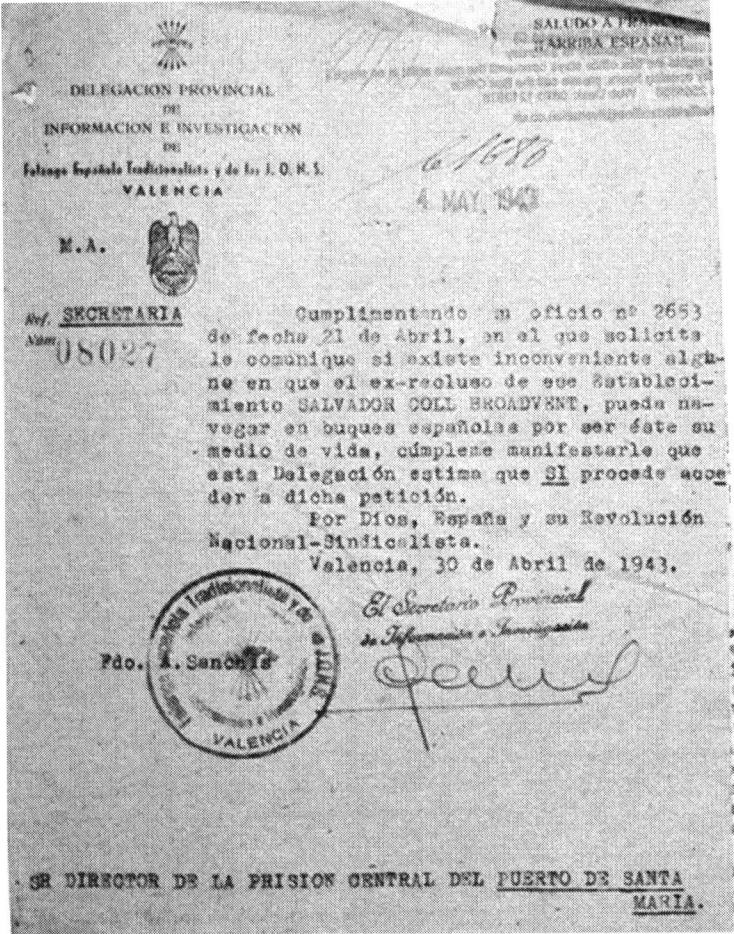

Figure 4.3

ably, fate was not entirely unkind to him since shortly after he moved to the *Isla de Tenerife*, the *Ciudad de Cádiz* was torpedoed by a Nationalist submarine in the Adriatic Sea in August 1937.[75]

Pons Abelló was ordered to embark on the *Isla de Tenerife* on January 1, 1937 in order to relieve the captain who was ill. The prison files indicate that his first, second, and third officers had had affiliations to the UGT or CNT, as had his two radio operators, first and fourth engineers, waiter, and cook. The *Isla de Tenerife* had earlier been involved in sailing from Las Palmas in the Canary Islands to the port of Ciudad Condal, Barcelona. The duties of this ship had involved the transportation of troops

---

75. *La Vanguardia*, August 25, 1937.

for the Catalan government in its abortive attempt to reconquer Majorca. On August 13, 1937 the vessel set sail from Santander to France with an assorted cargo of soda, iron, and other cargo for the Republican war effort only to be intercepted by the Nationalist cruiser *Almirante Cervera*. The prison files give an account of this interception in which the Republican ship tried to trick the cruiser by sailing without lights and replying in English. Ordered not to use radio, the *Isla de Tenerife* was eventually captured by the *Almirante Cervera*.

Pons Abelló was charged with *adhesion a la rebelión* and sentenced to thirty years' imprisonment in Valladolid. This imprisonment started on November 30, 1938, and he was subsequently admitted to the penitentiary of El Puerto on April 25, 1939. Other members of the crew were sentenced to imprisonment ranging from fourteen to thirty years. Subsequent to his release and resumption of his duties, on August 11, 1950 Pons Abelló was welcomed at a ceremony in the City Hall of Ibiza as the captain of the merchant ship with the same name.

A third naval case concerned Serafín Navarro Oliver, aged twenty-two, who was a former farmworker turned sailor, from Murcia.[76] In this instance, his prison file (most unusually) contained legible personal details of his appearance that described him as a person "with a round face, thick beard, and blue eyes." Earlier, Navarro Oliver was indirectly associated with the large-scale naval violence in Cartagena in August 1936. The last city to fall to Franco in 1939, Cartagena was the leading Republican naval base and the evidence reflected the sharp division between officers and men in the Spanish navy. The former supported the Nationalists and the latter the Republic. It was estimated that some 34 percent of naval officers on active service were shot.[77]

The prison report stated that the ship carrying imprisoned Nationalist officers and other senior officials was *España nº 3*, originally called the *Roma*. At dawn, on August 15, 1936, the ship left Cartagena. Some twenty miles out, on their own initiative, the crew began killing the officers. The situation was exacerbated by the arrival on board of a group of crew members from the *Jamie 1* (a Republican battleship) who formed part of the execution squad. The first mate on the *España nº 3* was Cristano López Carrasco, who played a leading role in executing the captured officers, including Admiral Don Ramón Nevia Ossorio and Captain Don Vicente Gironella Ronquillo.

---

76. AHPC/PSM, Legajo 29347, Causa número 194 de 1939.
77. Ramón Salas Larrazábal, *Historia del ejercito popular de la República*, vol. 1 (Madrid: Editora Nacional, 1974), 163.

Navarro Oliver was charged alongside some fourteen other crew members, but he was the only one not condemned to death from this collective charge. The report found that although he had some responsibility for the custody of prisoners, on this occasion he was not found to be aboard. Nevertheless, tarred with guilt by association of the recent events on his ship, he was charged with *adhesión a la rebelión* and given the normal sentence of thirty years' imprisonment in Cartagena on May 24, 1939. He was transferred from the naval military prison in Cartagena to the central penitentiary in Chinchilla, Albacete, directly after sentence, and arrived at El Puerto on June 23, 1939.[78]

He never left prison, since the final entry concerning Navarro Oliver is a note from an official of the penitentiary of El Puerto on March 9, 1942, which confirmed his death in the prison hospital. (See figure 4.4) Here was an example of an innocent man, wrongly condemned, who was to die in prison at the age of twenty-five. He was not executed but died as a result of illness in a hostile climate.

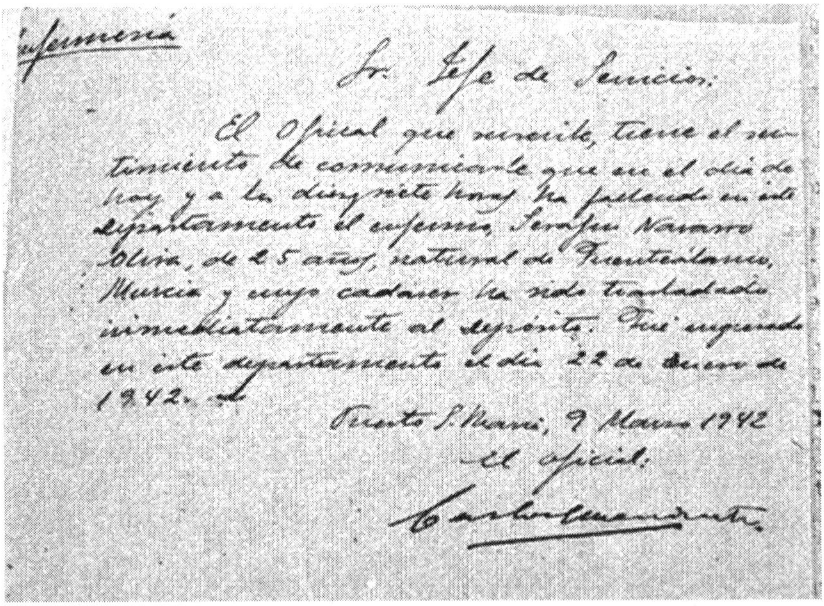

nfermería

Sr. Jefe de Servicios:

El Oficial que suscribe, tiene el sentimiento de comunicarle que en el día de hoy y a las diecisiete horas ha fallecido en este departamento el enfermo, Serafín Navarro Oliva, de 25 años, natural de Fuente Álamo, Murcia y cuyo cadáver ha sido trasladado inmediatamente al depósito. Fue ingresado en este departamento el día 22 de Enero de 1942.

Puerto S. María, 9 Marzo 1942
El oficial:

Figure 4.4

78. Ironically, the central pentitentiary in Chinchilla was closed down on February 23, 1946 and all prisoners moved to El Puerto.

It transpires that Navarro Oliver was not the only prisoner to have traveled on the *Isla de Tenerife* when it was intercepted by the *Almirante Cervera*. Zoilo Sánchez Herrera from Sestao, Bizkaia, was a Basque soldier who was a passenger on the vessel. His file suggests that he may have subsequently escaped to France.[79]

Chief production manager/boiler maker/industrial worker/machinist (Sestao, San Salvador del Valle, Zarautz, and Arrigorriaga)

Although Bilbao had perhaps the largest iron and steel presence in Spain in 1936, I have only found one detailed example of a prisoner who was involved there. Casáreo Zaro Alava, aged thirty-three and from Sestao, worked for Altos Hornos de Vizcaya (AHV).[80] Sestao was an important industrial location and was essentially a steel producing unit. It was also a Socialist stronghold due to large numbers of workers in AHV.

In the case of Zaro Alava, he was a chief production manager, responsible for the lamination of garages and workshops. Highly unusual for a prisoner's file, his jailers have included his previous monthly salary that was allegedly 500 pesetas per month. (The economic historian Pedro Pérez Castroviejo rates AHV skilled workers as possibly the highest paid Spanish workforce in the early 1930s).[81]

He was accused of being a strong Marxist ideologist and at the first meeting after the rising in July, he showed great enthusiasm for the red cause. He enrolled voluntarily in the red militia and became a lieutenant of the Sexta Battalion of the UGT. Later he became a commander and was evacuated to Santander and Asturias. Finally, he was captured on the high seas and was taken onboard the *Margarita*.[82] At his trial, Zaro Alava was charged with *adhesión militar* in Bilbao and was sentenced to thirty years' imprisonment on April 25, 1939.

Francisco Alcazar Barral, aged thirty-five, was a boilermaker from San Salvador del Valle (today, Trapagaran-Valle de Trápaga), Bizkaia and was a member of the UGT, the JSU, and the PSOE. He had some involve-

---

79. AHPC/PSM, Legajo 29285, Causa número 3241.
80. AHPC/PSM, Legajo 29354, Causa number 14568 de 1939.
81. See P.M. Pérez Castroviejo, *Clase obrera y niveles de vida en las primeras fases de la industrialización vizcaína* (Madrid: Ministerio de Trabajo y Seguridad Social, 1992), 115, 122.
82. His prison file also includes a note from the provincial examining judge for political responsibilities in Bizkaia on October 20, 1941 (número 503) stating that Zaro Alava could not be found in the prison of El Puerto. In fact, he did not leave there until November 8, 1942. This is the second occasion that the prison authorities made this mistake about a Basque prisoner.

ment in the October Revolution of 1934 but was not detained. In the 1936 elections he was an agent of the Popular Front and was an active supporter of the Republic on the rising the following July. Allegedly, he assisted the police in detaining señores Molinero, Alegría, and Niexa in Bilbao. He returned to his work as a boilermaker but later volunteered to serve with a UGT Battalion that could have been UGT 3. He was then involved in active service on various fronts and was taken prisoner at Avilés, Asturias. In this case, his prison file also contains details of his trial in Bilbao in which the public prosecutor asked for the death penalty and his defense successfully asked for a reduction of sentence. He was sentenced for *adhesión a la rebelión* with a reduced sentence of twelve years and one day on April 17, 1939.[83]

Another case of a prisoner with an industrial background was that of Santiago Arruti Gurmendi, whose prison file simply shows him as "an industrial worker." He was aged thirty-two and came from Zarautz.[84] A Basque nationalist, he was a member of the SOV (Solidaridad de Obreros Vascos, later renamed Solidaridad de Trabajores Vascos, STV).[85] He held the position of treasurer at his local Batzoki. Arruti Gurmendi had responsibilities for the requisitioning of mattresses, blankets, and other utensils from abandoned houses on behalf of the Republican cause. This was allied to confiscating telephones in Zarautz and acting as a tribunal member to the local war commission. He subsequently went to France for six months and was called up to an artillery unit. Part of his duties involved the supervision of prisoners in the construction of trenches. Promoted to lieutenant and then captain, Arruti Gurmendi was involved in the battle of Sollube from May 6 to 14, 1937.[86] He was wounded and transferred to Basurto (Bilbao) and then Santander, where capture followed. He was charged with *adhesión a la rebelión* at Santoña on September 11, 1937 and sentenced to thirty years' imprisonment. A transfer followed to El Puerto on August 8, 1938.

A final example of a Basque prisoner involved in the industrial sector is provided by Cesário Setién Garrido, aged thirty-three, a Socialist and machinist from Arrigorriaga, Bizkaia.[87] An executive member of the

---

83. AHPC/PSM, Legajo 29268, Causa número 17547 de 1939.

84. Ibid., Legajo 29272. Causa número 6 de 1937.

85. The SOV was a Catholic and Basque nationalist labor union established in 1911.

86. The Battle of Sollube was a defense for Bilbao, involved José Antonio Aguirre, the Basque *lehendakari* (president), and Basque, Asturian, and Cantabrian contingents; on the other side, it also involved the Italian Black Arrows and the German Condor Legion. Initally there were some one thousand deaths. See Vargas Alonso, *Bermeo y la Guerra Civil*.

87. AHPC/PSM, Legajo 29351, Causa número 14505 de 1938.

Casa del Pueblo, Gernika, he was imprisoned for taking part in the rising against the then Spanish government in 1934. He was subsequently involved in preparation of propaganda material for the PSOE for the general election of February 1936. During the period of Basque rule after the outbreak of the war, he was elected as a councilman in Gernika. Setién Garrido was also a UGT representative on the Gernika trades council and was involved in the removal of factory machinery that could have been of use to the Nationalists.[88]

He also participated in a commission that had responsibility for identifying pro-Franco local supporters. There are no details about his capture but his report indicates that Setién Garrido was sentenced to thirty years' imprisonment on the charge of *adhesión a la rebelión* in Bilbao on December 22, 1938. He was later transferred to El Puerto on April 26, 1939.

Elderly prisoners (Huelva, Grazalema, and Seville)

When visiting Grazalema a few years back I observed that people who live there spelt it as above.. My wife and I have visited Andalusia over a period of 15 years and have not noticed a name change. I suggest that it will also be confusing for people in Spain and UK to spell the name Grazaelema.

As indicated by the execution of elderly people in Chapter 2, the military tribunals were no respecters of age; there were at least three people over seventy in El Puerto prison. The first example was that of Cirulo López López from Huelva, aged seventy-one.[89] He was to be convicted with eighteen others, some of whom were suspected of participating in demonstrations; there were members of the local Defense Committee, members of the UGT or FAI (Federación Anarquista Ibérica, Iberian Anarchist Federation), those who had supported the Popular Front or were deemed to have Marxist sympathies. Others in the group took up arms. Another defendant in this hearing, José Villegas, boasted of taking part in an assault on the Civil Guard barracks; this was proved to be false. All of this inevitably conditioned the reaction of the tribunal to López López and must have affected his long sentence. He was charged with *rebelión militar* and sentenced in Valverde to thirty years' imprisonment on October 25, 1937. In his case, he was found guilty of involvement in distributing propaganda against the Movimiento Nacional. He was admitted to the

---

88. His prison report states that this was in anticipation of the approach of the Nationalist destroyer, *Armu*, to the Port of Gijón.

89. AHPC/PSM, Legajo 29287, Causa número 623 de 1937.

penitentiary of El Puerto on November 29, 1938.

I discovered two more elderly prisoners in El Puerto although there was comparatively little detail available. One was Francisco Castro Córdoba, an illiterate agricultural laborer from Grazalema.[90] He was aged seventy-one and charged with *adhesion a la rebelión* in Ubrique, where he was sentenced on May 21, 1937. The court was told that he always appeared to be a dangerous anarchist with CNT connections and he was sentenced to thirty years' imprisonment in Ubrique. He was admitted to the penitentiary of El Puerto on September 23, 1938.

The other elderly prisoner was Rafael Nogales Rivera, a builder from Seville, who had been a guard at a local school and had connections with the Popular Front.[91] He was sentenced thirty years for *rebelión militar* in Badajoz on August 3, 1938. (However, although the front of his prison file indicates that he was aged seventy-three, this is contradicted in the later part of his file).

There is also a poem by the *abuelo* (grandfather) in the prison mentioned in Chapter2; unfortunately, efforts to find out more details about him proved unsuccessful. The poem gives us more personal data than the files as it outlines the way in which a rather elderly inmate deals with incarceration in El Puerto.

There was an enormous disparity between the ages of the elderly prisoners and the other prisoners, since the average age of captives in El Puerto was around thirty-six in 1940.

A former Spanish Legionnaire serving in the Basque Army (Donostia-San Sebastián)

José Expósito Gardiaga from Donostia-San Sebastián had been a Basque member of the Spanish Foreign Legion.[92] The prison file states that he had previously served in the Legion but gives no details. At first sight, this background of service in the Republican cause may appear somewhat unusual. An explanation of why a member of the crack Nationalist force should change loyalties is partly explained by Matthews "The greatest percentage of [Republican] defectors is from the *Tercio* [Spanish Foreign Legion], with 70 percent of the defections."[93]

---

90. AHPC/PSM, Legajo 29295, Causa número 175 de 1937.
91. AHPC/PSM, Legajo 29295, Causa número 186 de 1938.
92. AHPC/PSM, Legajos 29308, 29314, Causa número 1575 de 1938.
93. Matthews, *Reluctant Warriors*, 194–95. Has cited extract from Archivo General Militar, Ávila Zona Roja. 58, 1.631, 1, d 3/8.

It is from Matthews's book Reluctant Warriors on the pages stated below. He in turn has taken it from Archivo General Militar. Ávila, Zona Roja a.58,1.631,1,d.3/8.

A member of the UGT, he was evacuated to Durango at the onset of the Nationalist troops' advance and joined an unidentified Basque battalion. Here, he was elected sergeant for his previous service in the Legion and took part in action in Aretxabaleta (Arechavaleta), Gipuzkoa. On regrouping, he moved battalions and was elected captain of a UHP Battalion.[94] Expósito Gandiaga fought in the campaigns of Elorrio, Eibar, and Gernika in the spring of 1937. Wounded, he withdrew to Santander where he attempted to escape by sea but was intercepted, Expósito Gandiaga was subsequently charged with *rebelión militar* and sentenced to thirty years' imprisonment in Bilbao on April 20, 1938. He was transferred to El Puerto on July 17, 1938.

An Assault Guard (Elgea, Araba)

The next cases relate to a paramilitary force, the Assault Guard, which had been established only four years earlier by the Republic in January 1932. Its role was to deal with urban violence; and enlistment was only open to known Republican sympathizers. According to Thomas, some 12,000 of its number supported the government while some 5,000 supported Franco on the outbreak of the Civil War.[95] The cases of Felix Iñurrieta Inguida and his colleagues were part of the majority of the Assault Guards who continued to support the Republic

Iñurrieta Inguida, aged twenty-nine and from Elgea, Araba, served alongside three other Assault Guards, Joaquín Ruiz Pérez, José Gomara Fernández, and Marcelino Crespo Lavin.[96] Iñurrieta had had an active and varied career in the service of the Republic. In his case, he served as an Assault Guard in Bilbao until July 23, 1936, a week after the outbreak of the Civil War when he was then transferred to Urduña and Eibar. He subsequently joined the barracks at the University of Deusto, where he volunteered to act as an instructor from November 1936 to February 1937. Here, Iñurrieta was promoted to the rank of captain, but was unfortunately moved before receiving the emolument due to this rank. He then moved again, this time to Bilbao and then Santander, arriving in Gijón. Here, he fought with a Marxist battalion in which he became lead corporal in the Assault Guard.

---

94. See the case of Marcelino Astizaran ealier in this chapter. He was also in the UHP.
95. Thomas, *The Spanish Civil War*, 29.
96. AHPC/PSM, Legajo 29286, Causa número 1898 de 1938.

Later captured in December 1937, he arrived at the penitentiary of El Puerto on May 24, 1938 after a sentence by Don Valeriano Pena Gonzalez, authorized secretary of military court number 1 in Bilbao, on December 9, 1937. The court decided that his behavior "constituted *rebelión militar* in view of his momentous and significant activity as captain in the rebel army." He was freed from El Puerto on July 2, 1940. His other Assault Guard colleagues were charged for similar offenses, attracting the same length of sentence. Like Iñurrieta Inguida, they had been involved in evacuation and fighting the Nationalist army; one had also guarded prisoners on the prison ship *Luis Caso de Cobos*, moored in El Musel, off the Port of Gijón, Asturias. All were condemned for "supporting the ideology of the Popular Front."

Teachers (Granada, Seville, Huesca, and Vallejo de Mena, Burgos)

Beevor writes that "this [teaching] profession was one of the most heavily punished in the Nationalist repression. Several hundred were murdered in the first few weeks including fifty in León, thirty-three in Zaragoza, twenty-one in Burgos, and twenty in Huelva."[97] Verified, 460. Chapter 9 The White Terror. Note 5.They were perceived to be enemies of Nationalists and committed to liberal views that would influence the young.[98] One of the groups that strongly supported the Republic was the *Institución Libre de Enseñanza*, the Free Educational Institute, founded in 1876.[99] This was an organization of liberal educationalists and teachers dedicated to modernizing and secularizing Spanish education. It was dissolved by Franco in March 1940 and all its facilities confiscated; there were also purges of schools and the educational system from 1936.[100]

As indicated in chapter 2, one of those likely to have been associated with the *Institución Libre de Enseñanza* was Juan López Tamayao, a school inspector from Loja, Granada in El Puerto. He was executed on August 13, 1936.

A primary school inspector in the prison, Luis Fernando Pérez, aged forty-two, married and from Seville, was not executed, but suffered the maximum sentence of confinement.[101] The government issued a decree

97. Beevor, *The Battle for Spain*, 460.
98. See the Spanish 2000 Goya Award film *La lengua de las mariposas* (Butterfly, dir. José Luis Cuerda, 1999), which shows a most realistic depiction of a relationsip between a liberal teacher and pupil in Galicia in 1936, curtailed by Nationaists.
99. See Antonio Jiménez-Landi, *Breve historia de la Institución Libre de Enseñanza, 1896–1939* (Madrid: Tébar, 2010).
100. See "Represión contra los maestros en la Guerra Civil," *El País*, January 27, 2003, 33.
101. AHPC/PSM, Legajo 29357, Causa número 54 de 1937.

ending the independence of primary school inspectors who had enjoyed independence and long tenure of office since 1913. Now they could be transferred or removed at the request of local authorities.[102]

In the case of Fernando Pérez, it was alleged that on February 9, 1936 he had attended a meeting in the Monumental movie theater in the district of San Fernando, where he advised the local branches of the tobacco union and the metalworkers' union. He had also taken part in other political acts in the province of Cádiz. It was also alleged that he had joined the Freemasons during 1929 and had attended meetings up to 1935. Fernando Pérez had belonged to the Casa del Pueblo in Madrid until 1934 and admitted to accepting Marxist propaganda prior to 1936. The tribunal in Seville on March 31, 1937 charged him with *rebelión* and accepted that, through his associations and behavior, he had demonstrated hostility to the Glorious Movement. Sentenced to thirty years' imprisonment, he was eventually admitted to the penitentiary of El Puerto on May 20, 1938.

Two other cases with Basque connections relating to teachers were discovered among the prison population of El Puerto. Antonio Allue Herranz, a single man, aged twenty-five, was originally from Huesca.[103] A teacher in Soraluze (Placencia de las Armas, Gipuzkoa), he moved nearer to Bilbao on outbreak of hostilities and became a primary school teacher in Arrigorriaga (Bizkaia). In November 1936 he became a second lieutenant in an artillery regiment destined for Durango. He was involved in action but withdrew following the fall of Bilbao on June 19, 1937. Promoted to full lieutenant, he moved to Santander where he embarked on a small coastal vessel bound for France, but was arrested. It may well have been the vessel *Aller*, as this was the vessel used by his codefendant, Vicente Alvares, when he was captured.

The Basque naval historian Juan Pardo San Gil writes: "During the evacuation, the Francoist boats took a good number of prisoners in their effective small coastal boats like the *Aller*, which took many Republican soldiers."[104] (The owner of the boat in this instance was Nicolás Lafuente y Suiza from Santander). The case of Allue Herranz was heard by a Bilbao tribunal on September 25, 1937, when he was charged with *adhesión a la rebelión* and sentenced to thirty years' imprisonment.

---

102. Dealt with by Commission C of the purging of teachers, which covered teacher training institutions and primary school inspectors. Orden del Ministerio de Educación Nacional del 11 mayo 1938.
103. AHPC/PSM, Causa número 1054 de 1937.
104. Pardo San Gil, *Crónica de la Guerra en El Cantábrico*, 187.

The other teacher imprisoned in El Puerto was Teodimiro Villate Arena, aged twenty-eight, from Vallejo de Mena, Burgos.[105] Villate Arena was a member of the Federation of Teachers that was affiliated to the UGT. He was regarded as a propagandist and joined the "Red Army" on August 25, 1936, and thereafter he presented himself, without arms, in Portugalete in September 1937. The tribunal tried him alongside seven others in Bilbao on November 4, 1937, when he was charged with *adhesión a la rebelión*. He was sentenced to thirty years' imprisonment. Villate Arena was transferred to El Puerto on July 29, 1938.

These examples were taken from a profession that had attracted the first purging *depuración* framework by Decree 66 on November 10, 1936. In these three cases, the picture is complicated in that although the teachers were imprisoned, they also were active soldiers at the time of their arrest. If they wished to return to a teaching career after release from prison, they had to appear before a purging commission, Commission D, which investigated primary and secondary school teachers.[106] These provincial commissions included a school head, a primary school inspector, the president of the local parents' association, and two persons of "the highest moral and technical ability." Ruiz reminds us that after the war, "the number of commissioners was later increased to seven by the inclusion of two Falangists."[107] This change had the obvious punitive intent of making the commission even more political and was enforced by decree.[108] It also undoubtedly contributed to a situation whereby a quarter of all teachers in Spain lost their right to practice as teachers.[109] It is interesting to note that teachers were one of the very few professions to attract their own purging security mechanisms.

A student (Algorta, Bizkaia)

Juan Antonio Langurica Eizaguirre, aged twenty-two and from Algorta, Bizkaia, was a student.[110] This was a somewhat unusual occupation for prisoners in El Puerto between 1937 and 1942. He was studying pharmacy and was a Basque nationalist. Langurica Eizaguirre had not participated in the Civil War until Algorta (in the municipality of Getxo) was shelled

---

105. AHPC/PSM Legajo 29294. Causa número 1112 de 1937.
106. See Fraser, *Blood of Spain*, 204-5 for examples of cases of application of purges of teachers.
107. Ruiz, *Franco's Justice*, 174 n. 46.
108. *BOE*, November 8, 1939.
109. Graham, *The Spanish Civil War: A Very Short Introduction*, 132.
110. AHPC/PSM, Legajo 29286, Causa número 35 de 1937.

by the Nationalist destroyer, the *Velasco*.[111] Langurica Eizaguirre enlisted in April 1937 and enrolled at a nearby academy. He participated in some conferences and reached the rank of captain; surrendering to Nationalist forces in Santoña. His case was heard by a Bilbao tribunal in which he was sentenced to thirty years' imprisonment for *adhesion a la rebelión* on October 4, 1937. Initially imprisoned in El Dueso, he was transferred to El Puerto on October 8, 1938.

Political activists (Seville, San Juan de Aznalfarache, and Alcalá de Guadara)

The cases relating to the codefendants of Luis Fernando Pérez are also quite significant in the context of a study of the prison files in El Puerto, for a variety of reasons. Not only do they provide a detailed and legible account of the charges against individual prisoners, they also contain a very good example of a collective hearing with an unusual amount of information relating to each prisoner.[112] All prisoners quoted in this example were charged under the same *causa número* or indictment number.[113] They also provide interesting background information about some of the Republican sympathizers in Seville, one of the most prominent Andalusian cities in 1936.

The other prisoners charged with Fernando Pérez were alleged to be Communist sympathizers, staying at the home of a corporal in the Assault Guard prior to an attack on the Civil Guard, belonging to the olive pickers' union, the CNT, acting as a delegate to the waiters' union, involvement with the tobacco union that had suspicious links with the *Socorro Rojo Internacional* (International Red Aid), and participating in the bloody defense of Triana, a working-class district.[114] The fact that the group included a Communist sympathizer and a CNT member may be regarded as somewhat unusual in that there was usually a considerable amount of antipathy between the two in this part of Andalusia. However, a local Andalusian historian from Vejer de la Frontera, Antonio Muñoz Rodríguez, considers that this could have been quite understandable. He expresses the view that, "there was rivalry between anarchists and com-

---

111. Pardo San Gil, *Crónica dela Guerra en el Cantabrico*, 112–19. The *Velasco* had been seized by Nationalist forces in Ferrol early in the war. It bombed Bilbao, Santander, and Gijón.
112. AHPC/PSM, Legajo 29357, Causa número 54 de 1937.
113. Ibid.
114. Ibid.

munists but from time to time there was collaboration in Andalusia."[115] All those charged with Fernando Pérez were either convicted of *rebelión* or *auxilio a la rebelión* and were sentenced on March 31, 1937.

Juan Gómez Guerra had been a member of the Communist Party before July 17, 1936 and was regarded as one of the leaders of the "revolutionary Marxist movement" in San Juan de Aznalfarache (some two miles from Seville). He had been heard calling out in a very loud voice that the Nationalists should not enter the town. A workman had reported to the Civil Guard on July 18, 1936 that he saw a group patrolling the streets with shotguns, affirming the same message. The Civil Guard in their report confirmed that Gómez Guerra was considered to be "a dangerous individual of the left." He was condemned to death, a sentence that was later commuted to thirty years' imprisonment.

Ramiro González Cruz was reported to have left his work in Seville on July 18, 1936 in order to return home. However, he did not return, but went to a place known as La Almeda where he spent two nights in the home of a corporal in the Assault Guard. He did not return to his own house until three days later. The head of the invesitigative brigade of the Falange considered that that he was involved with those who fired on the Nationalist army; he also considered him to be a member of the revolutionary Marxist movement. The tribunal was not of the view that he had actually taken up arms against the Nationalist forces. In January 1936 he had been admitted to the mental hospital of Miraflores for psychological disorders and the tribunal considered that he might not be fully recovered. Despite this medical history, he was charged with *rebelión militar* and was sentenced to thirty years' imprisonment.

José Rugateiro Bozada came from near the large town of Alcalá de Guadaíra (some seven miles from Seville). He was detained by the Civil Guard, who indicated that they were seeking men who had left three shotguns that had been obtained from police barracks. However, the evidence given to the Civil Guard by the local head of the Falange indicated that Rugateiro Bozada was not a member of any political party and had demonstrated good behavior before the outbreak of war. The sergeant of the Civil Guard, Manuel Espinosa, stated that although Rugateiro Bozada knew about the arms, there was no evidence that he intended to use them. Surprisingly, the case against him was dismissed for lack of evidence. This may have been due to the fact that this accused had no previous political

---

115. Interview with Antonio Muñoz Rodríguez, May 19, 2004. Also see Antonio Muñoz Rodríguez, *Vejer de la Frontera* (Cádiz: Diputación Provincial De Cádiz, 1996).

affiliation and the case was heard on March 31, 1937, as opposed to six months earlier, when the climate of sentencing was influenced by a proximity to the outbreak of the war in July 1936.

On the other hand, Diego Carrillo Jurado, also from Alcalá de Guadaíra, had a record of violence and political affiliation. The Civil Guard alleged that he held anarchosyndicalist ideas and that, during the "days of Marxist domination" in the town of Alcalá de Guadaíra, he had been seen in streets with the mobs. He had carried an iron bar and participated in the burning of the church, the Parroquia de Santiago. From reports collected, he had been a prominent member of the olive pickers' union and was regarded as a disturber of law and order. Condemned to death for *rebelión militar*, this was later commuted to imprisonment for thirty years.

Luis Rodríguez Delgado belonged to the CNT and was regarded as one of its leaders. He was also secretary of the metalworkers' union and was accused of being at the barricades of the working-class district of Seville, Triana, between July 18 and 20, 1936 against the troops of Queipo de Llano. This would have been hard to establish since the prison reports indicate that several of the prisoners alleged that large numbers of outside volunteers came to Triana after a request from Radio Sevilla. However, if one accepts that this is the case and the fact that the majority of the defenders were massacred by the Spanish Foreign Legion, it would have been difficult to establish the identity of all the defenders. In the case of Rodríguez Delgado, he claimed that he only left his house to buy bread for his family. The tribunal did not believe him and he was sentenced to death for *rebelión militar*, which was later to be commuted to thirty years' imprisonment.

On the other hand, Antonio Ochoa Ruiz admitted that on the afternoon of July 18, 1936 he left his place of work in Seville, definitely stating that he was going to join the barricades of Triana. The tribunal accepted he had been present and had taken part. Ochoa Ruiz had been president of the Federation of Spanish Tobacco that was affiliated to the local labor unions. He was regarded as a person who had political sympathies with the Communist Party, having expressed support for "the red cause" and a successful outcome of the war for them. These comments were expressed to the director of the local tobacco factory. He was also connected with the *Socorro Rojo Internacional*. The military tribunal sentenced him to death, but later commuted the sentence to thirty years' imprisonment.

*Basques who had been Presidents of Batzokis (*Portugalete Ortuella in Bizkaia, and Tolosa, in Gipuzkoa*)*

Two Basque cases have been included here since they relate to former Batzoki presidents. One was Juan Arrien Utriaga, an elected president of a Batzoki.[116] Aged twenty-nine, he was an accountant from Portugalete, part of Greater Bilbao. A member of a *partido separatista* (unspecified) from 1931, Arrien Utriaga was also a labor union activist from 1934 on. He was then elected president of the Batzoki of Santurtzi during the time of an autonomous Basque government.[117] A PNV club, this was not unlike the Spanish Casa del Pueblo affiliated with the PSOE, workers' clubs that were often political educational centers (presidents of both institutions were often prime targets for Nationalists). Arrien Urtiaga also had an involvement with the committee of Popular Front sympathizers who had responsibility for interrogation and detention of those people "considered to be unsympathetic to the Republic."

During the war he served in the PNV's Gordexola and Ibaizabal Battalions and was promoted to lieutenant and then captain. The prison report alleges that he was "sufficiently qualified to be a political commissar" in one of the battalions. It is likely that he was involved in the unsuccessful Basque defense of Bilbao, the *cinturón de hierro,* and the subsequent surrender to the Italian *Freccie Nere,* the Black Arrows, on August 26, 1937 in Santoña. He was sentenced to thirty years for *rebelión militar* in Bilbao on November 4, 1938 and transferred to El Puerto on December 10, 1938. Released on September 17, 1941, he obtained employment soon afterward.

This employment was in Bermeo with Ruperto Omaza, the owner of a firm that dealt with exported salted and preserved fish. (See figure 4.5.) In his case, the fact that he was able to find employment in a small town some twenty miles from home could partly be explained by his professional qualification as an accountant, and his former political connections such as being president of the Batzoki of Santurtzi. Generally speaking, this had not been the usual experience of most prisoners, as related by their relatives in other chapters.Another prisoner who was also president of a local Batzoki was Martín Arrieta Calleja. He was thirty years old and was a draughtsman from Ortuella, Bizkaia. A Basque nationalist, he belonged to the Basque labor union, the SOV and had had some involvement in the

---

116. APHC/PSM, Legajo 29308, Causa número 12422 de 1938.
117. An autonomous Basque control under PVV leadership set up on October 7, 1936.

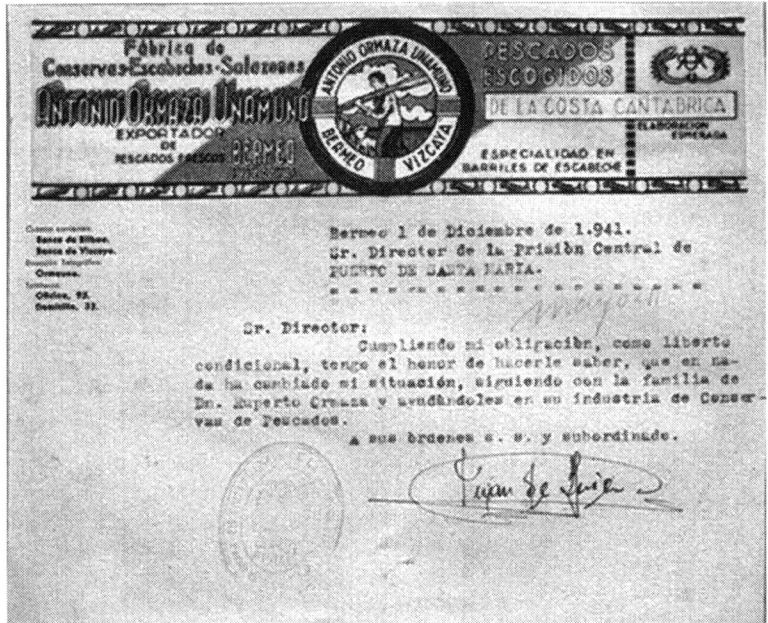

Figure 4.5

1936 elections. After the rising he was spokesman for the first committee of Ortuella and allegedly involved with the first fourteen Nationalists detained in the town and their interrogation; four of them were executed. Arrieta Calleja also negotiated for the release of others with variable success. Moreover, he was responsible for transportation in Ortuella. On the fall of Bilbao, he was involved in the moving of war materials. He worked with the Arana Goiri Battalion and the motorized police. He was subsequently captured on the high seas and was sentenced by a Bilbao tribunal to thirty years for *rebelión militar* on April 25, 1939.[118]

A Writer, Poet, and Storyteller (Tolosa, Gipuzkoa)

Luis Rezola Arana was a writer, poet, storyteller, and soldier.[119] He started work at age of thirteen for the Goñi firm making screws and bolts.[120] Aged twenty-three at the outbreak of war, he joined the PNV's Loyola Battalion and then moved to the Jagi-Jagi faction.[121] Captured by the Italians in 1937

---

118. Ibid., Legajo 29272. Causa número 1458 de 1939.
119. Ibid., Legajo 29299, Causa número 63 de 1937.
120. Email from Joxemari Mendizabal Sarasua, February 23, 2015.
121. Originating in the PNV's Mendigoxales (mountaineers) group, Jagi-Jagi emerged as a pro-Basque independence faction within the party and raised two units in the Spanish Civil War.

and later sentenced to thirty years' imprisonment in Santoña for *adhesión a rebelión,* he arrived at El Puerto on August 12, 1938. During his imprisonment in El Dueso and El Puerto he wrote poetry, some examples of which are used in chapter 2. Released from El Puerto on August 12, 1940, he continued to write and his work was published in the Basque journals *Zeruko Argia* and *Príncipe De Viana.* He was detained again in the prison of Ondarreta (Donostia-San Sebastián). Rezola Arana was later honored at the Bertsolari Eguna (day of Bertsolari) in 1994.

Socorro Rojo Internacional (Arcos de la Frontera, Seville, and Málaga)

Several prisoners of El Puerto had been involved with the *Socorro Rojo International* (SRI), which was a proscribed organization by the Nationalist authorities. Essentially an important political pressure group and a social service during the Spanish Civil War, the SRI was organized by the Communist Party in 1922. There were branches in some nineteen countries, with a significant intervention in Spain during the Asturias rising in 1934. It was particularly relevant to prisoners and their insignia consisted of the letter S behind the bars. The SRI organized soup kitchens, transformed buildings into makeshift hospitals, created a school and a park for children in Madrid, created an ambulance service, blood banks, dental clinics, and a mini library for soldiers. The SRI also conducted campaigns for Communist soldiers. (The communist POUM party also organized a parallel organization, *Socorro Rojo,* in competition with SRI, mainly in Catalonia).

Richards considers that "the most direct instrument of this solidarity between prisoners and their families and supporters was the so-called Socorro Rojo . . . the mutual assistance organisation that . . . saved many lives."[122] Membership was regarded as resistance to the Nationalist state. The most infamous case related to "*las trece rosas*" or "thirteen roses" involving thirteen young women who were members of the PSOE youth section, the JSU , and who had organized material help for families of prisoners.[123]

Some prisoners in El Puerto were imprisoned as a result of support for this organization. The case of Jenaro Iglesias Martínez provides an excellent example of SRI involvement prior to imprisonment. Iglesias Martínez, a carpenter, aged forty-five, from Arcos de la Frontera, Cádiz,

---

122. Richards, *A Time of Silence,* 159.
123. They were executed, along with some forty-three other prisoners, in Madrid on August 5, 1939.

was sentenced to thirty years' imprisonment for *rebelión* in Ceuta on June 7, 1937.[124] As was so often the case, his trial was a collective one and he was tried with some thirty-two others. Some of his associates were regarded as Communist sympathizers and had known contacts with the SRI. The collective trial ended with all defendants being sentenced to between twenty and thirty years. As reported, this trial proved to be a good example of the psyche behind Nationalist collective trials of the late 1930s. This was an extremely interwoven and complicated case and it was inevitable that this particular batch of prisoners would suffer from guilt by association and the fact that they were all grouped together.

Books on Communism had been found in houses, as had two pistols and a revolver. There was evidence of Popular Front support and there was a Freemasonry connection; Lenin was mentioned; a rising in El Rincón del Medik (today M'Diq, a town in Spanish Morocco) was discussed; one of the defendants had been discharged from the Hispano American bank for participating in a bank strike in 1931 and the events of 1934; while another had been dismissed from the army for his socialist beliefs; some allegedly had masonic connections; others had been connected with José Jiménez, who had been executed and had denounced two members of the pre war Spanish consulate for their Nationalist sympathies. Meetings had been mainly held in a bakery by the name of La Espiga de Oro, in Tétouan, where monies had been collected for arms and the SRI. A prominent person here was Mohamed Ben Hamed Ramu, from Morocco, who had responsibility for the collection of the agreed one peseta a week.

However, the central theme appears to have been the *Socorro Rojo Internacional*. At least thirteen defendants in the collective trial were said to have SRI involvement. Sergeant Emilio Safón Carvert of the local security forces liaised with the police for their contributions. Some, like Jenaro Iglesias Martínez and José Muñoz Espinosa were accused of being involved in the SRI organization, while Isaac Cohen Bentata, Ramón Nuñez de Castro Caudil, and José Sanmartín were accused of raising funds for the SRI. Alejandro Sánchez Sánchez was accused of raising money for Republican families of prisoners and those shot.[125] There were also some twelve or more who were either connected with the SRI organization or helped to raise money to help prisoners or the families of those executed.

This military tribunal in Ceuta, presided over by the examining judge

---

124. AHPC/PSM, Legajo 29263, Causa número 280 de 1937.
125. This shows a further inconsistency in Nationalist punishments.

Colonel Don Ramón Buesa Arguinchoa, specifically included an attack on the SRI in its court ruling: "the *Socorro Rojo Internacional*, whose ideology is publicly and notoriously in all matters opposed to the Glorious Movement that sustains Spain . . . contribute[s] to the acquisition of arms and give[s] encouragement and aid to political prisoners and their families."[126]

There were two other cases relating to active membership of the SRI. Antonio Ochoa Ruiz of Seville was charged with *rebelión* and sentenced to thirty years' imprisonment on March 31, 1937 in Seville.[127] In a smaller collective case, Ochoa Ruiz was identified as an active labor union member who sympathized with the Communist Party. His "crimes" consisted of serving as president of the federation of Spanish tobacco with known links to the SRI. His prison file states that "on the afternoon of July 18 he left his work with a message for the director of the local tobacco factory. The message was that he was going to join the barricades at Trianaa workers' district in Seville then under heavy Nationalist fire." Another prisoner convicted for involvement with the SRI was José Calvente Apanda, aged thirty-four and a chauffeur from Málaga.[128] He was charged with *rebelión militar* and sentenced to thirty years' imprisonment in Ceuta on January 28, 1937. He belonged to the SRI directorate and was reportedly the secretary of the local Communist Party (cell number 13). The tribunal considered that this joint membership left no doubt about "his revolutionary tendencies." Initially imprisoned in Hacho prison, Ceuta, he was transferred to El Puerto on July 13, 1937.

Basque and Galician doctors, nurses, and hospital workers
(Orozko, Oñati, Donostia-San Sebastián, and Galicia)

The role of prisoners in the penitentiary of El Puerto who were doctors was an extremely important one, especially in view of the scarcity of prison medical staff and resources available. The examples quoted here are mainly drawn from Basque medical staff. Mention has already been made of the particular contribution of Dr. Julián Guimón Rezola, originally from Bergara, Gipuzkoa, who was the Bilbao doctor who operated on fellow prisoners in El Puerto and helped to provide a few with work on release. In the previous chapter, he is mentioned in the testimony of relatives of Basque prisoners. He is included here as a case study relating

126. AHPC/PSM, Legajo 29263, Causa número 280 de 1937.
127. AHPC/PSM, Legajo 29357, Causa número 318 de 1937.
128. AHPC/PSM, Legajo 29275, Causa número 1197 de 1937.

to him and his colleagues at the Basurto hospital in Bilbao. Dr. Guimón Rezola was an extremely well-known person at the time of his detention, when he was a prominent surgeon and assistant director of this hospital.[129] His trial was a collective one with some twelve other hospital staff ranging from the director (who held the rank of captain) to the typist (who was a Basque nationalist who had spoken against the *Movimiento Glorioso*). Others were alleged to have some affiliation to the UGT, the CNT, or the PNV.

In the case of Dr. Guimón Rezola, the tribunal heard that he had made a contribution to the creation of a Basque university and had helped many people. Yet the military tribunal in Bilbao was of the view that there were "no modifying circumstances" in his or any other of the medical cases. Guimón Rezola was convicted of *rebelión militar* and sentenced to twelve years' imprisonment.

This collective case serves as a good example of the Nationalist attitude toward Basque medical staff in Basurto hospital. According to the prison files of El Puerto, sentencing was handed out to some thirteen Basurto hospital staff of varying grades, ranging from senior director to hospital typist. Three were sentenced to death, others were sentenced to between twelve and thirty years' imprisonment in Bilbao on July 12, 1937.[130] They included:

1. Dr. Alfonso García Borreguero. Confirmed by prison file Senior doctor. He had previously worked in Asturias, Santander and Vizcaya. He had been a hospital director in Gijón. No political affiliation but known for his left tendencies. Sentenced in Plaza of Bilbao on July 12 and executed on 22 July 1937.

2. Dr. Francisco Pérez Andrés. Head of urology department. Sympathetic to the UGT. Allegedly prevented colleague from speaking about victories of Nationalist forces.

3. Dr. Julián Guimón Rezola (mentioned above). A leading Basque urologist and assistant director of the hospital. He was an important Basque doctor in the penitentiary of El Puerto.

4. Juan Conde Hernando. Barber of the hospital. CNT sympathizer

---

129. AHPC/PSM, Legajo 29267, Causa número 53 de 1937.
130. Ibid.

and allegedly threatened the religious community of the hospital. Sentenced in the Plaza of Bilbao on July 12 and executed on September 6 1937.

5. Anastasio Gonzálelz Palacios. A laboratory porter. President of the Agrupación Enfermeras since 1931. Allegedly had a black list of Nationalist supporters. Sentenced in the Plaza de Bilbao on 12 July and executed on July 22 1937.

6. Juan Vadillo Cuevas. A nurse with UGT sympathies, he allegedly refused to treat a wounded soldier from a disciplinary unit, not the most popular branch of the Republican army. James Matthews writes "These [security] units were created in response to the increasing problems the Republic faced with its troops' discipline. Initially there was one battalion per army corps, but more were created as increasing numbers of men were punished."[131]

7. Elias Adell Gargallo, a nurse with UGT sympathies. Allegedly would not treat persons of rank.

8. Pilar Ruiz Martín, a nurse with UGT sympathies. Allegedly would not treat persons of rank.

9. María Ceniceros Dufós, a nurse with PNV sympathies. Allegedly used to talk about fifth columnists.

10. María Luisa Goicoechea Guezurraga, a volunteer nurse and Basque nationalist since 1931.

11. Pilar Urrutia Alvarez, a hospital typist and Basque nationalist. Allegedly had spoken against "the Glorious Movement."

12. Elías Bernota López, occupation unclear. Allegedly a UGT member since 1931 and a Socialist supporter.

13. Segundo San Martín Sáenz, a nurse. Allegedly had participated in street demonstrations, wearing emblems of a hammer and sickle.

---

131. Matthews, *Reluctant Warriors*, 57. Also see *Gaceta de la República. Diario Oficial*, June 29, 1937.

The execution of a senior doctor does not support the trend identified by Ruiz in his Madrid study in which he writes that, "those with a middleclass background were more likely to have their death sentence commuted."[132] This safeguard did not however apply to those doctors who were perceived to have extreme left-wing connections.

The case of the aforementioned doctor, Julián Guimón Rezola, also revealed a certain amount of chaos in prison administration, since it appeared that they had difficulty in keeping track of their prisoners. The problem arose following a request for a prisoner exchange. It is also likely that the doctor was in the Andalusian prison, but prison bureaucracy showed him to be elsewhere.

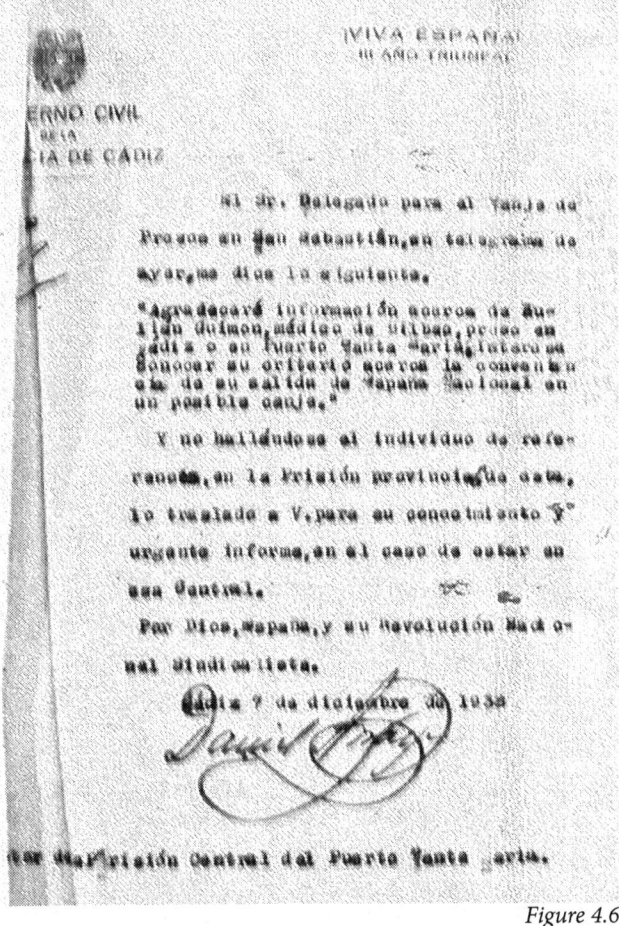

Figure 4.6

---

132. Ruiz, *Franco's Justice*, 104. This is also borne out by the occupations of those executed in El Puerto from 1937 to 1939.

This communication from the Gobierno Civil (central government representative in the provinces) headquarters in Cádiz on December 7, 1938 to the delegate for prisoner transfer in Donostia-San Sebastián admitted that Dr. Guimón could not be located in the penitentiary of El Puerto. Yet it was most likely that he was there because he operated on some of the prisoners of relatives interviewed around this time (see chapter 3). The only other document in the prison file of Guimón Rezola relates to a letter from a military judge on April 22, 1940 (figure 4.7) stating that while this Basque surgeon could practice medicine on his release, he was barred from any political activity.

This document provides another example of the control exerted by

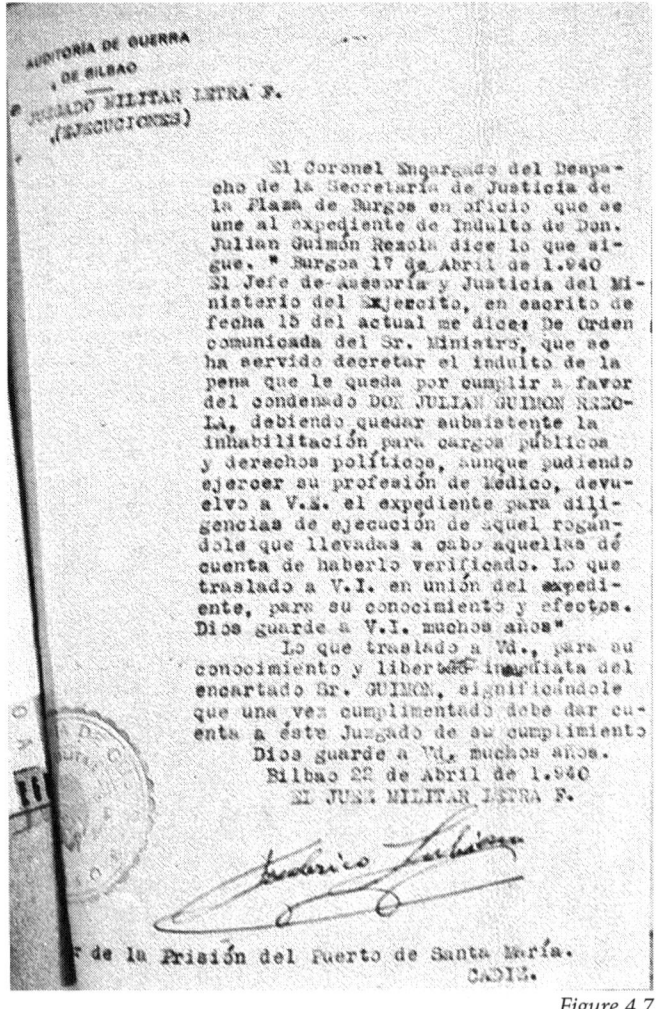

Figure 4.7

the Franco regime over released prisoners concerning the resumption of their profession, even after parole conditions had been met. In the case of Dr. Guimón Rezola, although he had permission to resume his medical career, he was expressly barred from holding a political post or exercising any political rights. Failure to adhere to these requirements would result in a recall to prison.

As far as can be ascertained from the prison files, there were at least five other Basque doctors who were prisoners in El Puerto. There is hardly any information on two of them, namely Dr. José Ibarrola Echeverria from Orozko (Bizkaia)[133] and Dr. José María Inurriaga;[134] they were among the many Basques captured and imprisoned following the Santoña agreement on August 28, 1937. They were both sentenced to thirty years' imprisonment for *adhesion a la rebelión* on October 11, 1937. In the case of the remaining two doctors, one, José María Galarza Zulueta, could well be from Oñati (Gipuzkoa), had a prison file that states that he was a Basque nationalist and had an important medical post in Basurto hospital.[135] He was sentenced to twenty years one day for *adhesión a la rebelión*. Meanwhile, Eduardo Garbisu Llaguno from Bilbao was sentenced to twelve years and one day for *auxilio a la rebelión*.[136]

The file of Dr. Fernando Echaque Cerrajueria from Donostia-San Sebastián contains more information and his prison details appear to indicate that he was involved in a number of different incidents relating to the Civil War.[137] Aged twenty-nine, he was charged with *adhesion a la rebelión* and sentenced to thirty years' imprisonment in Bilbao on November 4, 1938. Before detention, he had been a member of "a radical party"[138] This is the exact term used taken from the prison file. 1934 and was a secretary of the National Committee of Young Radicals. In the revolution of 1934 he fought on the side of the government. He supported the Popular Front and the Basque *separatistas* and was known to be active in Villalba de Losa (Burgos) and Urduña (Bizkaia). The prison file of Echaque Cerrajuena contains an unusual amount of detail on his movements following the outbreak of the war. On July 22, 1936, on the pretext of taking a sick person to Bilbao, he returned to Urduña, where he was briefly detained.

133. AHPC/PSM, Legajo 29286, Expediente 7.
134. Ibid.
135. Ibid., Legajo 29280.
136. Ibid., Legajo 29258. Expediente 23.
137. AHPC/PSM, Legajo 29276, Causa número 11024 de 1938.
138. This could refer to Alejandro Lerroux and his Radical Republican Party (RRP) or a part of the Socialist Party. (PSOE). Basque industrialisation in Bilbao had led to politicisation and growth of trade unionism by the early thirties.

He was however able to offer medication to "the reds" on his release. Echague Cerrajueria then traveled to Berberana, Burgos, where he was involved in the transportation of 1,500 liters (approximately 400 gallons) of gasoline. He traveled between Urduña and Berberana, where he was also involved in transport issues. This was followed by a further detention, this time in Bilbao, for two days. At the beginning of "red domination" he was assigned to Orozko, where he became a medical lieutenant in the Rosa de Luxemburgo Battalion (Communist affiliation) on November 1, 1936; this was followed by promotion to the rank of medical captain on April 29, 1937. On being taken prisoner, he served as a doctor in the Workers' Battalion—battalions made up of prisoners of war forced to take part on the Nationalist side—at the Battle of Brunete, near Madrid, between July 6 and July 26, 1937, at which he treated wounded Nationalist soldiers then and also in the month of August. This, however, did not serve as a mitigating factor at his trial on November 4, at which he was charged with *adhesión a la rebelión* and sentenced to thirty years' imprisonment in Bilbao.

The cases of the doctors were not the same as those of the teachers because the Nationalist authorities did not establish a purging commission to deal with them. However, it would appear that if the doctors had any political connections, they attracted similar severe punishments. Apart from the Basque cases, in Galicia there was a record of Nationalist action against doctors in this context.[139] Carlos Reino Caamaño a member of Izquierda Republicana and mayor of Verín, was shot in Ourense on June 17, 1937. Other doctors who were imprisoned for lengthy periods included: José Meixengo Pereira, mayor of A Arnoia with Popular Front support; Manuel Peña Rey, director of the hospital of As Lagoas with Communist connections; and Manuel Vázquez Álvarez, from Espinosa-Cartelle, who helped Ourense Republicans with propaganda.

Cases that relate to Nationalist Prisoners

Clearly the jails of Franco existed to imprison his Republican enemies, but occasionally Nationalist supporters would be imprisoned for offenses that the Franco regime considered to pose any kind of threat. El Puerto was no exception and, on occasions, contained an admixture of different "crimes" against the Nationalist regime committed by its own supporters.

---

139. David Simón Lorda, "La medicina desterrada. Un repaso por la vihda de varios médicos ourensanos represaliados por el franquismo," *Auria. Revista de Caixanova* 46 (February 2001), 18–23.

A Republican salute by a member of the Falange (Cáceres)

This was an unusual case in that it involved a new Falange member, Sebastián Pantoja Puerto, a shoemaker aged forty-four from the Cádiz area. He gave the clenched fist salute of the Republic and faced the most serious charge, *adhesion a la rebelión*, which carried with it a sentence of between twenty and thirty years' imprisonment. But in this case Pantoja Puerto was sentenced to eight years in Cáceres on April 2, 1937.[140] His crime was to give a salute "in a Marxist style" to the town crier of Valdefuentes. Pantoja Puerto had previously been a member of the Izquierda Republicana, but joined the Falange only days before the outbreak of war. Testimony was given by the local head of the Falange at the tribunal and he testified that Pantoja Puerto was not "a reliable man." The sentence of this prisoner does not accord with the tariff for *adhesion a la rebelión*, which ranged from twenty to thirty years. If he had been charged with the lesser "crime" of *excitación a la rebelión*, with a maximum sentence of twelve years, the military tribunal could still have achieved its objective concerning length of sentence. This constitutes yet another example in which military tribunals ignored the charge guidelines stipulated by the Nationalist regime.

Desertion by a Nationalist Soldier (Badajoz, Logroño)

Michael Alpert writes about desertion but he is referring primarily to the situation faced by the Republican army, more especially at the time of the Battle of the Ebro that began on July 25, 1938.[141] A more detailed comparative analysis of desertion is provided by James Matthews, who examines the serious breaches of discipline in both Nationalist and Republican armies.[142] In the Spanish Civil War desertions and defections were common on both sides and involved volunteers and conscripts. However, in the cases cited here they refer to the desertion of Nationalist soldiers in the earlier period of the war.

Julián Hidalgo Martín, aged twenty-six, was a miner from Valencia del Ventoso, Badajoz.[143] Then a soldier in the Cazadores del Serrallo Battalion, number 8, Group C, he was based at Ceuta. Hidalgo Martín's attempt to escape to the French zone of Morocco was via a river, only to

---

140. AHPC/PSM, Legajo 29289, Causa número 39 de 1937.
141. Michael Alpert, *The Republican Army in the Spanish Civil War 1936–39* (Cambridge: Cambridge University Press, 2007). 68-71.
142. Matthews, *Reluctant Warriors*.
143. AHPC/PSM, Legajo 29319, Causa número 890 de 1937.

be apprehended by one Hamed Ben Mohamed, a local resident. He was sentenced in Ceuta on October 7, 1937 alongside another, to thirty years' imprisonment for *deserción al frente de enemigo*, desertion in the face of the enemy. Although he had deserted, he had not joined the Republican army at the time of his arrest. He was to be transferred to El Puerto on October 20, 1939.

Another case of desertion, this time from the army of Franco to Republican forces, is provided by Celestino Arenzana Ramón.[144] One would have expected the death penalty for Arenzana Ramón, since as a sergeant, his rank undoubtedly influenced the actions of others. However, desertion to the Republican army was not punished for treason since that would involve an official recognition that the Republican army was the legitimate army of the legitimate government.[145] As the Nationalist authorities did not recognize either, the charge for this offense was *adhesión a la rebelión* or *rebelión militar*.

In this case four soldiers and six civilians were involved; the report of events leading to their conviction involved more detail than was usually contained in prison documents. The trial was held in Vitoria-Gasteiz. The main accused was Arenzana Ramón, aged twenty-three and a builder from Logroño with no immediate family. He served as a sergeant paymaster in Company Number 1 of the Fourth Battalion of the Bailén Regiment. His company was in an advanced position at Mount Isuskitza (Isusquiza, Araba) near the "Reds" and he indicated to his comrades that he was going over to the other side, since the Nationalists had shot his brother. On January 14, 1937 he fled his position during the night and made toward Legutio, where he had breakfast in a farmhouse owned by Teodoro Beita. As from prison file..Arenzana Ramón was advised not to go to Vitoria-Gasteiz as it was too dangerous. However, he involved other civilians in his movements and returned to Vitoria-Gasteiz by night, where he was detained by a pair of *Requetés*, after his desertion. He gave them false information concerning his stay for three days behind Republican lines.

It was alleged that, during the three days he spent on Mount Isuskitza, Arenzana Ramón was involved, with three soldiers and six civilians, in persuasion to defect to the Republicans. The prison report then gives a very long and involved account of the actions of the main accused, which included connivance with one of the mothers of the soldiers in persuading them and the young men of the town to follow his example. Nevertheless, it was later not proved to the satisfaction of the military tribunal

---

144. AHPC/PSM, Legajo 29278, Causa número 103 de 1937.
145. Fernández Asiain, *El delito de rebelión militar*, 57–65.

that the soldiers Alberto Clemente Pantaleón and Santos Aldea Feliz had deserted the Nationalists. Their trial information included allegations that before the Civil War they used to go to meetings of the Popular Front.

On return to Vitoria-Gasteiz, all were arrested and placed on trial in Vitoria-Gasteiz. However it was accepted that Arenzana Ramón's flight and time spent on Mount Isuskitza did not constitute penetration of rebel territory as he returned to his base. Nevertheless, the tribunal in Logroño on July 28, 1937 found him guilty of *rebelión militar* and sentenced him to thirty years' imprisonment, as well as dismissal from the Nationalist army with a loss of all rights that he had acquired. The *Ministerio Fiscal* (Attorney General) argued that his actions were worthy of the death sentence. The other soldiers and civilians were sentenced to varying lengths of imprisonment, ranging from six to twenty years. One of them, Antonio Escribano Garrido, a soldier, was set free for lack of proof.

Negligence by a senior Nationalist officer (Castillo de San Francisco, Las Palmas de Gran Canarias)

Although his prison file contained relatively few details, this case was very interesting as it involved the imprisonment of the most senior Nationalist Army field officer found in El Puerto, Juan Montero Cabañas, aged fifty-two, from Las Palmas in the Canary Islands.[146] He was the actual commander of the Ifni Snipers' Battalion from May 15, 1935 to August 15, 1936.[147] Under suspicion for some time, Montero Cabañas had been suspected of some Republican sympathies and was perceived as reluctant to join the uprising. It was alleged that, in September, October, and November 1936, he neglected his correspondence and was absent from his place of work without authorization, disappearing to inspect the northern parts of his territory. He was relieved of his command and was sentenced at Castillo de San Francisco in Las Palmas de Gran Canaria on September 23, 1937, to imprisonment of six years and one day for *abandono de destino*, abandoning his post. Montero Cabañas was transferred to the penitentiary of El Puerto on February 18, 1938, where there would have been very few senior Nationalist officers. It also illustrates that the Nationalist authorities had no compunction in placing ex-Nationalist army officers in a prison that would have been a very hostile environment indeed.

146. AHPC/PSM, Causa número 347 de 1937.
147. Ifni at that time was a Spanish province, located on the Atlantic coast of Morocco, across from the Canary Islands. Spain returned the territory to Morocco in June 1969.

Cowardice by the Civil Guard (Villanueva de la Serrena, Badajoz)

An example of a different case brought against a serving member of the Nationalist forces was *cobardía ante el enemigo*, cowardice in the face of the enemy, leveled at Sebastián Rodríguez Pérez, a Civil Guard from Villanueva de la Serrena, Badajoz.[148] There were two other members of the Civil Guard involved and it was alleged that, on August 19, 1936, they were situated on the outskirts of the town of Santa Amalia on guard duties within a short distance of Nationalist *Regulares* (regular army). A "rebel" aircraft flew overhead and subjected them all to light bombing. The *Regulares* fired back, but the three Civil Guards withdrew to the interior of the town in the direction of the Miajadas road. Here, they commandeered a passing car, thus losing contact with the *Regulares*. Surprisingly, a plea of mitigation based on their previous contribution involving the defense of a factory in Miajadas was accepted and the military tribunal in Cáceres sentenced them all to imprisonment of one year and six months on January 23, 1937. One would have expected a far heavier sentence for this charge and, unusually, the tribunal accepted mitigating factors, albeit for Nationalist prisoners. Also unusual was the fact that there were three separate charge sheets, in three different prison files, repeating identical information. This was the first occasion that I have encountered this; certainly, it was not a common practice where Republican prisoners from the Basque Country and Cádiz province were involved.

Treason of a territorial Falange head and acolytes (León and Galicia)

By far the most serious case, as far as internal Nationalist security was concerned, in El Puerto involved the detention of three Falange heads, one more senior than the others. They were Mario González Zaera (territorial head of the Falange in Galicia), Eduardo Gómez Requejo Rodríguez (local Falange head in Sarria, Lugo, Galicia) and Luis López y López (local Falange head in Paradela, Lugo, Galicia).[149] Two ended up convicted for *traición* (treason) and were condemned to death, while the other was sentenced to thirty years' imprisonment. While it is certainly not the purpose of this work to delve into the early struggles of Franco and the Falange, the imprisonment of these three inmates in this prison provide an excellent example of the attitude of the Franco regime toward its enemies, the Republicans, and opponents among the Nationalists themselves.

---

148. AHPC/PSM, Causa número 475 de 1937.
149. AHPC/PSM, Legajo 29266, Causa number 1 de 1938.

The cases of the three Falange heads concerned matters that directly related to Franco since the three were acolytes of Manuel Hedilla, for a short time national head of the Falange, and described by Paul Preston as "an unsophisticated Fascist thug."[150] The involvement with Hedilla became extremely complex with a multiplicity of plots and goes far beyond the study of prison reports of an Andalusian penitentiary. González Zaera, as the Galician territorial head of the Falange, was one of those who had responded to the situation in which Hedilla had been drumming up support in the provincial capitals in the north. The struggle for control of the Falange involved Hedilla and his acolytes against Franco's brother-in-law, Ramón Serrano Suñer, brother, Nicolás Franco, as well as Franco himself. The outcome was predictable with Hedilla and González Zaera charged with "trying to overthrow *the Caudillo*." They were condemned to death, but the sentences were later commuted.

In this particular case, the prison files contained far more detail than any other prison documents in El Puerto. There appears to have been a determination on the part of the Franco regime to openly establish the guilt of the three charged, especially in the case of González Zaera. In fact, his prison file includes a unique plethora of crimes not seen in any other prisoner's documents in El Puerto. Aged thirty-seven from the León area, he was described as an industrial worker. Together with Eduardo Gómez Requejo Rodríguez, wearing the "sublime blue shirt," they terrorized the region, appropriating an absolute power that they exercised over life and property and covering their activities with "a black veil." They abused the "glorious dawn of our Spain, contrary to the spirit initiated by our glorious army and the justice brought by our leader." Their activities involved trying to use influence to obtain posts such as municipal judges in the town of Sarria, also clashing with the local boss Señor Saco, in order to obtain local political control.

González Zaera became involved in local commerce with one Victoriano Díaz Vázquez, and the Bank of Coruña and its branch in Sarria. He gave false information that resulted in defrauding people and feathering his nest at the cost of bankruptcy and financial loss to others. Other people were swindled as a result of his involvement with a pharmaceutical product and then buying and selling furniture. González Zaera was involved with the local post office and the communications department with a view to illegally using exempted postal services. He also defrauded the industrial office.

---

150. Preston. *Spanish Civil War*, 13.

On the outbreak of war, he surrounded himself with prominent Falange members, including Gómez Rodríguez. He made financial contributions to the Falange and used the car and gasoline of the Falange and the state during his visits to Portugal. Freemasonic membership is also mentioned. González Zaera adopted an ostentatious life style and aroused the suspicion of the general of the division. He is alleged to have forged a close relationship with Manuel Hedilla, presenting him with a car and 20,000 pesetas. The Nationalist authorities clearly made every effort to discredit the accused in this case. However, despite all these alleged criminal activities, González Zaera became territorial head of the Falange in Galicia, with the local head of the Falange in Sarria, Eduardo Gómez Requejo Rodríguez. Both became involved, at a lower level, in the power struggle with Hedilla and Franco concerning the future independence of the Falange. Ultimately, both Falange heads were condemned to death for treason by a tribunal in León on July 28, 1938, which was later changed to a thirty-year sentence each. Luis López y López, the local Falange head of Paradela, was also condemned to a thirty-year sentence. After his sentence, González Zaera was admitted to the penitentiary of El Puerto on September 8, 1938. He was to receive his certificate of liberty on April 14, 1942. It is interesting to note that, while these gangster-type activities would have been well-known to the Nationalist authorities, apart from the intervention of the Civil Guard on the odd occasion, little was done to curtail such activities. One could argue that this provides an excellent example of abuse of power by the Falange, left unchecked by the Civil Guard and the military, until it constituted a danger to them.

*Death penalty carried out in the penitentiary of El Puerto (*Algeciras and Torre Alháquime*)*

The most serious category of sentences of prisoners is to be found in cases in which the death penalty was carried out in the penitentiary of El Puerto. Chapter 2 indicated there were at least fifty prisoners executed between1936 and 1939. Two different combinations of examples have been cited here: one was a connected spy case in which two prisoners were sentenced in Algeciras, while the other involved five other prisoners sentenced in Torre Alháquime.Manuel Tinoco Rodríguez, aged thirty-seven, was a chauffeur from Jerez de la Frontera. He was suspected of espionage and sentenced to death for treason by the military tribunal in Algeciras on December 28, 1938 (figure 4.8).[151]

---

151. AHPC/PSM, Legajo 29259, Causa número 444 de 1938.

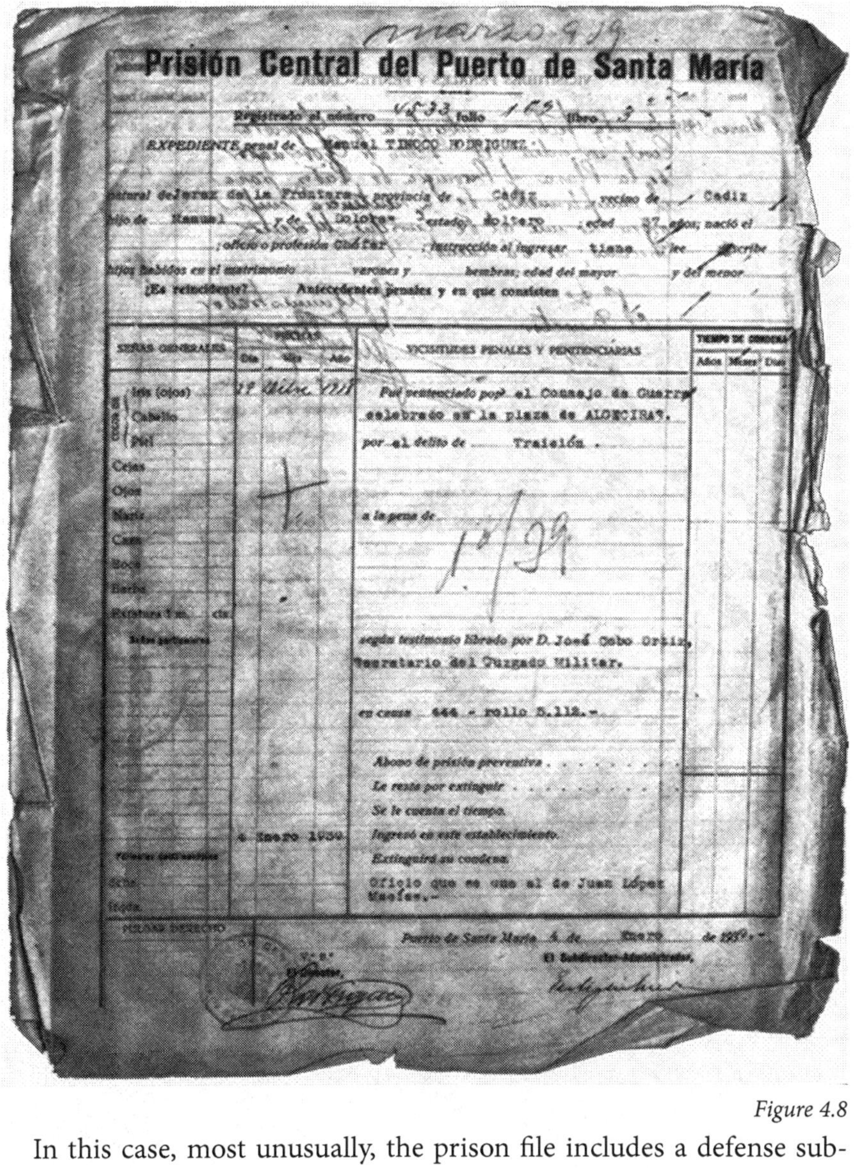

Prisión Central del Puerto de Santa María

Registrado al número 4533 folio 162 libro 3

EXPEDIENTE penal de Manuel TINOCO RODRIGUEZ

natural de Jerez de la Frontera provincia de Cadiz vecino de Cadiz

hijo de Manuel y de Dolores estado soltero edad 37 años; nació el

; oficio o profesión Chófer ; instrucción al ingresar tiene lee escribe

hijos habidos en el matrimonio varones y hembras; edad del mayor y del menor

¿Es reincidente? Antecedentes penales y en que consisten

SEÑAS GENERALES | FECHAS (Día, Mes, Año) | VICISITUDES PENALES Y PENITENCIARIAS | TIEMPO DE CONDENA (Años, Meses, Días)

Iris (ojos) — Cabello — Piel — Cejas — Ojos — Nariz — Cara — Boca — Barba — Estatura 1 m. cm.

Fué sentenciado por el Consejo de Guerra celebrado en la plaza de ALGECIRAS.

por el delito de Traición.

a la pena de

según testimonio librado por D. José Cobo Ortiz, Secretario del Juzgado Militar.

en causa 444 - rollo 5.112.-

Abono de prisión preventiva . . . .

Le resta por extinguir . . . .

Se le cuenta el tiempo.

4 Enero 1930. Ingresó en este establecimiento.

Extinguirá su condena.

Oficio que se une al de Juan López Macías.-

Puerto de Santa María 4 de Enero de 1930.-

V.º B.º

El Director,

El Subdirector-Administrador,

Figure 4.8

In this case, most unusually, the prison file includes a defense submitted by the accused to the chief of police in Algeciras. An abbreviated translated version provides the sense of the undated letter.

Undated.

To the Chief of Police in Algeciras,

It appears that it is thought that I am K17 of the band in the cell of
spies that conspire against Spain. I was wrongly identified by Juan
López Macías: Justice is necessary because I am a man of honor.
I cannot have belonged to this group because I helped Father
Prior of Santo Domingo, Cádiz, by lending him my uniform as a
chauffuer, before he was taken out of number 10 Sopraná Street
and lynched by the Popular Front. When they burned the Convent
of María, I looked after some of the instruments of worship used
on the altar of the church.

I ask you to bring this information to the attention of the
authorities.

Manuel Tinoco Rodríguez.

This document was submitted as Tinoco Rodríguez may well have felt
that that the naming of his denouncer, Juan López Macías, would have
helped him (figure 4.9). This counter-denunciation failed because they
were both sentenced and executed on the same day; it indicated that the
authorities already knew about López Macías. More important was the
attempt by Tinoco Rodríguez to establish a connection with the Catholic
Church when he claimed to have tried to help a priest evade execution by
the Popular Front and hid some of the instruments of worship. His claims
were investigated by an investigating agent, who confirmed his guilt on
February 3, 1939.

Juan López Macías (mentioned in the plea statement of Tinoco Rodríguez) was a tailor, aged thirty-three, from San Fernando, Cádiz.[152] He
was also charged with espionage and tried for treason. The military tribunal sentenced him on December 29, 1938, and he was executed at the
penitentiary of El Puerto on March 28, 1939.

There were very few accompanying documents of note concerning
his case, but there is a document recording the possessions of the deceased, which were collected by his wife. This is a poignant legacy of a
man's life and gives an indication of the final possessions of one of the
more unfortunate internees of Franco's prisons (figure 4.10).

---

152. AHPC/PSM, Legajo 29259, Causa número 444 de 1938.

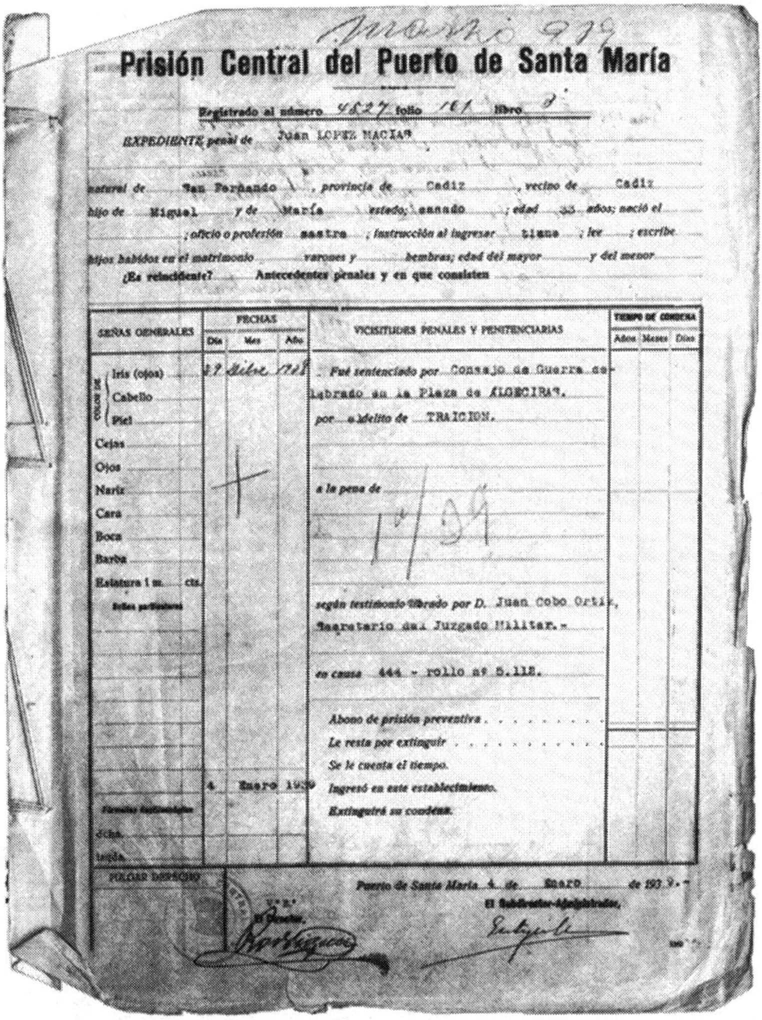

Prisión Central del Puerto de Santa María

Registrado al número 4527 folio 101 libro 3

EXPEDIENTE penal de Juan LOPEZ MACIAS

natural de San Fernando, provincia de Cadiz, vecino de Cadiz

hijo de Miguel y de María estado casado; edad 33 años; nació el

; oficio o profesión sastre; instrucción al ingresar tiene; lee ; escribe

hijos habidos en el matrimonio varones y hembras; edad del mayor y del menor

¿Es reincidente? Antecedentes penales y en que consisten

SEÑAS GENERALES	FECHAS Día	Mes	Año	VICISITUDES PENALES Y PENITENCIARIAS	TIEMPO DE CONDENA Años	Meses	Días
Color de: Iris (ojos), Cabello, Piel	27	dbre	1938	Fué sentenciado por Consejo de Guerra celebrado en la Plaza de ALGECIRAS. por el delito de TRAICION.			
Cejas, Ojos, Nariz, Cara, Boca, Barba, Estatura 1 m. cts.				a la pena de			
Señas particulares				según testimonio librado por D. Juan Cobo Ortiz, Secretario del Juzgado Militar.-			
				en causa 444 - rollo nº 5.112.			
				Abono de prisión preventiva			
				Le resta por extinguir			
				Se le cuenta el tiempo.			
	4	Enero	1939	Ingresó en este establecimiento.			
				Extinguirá su condena.			

Puerto de Santa María 4 de Enero de 193 9.-

V.º B.º
El Director,

El Subdirector-Administrador,

Figure 4.9

The list also refers to *dinero en peculio*, one's own money, which was a system used in the prison of El Puerto. This involved the payment of monies by families and friends to the account of prisoners, who were subsequently able to draw on their accounts. (This would have greatly reduced the amount of cash in circulation at the prison). Other possessions returned to the widow in this case included one suit, one beret, one pair of glasses, one fountain pen, letters and documents, and one peseta worth of prison voucher.

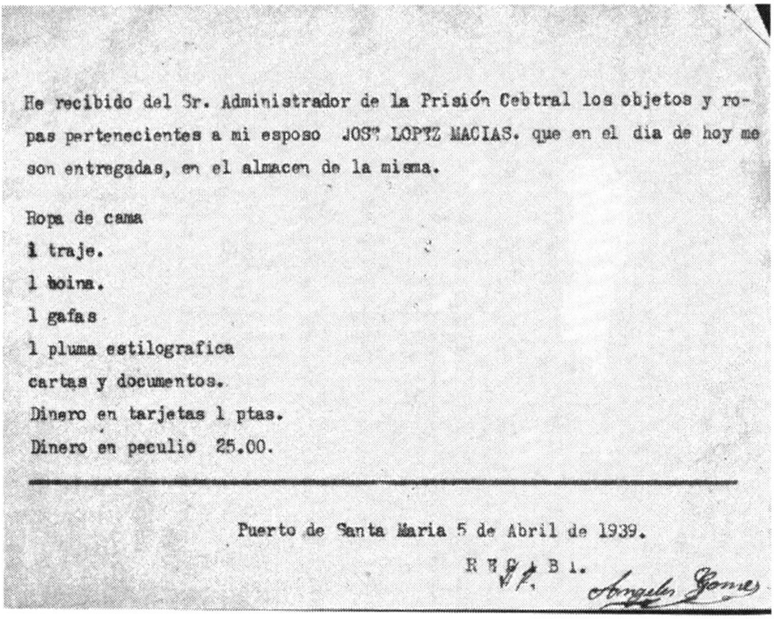

He recibido del Sr. Administrador de la Prisión Cebtral los objetos y ro-
pas pertenecientes a mi esposo JOSÉ LOPEZ MACIAS. que en el dia de hoy me
son entregadas, en el almacen de la misma.

Ropa de cama
1 traje.
1 boina.
1 gafas
1 pluma estilografica
cartas y documentos.
Dinero en tarjetas 1 ptas.
Dinero en peculio 25.00.

                    Puerto de Santa Maria 5 de Abril de 1939.

                         R E C I B i.

Figure 4.10

The other examples of cases in which prisoners were executed in
the penitentiary of El Puerto have been drawn exclusively from Torre
Alháquime, where some nine of its inhabitants were executed on July 2,
1937 (see chapter 2). The small town was very near to El Gastor and Olvera, both with active anarchist groups in 1936, and located in the Sierra
de Cádiz where at least sixty-three people were executed between 1936
and 1939.[153] In addition, it had a militant history in its own right with the
first collective of agricultural workers in May 1931, affiliated to the UGT.
Worsening unemployment was accompanied by sympathy strikes by
workers in Villamartín and an Izquierda Republicana branch in 1935.[154]
In the Civil War, Torre Alháquime was captured by Nationalist forces on
July 31, 1936.

In the case of some of those executed, an Andalusian historian, Fernando Romero Romero, provides a background to their cases that is simply not available in any of the prison files cited in this chapter. Five cases
involved agricultural laborers from Torre Alháquime who were charged
with treason, condemned to death by the military tribunal in Algodonales
on December 28, 1936, transferred to the penitentiary of El Puerto on
June 19, 1937, and all executed there on July 2, 1937. Some had clearly a

153. Romero Romero, *Socialistas de Torre Alháquime*, 146.
154. Ibid., 27, 36.

history of more "criminal behavior" than others, but it was clear that guilt by association was the overriding factor.

Diego Medina Guerra, aged thirty-three, was considered to be a militant agricultural worker and had been vice president of the local UGT since February 1936.[155] In July 1936 he was involved in Republican security and when the town fell at the end of the month, he became engaged in making explosives and cartridges. He then moved to a farm in Setenil de la Bodegas, which he helped guard. After Ronda fell on September 16, 1936 he went to San Pedro Alcántara, and then joined the *Méjico* militias and returned to his town via El Burgo. On his return, he found that his companion Ana had been raped and murdered and he then shot two local people. Medina Guerra was condemned to death, a victim of the double standards of the judicial system of Franco.

Juan Medina Guerra, aged forty, was born in Torre Alháquime but lived in nearby Barrio de San Roque with his partner Dolores and their six children. He was a member of the UGT. Here he undertook guard duties for the Republic.[156] .His house was near a road and used as a vantage point for anti-Nationalist forces. Working in agriculture in August 1936, he moved to Ronda and Alhaurín el Grande, both in Málaga, where he worked harvesting olive trees and in a tile factory. He formed part of a group on the run that went back to Torre Alháquime on Christmas night 1936 to see their families. Returning on February 14, 1937, he was detained in the municipal prison and later accused of carrying out guard duties and of looting barracks He was executed soon after. It would probably be true to say that, of all the cases cited in Torre Alháquime, he was the least culpable, suffering by association in a collective trial.

Roque Morales Guerra was fifty-five and had two sons, Antonio, aged twenty-five, and Trinidad, aged twenty.[157] All were UGT members who were forced to flee in the face of a Nationalist advance. They took refuge in a nearby olive grove and Trinidad found refuge in the Convent of San Carlos. They returned to their native town after the fall of Málaga in February 1937. According to the head of the Falange, "they held Communist ideas and held ready ideas for disturbances and were the soul of all street movements in favor of the Popular Front."[158] He said that the two youths had seen armed service and their father was "head of the riflemen" and had alerted *milicianos* of Nationalist movements. It was alleged that they

---

155. Ibid., 181. AHPC/PSM, Legajo 29249, Expediente 62.
156. Ibid., AHPC/PSM, Legajo 29249, Expediente 63.
157. AHPC/PSM, Legajo 29248, Expediente 63.
158. Romero Romero, *Socialistas de Torre Alháquime* 184.

were involved in the sacking of a barracks and a church. Moreover, the father Roque was reported as having walked through the town wearing a Civil Guard's jacket and the priest's hat; he conceded that he had removed some of the images from the church. The local Falange head also alleged that, in some way, Trinidad was involved in the killing of Manuel Vilches Guerra. Trinidad maintained that he was only once in El Barracal (known to be a meeting place of *milicianos*), where he was given a damaged revolver. The other son, Antonio, accepted that he had been present for some of the looting, but that he did not participate. The three were condemned to death, but the sentence for Trinidad was commuted to thirty years' imprisonment.

Pedro Pérez Álvarez, aged forty-six, lived with his wife and five children in the area and was a prominent member of the UGT.[159] He later became president of the local branch of the PSOE. In 1932 and part of 1933 he was union spokesman on the rural police commission. This would have given him a very high profile with his Nationalist captors, since this was a body established on July 10, 1931, soon after the establishment of the Republic on April 14, 1931.[160] These local commissions dealt with rural matters, consisted of three employers and three employees, and were chaired by the local mayor. They concerned themselves with such matters as ensuring that plans relating to farmwork were in accordance with local customs, with powers to administrate or even confiscate farms not complying. Pérez Álvarez became mayor of Torré Alháquime in October 1933, returning after the Popular Front success in February 1936. After the outbreak of war in July, he was actively involved in food rationing, disarming local Nationalist supporters, and quartering Republican troops. He left Setenil de la Bodegas before enemy occupation, took refuge on the *Las Hormigas* farm, and formed part of an armed *milicianos* group. Eventually returning to his local town, he surrendered on March 27, 1937; he was tried and executed in Andalusia.

Fernando Barriga Galán, aged thirty-one and a UGT member, had the dubious reputation of being the son whose father was the first victim to be killed by Nationalists when they occupied Torre Alháquime on July 31, 1936.[161] Fernando was the spokesman of the Young Socialists' executive council and a local committee member of the Popular Front. Organizing resistance against the uprising; he helped to requisition arms and

159. Ibid., 42, 191. AHPC/PSM, Legajo 29248, Expediente 34.
160. Antonio Florencio Puntas, "Patronal y sindicatos ante la legislación agraria de la II República. Sevilla (1931–1933," *Historia Contemporánea* 1 (1988), 121–40.
161. AHPC/PSM, Legajo 29249, Expediente 31.

to recruit agricultural workers from the orchards and the countryside. It was alleged that, when the Republican troops passed through the area, he was the one who sounded a horn as a call to arms. Involved in the looting of the church, Barriga Galán was part of the *milicianos* group that held Nationalist supporters hostage until the fall of Ronda forced him to retire through various parts of Málaga province, ending up in El Burgo. Allegedly he then joined the Battalion of Machine Gunners and, while in Málaga, was billeted in the church of San Carlos and the barracks at the residence of the Capuchin friars. He returned to his local town in February 1937 and was tried and executed.

These individual case studies of prisoners and their sentences in the penitentiary of El Puerto between 1936 and 1945 provide an interesting cross-section of the impact of the Spanish Civil War on its citizens. The sentences of the eighteen different military tribunals examined indicated that different offenses attracted dissimilar sentences and charges, depending on the individual military tribunals, which were in a particularly strong position before 1940. Arguably, they were the primary mechanism for Francoist repression at this time. Collective trials meant that guilt by association was commonplace and this is evidenced by the death sentences relating to Torre Alháquime, in which all the condemned had not been equally politically active. The cases of those guilty of genuine crimes, like that of Antonio García Benítez who was condemned for just over two years for a second offense of robbery, compared to those of political prisoners, in which the usual sentence of thirty years given to the vast majority of Basque soldiers, illustrates the point. On examining the prison archives, I have been surprised at the heterogeneity of the prison of El Puerto. The imprisonment of a senior military Nationalist commander and a regional Falange head alongside a large number of Basque soldiers from widely different occupations is an indication of how far the regime went to purge Spain.

Lengthy sentences applied to the vast majority of all the Basque inmates who were political prisoners and received thirty years' imprisonment, in contrast to inmates from the province of Cádiz. Here, the large number of nonpolitical prisoners received lesser sentences. There appeared to be a lack of consistency of sentences for lesser charges, and individual military tribunals seem to have applied military justice in a somewhat arbitrary and capricious fashion, especially between late 1936 and early to mid-1938. Sentences laid down by the Nationalist authorities were not always followed and charges did not always match the alleged offenses. These are well illustrated by the examples already cited. This important theme is revisited in later chapters.

The evidence was frequently flimsy or nonexistent, and often based on anonymous denunciations until 1941. Anderson writes that "[the Nationalist regime] made it very much in the interests of its supporters to incriminate neighbours . . . those who . . . [had] suffered for the Francoist cause now stood ready to inherit the burgeoning patronage of the new state."[162] Defendants could be retrospectively charged with incidents that had been legal at the time, as noted earlier, and collective trials could involve up to fifty people that finished within a very short time; the defense was virtually nonexistent and sometimes even hostile and pleas to Franco for clemency went to him after the appellant had been executed.

With military jurisdiction at maximum influence, a cold, administrative and routine terror was imposed by their tribunals, through which tens of thousands of people passed between 1939 and 1945, they were merely legal farces . . . Nothing had changed despite the end of war, the same ritual of death, the same desperation of prisoners, indefensible before the justice of Franco.[163]

The sentences of the military tribunals purged Spanish society under the banner of "Justice for God and Spain." They institutionalized and, in the eyes of some, legitimized the repression. The Historical Memory Act of 2007 acknowledged the right of those who suffered persecution during the Civil War to an entitlement of recognition and moral restitution.[164] This is also accompanied by the caveat that such recognition does not carry any compensation entitlement. The sentences of the military tribunals continue to be a source of deep-seated unhappiness to many in Spain today in that these illegal sentences have never been revoked. Sadly, the general amnesty of the kind offered by Manuel Azaña on February 21, 1936, for all those imprisoned for "political and social crimes" under the previous Radical-Ceda regime of Alejandro Lerroux, never seems to have been a factor considered by subsequent PSOE administrations.

---

162. Anderson, *The Francoist Military Trials*, 79.
163. *Morir, matar, sobrevivir*, ed. Casanova, Espinosa, Mir and Moreno Gómez, 20–21.
164. See "La Ley de Memoría se aprueba entre aplausos de invitados antifranquistas," *El País*, November 11, 2007.

5

The Penal Policy of the Franco Regime:
Charges, Sentences, Transfers, and Release Conditions of Prisoners in El Puerto de Santa María

Cierra las puertas, echa la aldaba, carcelero,
Ata duro a ese hombre: no le ararás el alma,
Son muchas llaves, muchas llaves, muchos cerrojos, injusticias

—Miguel Hernández, *El Hombre Acecha*

This chapter seeks to examine allegations of inconsistencies in charges, sentences, and release conditions for similar "crimes" affecting prisoners in El Puerto from the Basque Country and the province of Cádiz. The review of comparative charges and sentences focuses on "political crimes" carried out between 1936 and 1939 (tables 5.1 and 5.3) and the nonpolitical "crimes" dating from 1934–1949 (tables 5.2 and 5.4).[1] Based on the evidence of prisoners' files from El Puerto, there does appear to have been discrimination against Basques. These files also indicate that the Nationalist penal authorities used El Puerto partly as a local prison for Cádiz province (tables 5.6 and 5.7) and partly as an isolationist prison for Basques (table 5.8). Finally, an analysis of the conditions of release as applied to the two regions does provide further evidence of incongruity (table 5.9).

After the termination of the Civil War on April 1, 1939, important revisions affecting the penal system took place. This marked a clear distinction between events that occurred during the war and those that followed the Nationalist victory. One such major change involved the rationaliza-

---

1 AHPC/PSM, Legajos 29246–29446. Also interviews with archive director Manuel Ravina Martín, in Cádiz, May 21 and 24, 2007; May 28, June 2 and 10, 2008; and June 17, 2009.

tion of the powers of the military tribunals and the reassertion of central control in 1940.[2] This also included substantiation of all new denunciations in September 1941, after which no further anonymous denunciations were accepted. [3] These revisions also led to the decline in punitive sentencing, another major change.[4]

As far as the Basque prisoners in El Puerto were concerned, the effects of the Nationalist revisions to the penal system after 1939 were to mainly affect the large majority who had found themselves imprisoned en masse after the fall of Santander in August 1937. The point is perhaps worth laboring that Javier Rodrigo considers this capture involved approximately 50,000 men, "taken in the space of a few weeks [and was] the largest and most important surrender of the war."[5] Many of the Basque prisoners had arrived in El Puerto between June and August 1938 in order to serve maximum periods of detention. Table 5.3. shows that a majority of Basque prisoners had been sentenced to this maximum sentence of thirty years' imprisonment as a result of facing charges of the more serious "crimes," *adhesión a la rebelión* and *rebelión militar*.

Perhaps one of the most important postwar revisions of the Nationalist penal system that influenced the history of this case study related to early release and widespread use of parole. This revised structure for parole introduction was determined by Franco in June 1940, when changes in release had most impact on those serving lengthy sentences.[6] Convictions for the "crimes" of the Spanish Civil War finally ended in 1945.[7] However, external pressures emanating from World War II had powerful effects on Spain; these could not be ignored and also affected Nationalist penal policy regarding parole.

Historians do not appear to agree on reasons for the changes in the parole policy adopted by the Francoist penal authorities at this time. For example, Sabín argues that, from 1943 on, Franco felt that the Allies were more likely to win and sought to curry favor by placing repression in a more favorable light.[8] Richards believes the first substantial reprieve was

2. *BOE*, January 26, 1940.
3. *BOE*, September 5, 1941.
4. For example, nine prisoners from the Cádiz area were executed for treason in March 1939. (AHPC/PSM, Legajo 29259), but two prisoners from Cádiz were not executed for the same crime and were released in August 1941 and November 1942 on conditional liberty (AHPC/PSM, Legagos 29323, 29353).
5. Javier Rodrigo, "Campos en tiempos de guerra," in *Una Inmensa Prisión*, ed. Molinero, Sala, and Sobrequés, 24.
6. *BOE*, June 1940.
7. *BOE*, December 20, 1945. Martial law in force.
8. Sabín, *Prisión y muerte en la España de postguerra*, 21.

not granted until October 1945, and then under pressure from the Allies after the end of the World War II.[9] Ruiz, on the other hand, writes that prisoners were released in significant numbers in 1941 when Germans dominated the European continent (47,234); this was followed by the year of maximum release in 1943 (57,549).[10] In this instance, my evidence strongly accords with the view of Ruiz since the prison records relating to El Puerto leave no doubt that the peak years of prisoner release were 1941 and 1942.[11]

My view is that the pressures on the authorities for prisoner release were complex and decisions were often influenced by other pressing pragmatic reasons that contributed to a revision of Nationalist penal policy. A basic reason involved the cost of feeding an enormous prison population in the early 1940s when Spain itself was starving.[12] Much of the response of the authorities was determined by grossly overcrowded prisons that led to outbreaks of contagious diseases and extremely severe disciplinary problems. Certainly, the fear of epidemic outbreaks in confined spaces, allied to the possibility of such outbreaks affecting areas outside, made the authorities desperate to reduce the prison population. The unresolved build-up of tension was an important contributory factor. The fact that so many were on death row led to riots and other acts of indiscipline. Máximo Cuervo, director of prisons at this time, informed Franco on October 29, 1940 that Spanish prisons held 8,340 inmates who were condemned to death with 33,896 unconfirmed sentences and 92,286 awaiting trial.[13] This led to many prison escapes and he cites the escape of twenty prisoners in August 1940 from the makeshift prison in Hinojosa del Duque in the province of Córdoba;[14] several months earlier, on January 1, 1940, there had been a revolt leading to the deaths of a prison guard and fifty inmates in the prison of Almodóvar del Campo in Ciudad Real.[15] Almódovar del Campo is a town in the province of Cuidad Real.

9. Richards, *A Time of Silence*, 223. Also see Michael Richards, "The Limits of Quantification: Francoist Repression and Historical Methodology," *Revista de Historia Contemporánea*, 7 (2007), online journal.
10. Ruiz, *Franco's Justice*, 266–67; "A Spanish Genocide? Reflections on the Francoist Repression after the Spanish Civil War," *Contemporary European History* 14, no. 2 (2005), 189.
11. AHPC/PSM, Legajos 29247–29474.
12. Richards, *A Time of Silence*, 172–73. Richards makes reference to "unheard of levels of starvation and disease [in Spain] in the 1940s."
13. *Documentos inéditos para la Historia del Generalisimo Franco*, Fundación Nacional Francisco Franco (Madrid 1992), vol 1, 386–88.
14. Francisco Moreno Gómez, *La resistencia armada contra Franco, Tragedia del maquis y la guerrilla. El centro-sur de España, de Madrid al Guadalquivir* (Barcelona: Crítica, 2001), 3.
15. Ruiz, *Franco's Justice*, 128.

None of these releases was for humanitarian reasons and the pragmatism of the Nationalist penal authorities is well summarized by Vinyes, who believes that there were three main reasons for the extension of the parole system, none of which were humanitarian: "The first related to the collapse of penal administration, the second was based economic grounds, and the third stemmed from growing prisoner insubordination and unrest caused by saturated and overcrowded prisons."[16] All these factors would have exerted enormous pressure on the penal authorities to release rebellious and near mutinous prisoners, with the tremendously congested and overloaded prisons creating acute problems of health and penal control.

The fact remains that all those convicted for "political crimes" during the Spanish Civil War and its aftermath were victims of a judicial policy imposed by the Nationalists. The Francoists had asserted that the military rebellion of July 1936 was legal, accompanied by a declaration of martial law in all areas of Spain and a warning that anyone showing resistance to Nationalists would be sentenced for "military rebellion" by military tribunals.[17] It is worth repeating the highly relevant view of the Nationalist prosecutor, Eugenio Fernández Asiain, , who considered that "rebellion consisted of the defense of the Republican regime."[18] However even he conceded that Nationalist legislation had led to the possibility that "the same acts were judged in a diversified manner by different Spanish military tribunals."[19]

It is worth recalling that the most serious charge not always meriting the death penalty was *adhesión a la rebelión/ rebelión militar*, which carried a sentence of imprisonment from twenty to thirty years; this was followed by *auxilio a la rebelión*, which carried a sentence of six months and one day to twenty years; and the third of these charges was *excitación e inducción a la rebelión*, which carried a sentence of six months and one day to twelve years. They were by far the most important charges that led to conviction and imprisonment in El Puerto during the Spanish Civil War and immediately thereafter. Many other charges were different versions of the above; the powers of military tribunals extended to all aspects of Spanish life, and even such areas as excessive profiteering and responsibility for railroad accidents were subject to trial by court martial.[20]

---

16. Ricard Vinyes, "El universo penitenciario durante el franquismo," in *Una inmensa prisión*, ed. Molinero, Sala, and Sobrequés, 161–62.
17. *Boletín Oficial de la Junta de Defensa Nacional*, July 30, 1936.
18. Fernández Asiain, *El delito de rebelión militar*, 13.
19. Ibid., 175.
20. Even as late as 1974, some three hundred civilians appeared before military tribunals in Spain.

The different charges and sentences of those incarcerated in El Puerto reveal an inconsistency that gives rise to the question of whether a methodological plan existed in the allocation of prisoners to individual jails under Franco. The outcome resulted in a wide political, economic, and social mix in this prison during this time. This was compounded by the fact that, while around 20 percent of Cádiz inmates were transferred locally from El Puerto, fewer than 3.5 percent of Basque prisoners were moved north.[21] This confirms the impression that the Nationalist penal authorities were anxious to keep Basques in isolation in their far southern citadel in Andalusia for longer than other prisoners. Clearly, the impact of lengthy sentences would also have a far greater effect on them (and their families) than the other majority group in El Puerto, those from Cádiz province.[22]

Charges and sentences varied in different areas of Spain owing to the discretionary powers afforded to military tribunals under the Military Code of Justice.[23] Anderson writes that "[judges] had to plump for one of a number of specific charges . . . in practice the distinctions between 'joining the rebellion' (*adhesion*) ' and 'aiding and abetting the rebellion' (*auxilio*)*rebellion* were so blurred . . . It was this fluidity between tariffs that gave such influence to the Francoist neighbours of those on trial."[24] In El Puerto, 95 Basques were sentenced for *auxilio a la rebelión* while 751 were sentenced for *adhesión a la rebelión or rebelión,* mostly receiving maximum sentences of thirty years.[25] It would appear that many of the Basques in El Puerto attracted longer sentences than was usual, although Manuel Ortiz Heras considers that the most usual outcome of such charges was a prison sentence for Republican war prisoners of twelve to twenty years.[26] This view is largely shared by Julius Ruiz, who bases his estimates on research in the political responsibilities files in Madrid.[27]

At the time of conviction, the length of sentence affected the all-important issue of parole release.[28] Those who had been sentenced to a

21. AHPC/ PSM, Legajos 29246–29477.
22. I refer here to the visiting problems of Basque families facing a 500 mile journey.
23. Prison files of AHPC/PSM, 1937–43, show that El Puerto contained prisoners in receipt of sentences from eighteen military tribunals.
24. Anderson, *The Francoist Military Trials,* 108, 117, 118.
25. AHPC/PSM, Legajos 29246–29477.
26. Manuel Ortiz Heras, *Violencia política en la II República y el primer franquismo: Albacete, 1936–50.* (Madrid: Siglo XXI de España, 1996), 370–71. These views are based on research of prison files in Albacete.
27. Ruiz, "A Spanish Genocide? Reflections on the Francoist repression after the Spanish Civil War," 181.
28. After 1941, prisoners started to be released in large numbers and few prisoners actu-

maximum of six years and one day became eligible in June 1940.[29] This extended to those who had been sentenced to twelve years in April in 1941;[30] then to fourteen years eight months in October 1942.[31] The threshold was raised to twenty years in March 1943;[32] then to prisoners over seventy-years-old in October 1943.[33] Finally, parole was extended to all those who had been sentenced to thirty years, provided they had not been involved in "blood crimes," in December 1943.[34] The term "blood crimes" referred, specifically, to "any repugnant acts."[35] By 1945, around 47,000 remained imprisoned; some argue that the Civil Guard continued to arrest an average of 60,000 people a year between 1940 and 1943.[36]

The main sources for this chapter are files relating to 995 prisoners from Cádiz province and 1,047 from the Basque Country.[37] Additional evidence relating to a further 223 Basque prisoners has been obtained from the Provincial Historical Archive in Huelva.[38] In all cases, I have concentrated on political prisoners, but those charged with other minor offenses have been used for comparative purposes. Prisoners from Cádiz province in El Puerto were convicted on a very wide range of (mainly less serious) ninety-eight different charges, reflecting the fact that this prison was also used as a local prison accommodating inmates for less serious offenses. [39] The vast majority were convicted by 1940 and released by 1943; although most served around three years if convicted on the more serious charge, the sentence for those convicted of sedition could be nearer four years. Only ten of these charges could be said to relate directly to the Civil War. It is worth noting that not until November 12, 1966 were Spanish Civil War responsibilities removed from the list of offenses.[40]

ally served the full totality of their sentences.

29. *BOE*, June 6, 1940.
30. *BOE*, April 1, 1941.
31. *BOE*, October 22, 1942.
32. *BOE*, March 3, 1943.
33. *BOE*, October 30, 1943.
34. *BOE*, December 20, 1943.
35. Sabín, *Prisión y muerte en la España de postguerra*, 207–9.
36. Encarna Nicolás Marín, *La libertad encadenada. España en la dictadura franquista 1939–1975* (Madrid: Alianza Editorial, 2005), 17. See also Stanley Payne, "Gobierno y oposición (1939–1969)," in *La Época de Franco, 1939–1975*, coord. Raymond Carr (Madrid: Espasa Calpe, 2007), 114.
37. AHPC/PSM, Cádiz Province and Basque Country, Legajos 29246–29477.
38. AHPH/PPH, Signaturas 07516/021–07620/032.
39. AHPC/PSM, Cádiz Province, Legajos 29246–29474.
40. *BOE*, November 12, 1966.

Table 5.1 illustrates the political charges on which prisoners from Cádiz province were convicted between 1936 and 1939.[41] The major charge of *adhesión a la rebelión/ rebelión* was used to convict 149 individuals and resulted in three years maximum detention (following ease of parole conditions). There are also minor charges included.

Table 5.1. Prisoners from Cádiz province convicted on political charges, 1936–1939. Archivo Histórico Provincial de Cádiz.

Charges	Number convicted	Earliest year of admittance	Latest year of release	Maximum time in El Puerto de Santa María
Sedición (sedition)	5	1936	1939	4 yrs
Auxilio a la rebelión (assisting therebellion)	102	1937	1939	2 yrs
Rebelión militar (military rebellion)	77	1936	1947	3 yrs
Adhesión a la rebelión (aid, help for the rebellion)	72	1938	1946	3 yrs
Detenido gubernativo (preventive detention)	27	1936	1946	1 yr
Excitación a la rebelión (support for the rebellion)	23	1937	1946	2 yrs
Suplantación de la personalidad (deserter)	1	1937	1941	3 yrs 10 mnths
Provocación a la rebelión (inciting the rebellion)	2	1936	1941	1 yr
Insulto a Fuerza Armada (insulting the Armed Forces)	4	1936	1941	1 yr
Insultos a agencias de la autoridad (insulting agents of authority)	1	Not known	23 February 1938	Not known

41. AHPC/PSM, Cádiz Province, political charges 1936–39, Legajos 29200: 46, 52–53, 53–59; 61, 65–68, 70–79, 80, 82–89, 90; 29300: 8 , 22–43, 45–54, 56–64, 66–72, 76–81, 90–98; 29400: 6, 8 12, 16-20, 22–32, 51, 55, 76–77.

The mentality of the Franco regime toward defeated Republicans is evidenced by the enormous number of defeated who were imprisoned, although total figures for those imprisoned are debatable. Mirta Núñez Díaz-Balart quotes a figure of "280,000 prisoners in 1939";[42] however Julián Casanova puts this at "nearly half a million imprisoned in jails and concentration camps in the same year".[43]

Some of the charges border on the vexatious and indicate the determination of the victors to pursue their policy of "blanket punishment or penitence"[44] Examples of simple harassment included *insultos* for the defeated and a firm reluctance to "let the insultos (insults) and *injurias* (slander) stand. These dealt with perceived failure to show due respect to the *Nuevo Estado*. The prison files of El Puerto reveal a myriad of charges, some of them even against supporters of Franco; one example is a case of desertion, and another of a Nationalist soldier who had shown support for a guerrilla group in the mountains of Andalusia, where there was continued guerrilla resistance to Franco (concentrated in the Sierra Morena range from Huelva to Jaén).[45]

Table 5.2 illustrates again a further wide range of nonpolitical charges that led to imprisonment of those from Cádiz province. [46]

The charges listed in table 5.2 give further examples of just how far the influence of military tribunals extended into everyday life. Moreover, they give some indication of the drive to imprison enemies. Some of the charges like *amenazas* (threats) and *falsedad de documentos* (false documents) border on the trivial.

Table 5.2. Prisoners from Cádiz province convicted on nonpolitical charges, 1934–1951. Archivo Histórico Provincial de Cádiz.

---

42. Núñez Díaz-Balart, *Los años del terror*, 40.

43. *Morir, matar, sobrevivir*, ed. Casanova, Espinosa, Mir, and Moreno Gómez, 8.

44. Graham, *The Spanish Republic at War, 1936–1939*, 424.

45. Alfonso Domingo, *El canto del búho: la vida en el monte de los guerrilleros antifranquistas* (Madrid: Oberon, 2002), 203, 253. "El Lute" (Eleuterio Sánchez Rodríguez) was a notorious bandit in the Sierra Morena, imprisoned in El Puerto in 1965.

46. AHPC/PSM, Cádiz Province, nonpolitical charges 1936–39, Legajos 29200. 46–66; 29300. 4, 8, 21–25, 32, 44–45, 48, 50, 52–97, 99; 29400. 1–38, 41–74, 77.

Charge	Number convicted	Earliest year of prison admittance	Latest year of prison release	Maximum time served in El Puerto de Santa María
Hurto (theft)	101	1936	1951	2 years
Robo(robbery)	125	1935	1951	2 years
Atentado (assault)	15	1944	1951	5years, usually less
Homicidio (murder)	13	1936	1951	5 years, usually less
Ley de Vagos y Maleantes (law of vagrants and vagabonds)	10	1935	1947	1 year
Auxilio a *malchechores*(assisting criminals)	5	1944	1949	1 year
Atraco a mano armada (armed attack)	3	1945	1945	1 year or less
Asesinato (murder)	3	1935	1950	7 years
Falsification de documentos públicos (falsification of public documents)	3	1948	1948	Less than 1year
Fraude (fraud)	3	1946	1950	Less than 1year
Parrricidio (parricide)	3	1934	1949	2 years
Usurpación de funciones (usurpation of functions)	2	1944	1951	1 year
Injurias (insults)	2	1941	1942	Less than 1 year
Asociación transitoria para robar (accessory to robbery)	2	1944	1947	Less than 2 years
Amenazas (threats)	1	1944	1945	5 months
Atraco y elevación de precios (dealing in profiteering)	1	1945	1945	9 months
Contra los deberes de centinela(avoidance of sentry duty)	1	1949	1949	5 months
Desacato (contempt of court)	1	1944	1945	14 months
Encubridor de asesinato (harboring a murderer)	1	1945	1946	13 months

Falsedad de documento (false documents)	1	1948	1948	2 months
Malversación y Falsificación (embezzlement)	1	1947	1950	2 years 10 months
Quebrantamiento de consigna (breach of instructions)	1	1944	1944	7 months
Suplantación de la personalidad (deserter)	1	1937	1941	3 years 10 months
Sustracción de cable telefónico militar (robbery of military telephonic cable)	1	1945	1948	2years 7 months
Usurpación de funciones públicas (usurpation of public functions/office)	1	1945	1946	10 months
Inutilación voluntaría (attempts to avoid military service)	1	1945	1947	1year 7 months
Tenencia ílicita de armas (involved in illicit sale of arms)	1	1944	1946	2years
Venta a precios abusivos(excessive profiteering)	1	1943	1944	14 months

The climate of punitive pursuance of enemies was accompanied by postwar hardship allied to a scarcity of materials and food; black-market bread normally sold at 12 pesetas per kilo in Madrid, where wages for casual labor were 9.4 pesetas per day, and less in rural areas.[47] This inevitably led to the rise of corrupt dealings as "the black market sprang up in the 1940s."[48] Many high ranking officials were involved. In Bizkaia, the

---

47. Richards, *A Time of Silence*, 143.
48. Paul Preston, *¡Comrades! Portraits from the Spanish Civil War* (London: Fontana, 1999), 57.

black market in food was run by the head of the Civil Guard while "in Málaga, Córdoba and Gerona the Civil Governor was heavily involved in similar schemes . . . General Heli de Tella a pro monarchist. .(Richards mentions Civil Governors of Malaga on p138-9, Civil Governors of Córdoba and Gerona, General Heli de Tella p140 described as 'pro monarchist and therefore suspect and subsequently dismissed from the army") . was dismissed from the army . . . [for] producing black-market wheat from his mills."[49]

This was highly unusual because punishments normally depended on the status and allegiance of the culprit and only a handful of individuals were imprisoned for this offense in El Puerto. Eiroa San Francisco quotes an opposition member observing that, "when they catch a reactionary black marketeer nothing happens, but if he is a 'red' he ends up in a labor battalion."[50]

But Franco did eventually move against Nationalists involved in the black market and, in addition to Heli de Tella, he took action against the Falangist breakaway group Falange Española Auténtica (Authentic Spanish Falange);[51] indeed, one of its members was executed for illegal wheat sales. This was an extreme case as very few appear in the list of nonpolitical prisoners convicted for this offense in either the Basque or Cádiz lists, although Franco had made *estraperlo* (black market activities) a criminal offense in 1939.[52]

Table 5.3 relates to Basque prisoners who were convicted on political charges between 1936 and 1939.[53] It illustrates that 751 prisoners from the Basque Country were sentenced for the most serious offense, which did not always carry the death penalty, *adhesión a la rebelión /rebelión militar*, and received a maximum sentence of thirty years. This meant that there were far more Basques convicted for the same offense than those from Cádiz in this more serious category; the former were also detained for between sixteen and eighteen months longer.[54]

---

49. Richards, *A Time of Silence,* 138–40.
50. Eiroa San Francisco, *Viva Franco,* 120.
51. A clandestine organization founded in December 1939 by supporters of the disgraced Manuel Hedilla. Based on the premise of support for the Falange but not for Franco.
52. *BOE,* November 3, 1939.
53. AHPC/PSM, Basque Country political charges 1936–39, Legajos 29200. 47–49, 52–299; 29300. 1–38,11–12, 20–23, 26, 32, 36–37, 39–46, 49, 51–65, 67, 76; 29400. 1, 6, 12, 77.
54. Ibid.

Table 5.3. Prisoners from the Basque Country convicted on political charges 1936–1939. Provincial Historical Archive of Cádiz.

Charge	Number convicted	Earliest date of prison admittance	Latest date of prison release	Maximum time served in El Puerto de Santa María
Adhesión a la rebelión (attachment to rebellion)	570	1936	1946	4 years 4 months
Rebelión militar (military rebellion)	181	1937	1941	4 years 6 months
Auxilio a la rebelión (assistance to rebellion)	95	1938	1946	2 years 7 months
Excitación a la rebelión (incitement rebellion)	3	1938	1941	2 years
Sedición (sedition)	4	1936	1941	3 years 8 months

Table 5.4 lists the charges and dates of release of Basque prisoners between 1936 and 1947.[55]Although the charges listed in this table are numerous (twenty-two), they are fewer than those from Cádiz province (twenty-eight). The major crimes of robbery and theft saw 28 Basques sentenced for this crime as compared to 226 from Cádiz province, despite the fact there were roughly the same numbers imprisoned from the two areas. Nevertheless, here the maximum time for imprisonment for robbery could be over two years more in the Basque Country. This is another example that tends to confirm that Nationalists imprisoned Basques for longer periods.

---

55. AHPC/PSM, Basque Country nonpolitical charges, Legajos 29200: 46, 56–63, 65–99; 29300: 3–7, 15–17, 51, 53, 57, 61–62, 74, 76, 85, 87, 89, 91. 93; 29400: 3–7,10–15, 18–21, 27, 30–38, 40, 44, 53, 58, 60, 73–74, 77. They are not an exact match with Cádiz Province as table 4.2 and table 4.4 include slightly different years of admission and release from prison.

Table 5.4. Prisoners from the Basque Country imprisoned on nonpolitical charges, 1936–1947. Archivo Histórico Provincial de Cádiz

Charge	Number convicted	Earliest date of prison admittance	Latest date of prison release	Maximum time served in El Puerto de Santa María
Robo (robbery)	23	1947	1953	4 years 6 months
Abusos deshonestos (sexual assault, not including rape)	2	1945	1946	7 months
Robo y asociación para el robo (robbery and theft)	1	1946	1949	3 years 1 mnth
Robo y hurto (robbery and theft)	1	1944	1947	2 years 5 months
Asesinato (murder)	2	1938	1950	11 years 7 months
Hurto (theft)	4	1944	1948	3 years 2 months
Hurto, falsificación y amenanzas (theft, forgery and threats)	1	1946	1947	1 years 6 months
Hurto, abandono de servicio (theft and desertion of post)	1	1947	1947	4 months
Homicidio (homicide)	2	1946	1950	3 years 6 months
Homicidio y violación tentativa (homicide and attempted rape)	1	1947	1948	11 months
Deserción frente el enemigo (desertion in the face of the enemy)	3	1938	1945	2 years 11 months
Deserción y robo (desertion and robbery)	1	1945	1946	9 months
Estafa (fraud)	1	1946	1946	7 months
Falsificación de documentos (falsification of documents)	2	1943	1945	10 months

Ley de vagos (law of vagrants) *Ley de vagos y maleantes* (law of vagrants and criminals)	4	1936	1940	Up to 3 years 5months
Traición (treason)	1	1944	1944	2 months
Venta precios abusivos (black market activities)	1	1943	1943	6 months
Violación (rape)	1	1938	1941	2 years 11 months
Usurpación de funciones (usurpation of functions)	1	1943	1943	5 days
Malversación (embezzlement)	1	1943	1944	6 months
Infracción de la Ley de Tasas (infringement of tax laws)	1	1940	1940	7 days
Tenencia ilícita (illicit possesion)	1	1939	1939	2 months

As with the Cádiz examples, the charges listed in table 5.4 give an idea of just how far military tribunals extended into everyday life at this time. Some of the more trivial charges here included *tenenecia ilícita* (illicit possession), *infracción de la Ley de Tasas* (infringement of tax laws), and *usurpación de funciones* (usurpation of functions).

On the other hand, two charges of *asesinato* (murder) in this region involved a maximum stay of eleven years seven months in El Puerto. This was a much longer period of actual imprisonment than those associated with Civil War activities, with the exception of those convicted for "blood crimes." It is interesting that Richards considers that "the final pardon for those convicted of violence did not come until 1969 and the dubious category of 'blood crimes' appears to have included men whose only 'crime' had been to serve as Socialist local councillors."[56]

The Nationalist use of El Puerto penitentiary for Basque prisoners reflected the fortunes of the Republican / Basque Army in the north and

---

56. Richards, "The Limits of Quantification."

in many ways was a response to the fall of Santander on August 26, 1937. José Manuel Martínez Bande, the Francoist military historian, writes about the spectacle of some 30,000 Basques and 20,000 Santanderinos sitting around a bullring, waiting to be transported to prison.[57] This journey often ended up in Andalusia, with El Puerto as the most important southern prison between 1936 and 1943.

The earliest case I was able to find was one Basque prisoner who was sent to El Puerto in November 1936;[58] there were also a handful sent in August/September 1937.[59] The arrival of the majority in August 1938 was followed by the last in May 1953 (although this was a case that did not involve being convicted for civil war "crimes").[60]

One of the other Andalusian jails that included Basque prisoners was the provincial prison in Huelva, which included an intake of around 225 from the Basque Country. Although smaller than El Puerto, conditions were equally unhealthy and some thirty prisoners died in Huelva in March 1942.[61] Further details, obtained from the director of the Provincial Historical Archive in Huelva relating to Basque prisoners from 1937 to 1944, enables a comparison to be made regarding charges and sentences with El Puerto.[62] (Navarre is not included).

The earliest Basque war prisoner was admitted to Huelva in January 1937, a large influx (81) in August 1937, and an even larger intake (118) once again, mainly, in August 1938.[63] The last detained there for *rebelión militar* was in May 1949. Some prisoners were transferred in and out of Huelva several times; to concentrate only on the dates of the first admission and the last exit in these cases could sometimes give a misleading impression.[64] One interesting transfer was that of Antonio Basteguieta

57. Martínez Bande, *El final del frente norte*, 104.
58. AHPC/PSM, Legajo 29264. Prisoner sentenced for sedition from Zurien arrived on November 18, 1936. This is very real problem for me (as it has been throughout) since the archivos of Cádiz are the only ones in Spain that have the full details of El Puerto Basque prisoners in Spain as far as I know. Place and person names are in Spanish. The name Zurien is very clear on the prison file this time. I accept your point but suggest that in this case I should say something like Gulina Regino from Navarra was one of the few charged with sedition.
59. AHPC/PSM, Legajos 29267, 29272, 29276, Prisoners sentenced for *adhesión/auxilio a la rebelión* from Eibar, Bilbao, Mutriku, and Loiu arrived August/September 1937.
60. AHPC/PSM, Legajos 29246–29476. See also Pedro Barruso, *Verano y revolución. La guerra civil en Guipúzcoa (julio–septiembre de 1936)* (San Sebastián; R&B Editores, 1996).
61. Francisco Espiñosa, *La Guerra Civil en Huelva* (Huelva: Diputación Provincial, 1997), 676–78. AHPH/PPH, Signaturas 07516/021–07620/032.
62. Email from the director of the Provincial Historical Archive of Huelva, April 5, 2011.
63. AHPH/PPH, Signaturas 07516/021–07620/032.
64. Ibid.

of Kortezubi, Bizkaia, who was convicted for *rebelión*. Moved to Huelva from El Puerto on December 5, 1938, he ended up in the infamous penal colonies in Dos Hermanas, Seville.[65] In this particular case, the likelihood was that he was involved in the reconstruction of Dos Hermanas, rebuilt by prison labor. José Luis Gutiérrez Molina comments that, "this is what has come to pass as a symbol of the use of convicts in public works."[66] Two of the best examples of the projects that involved prisoners were the Bajo Guadalquivir Canal in Andalusia and the Valle de los Caídos near Madrid. Daniel Gatica estimates that 23 percent of prisoners from Cádiz province were transferred to penal colonies in Seville from El Puerto.[67]

I can find no such comparative figure for Basque prisoners who were transferred to Seville from El Puerto. The fact that a large majority from El Puerto were not moved elsewhere on arrival is almost certainly the reason.

There were over two thousand Basque prisoners in El Puerto during the peak years of 1940and 1941; although a study of individual Basque prisoners' files has been revealing, I am conscious of the fact that the whole picture is not available. However, my evidence is augmented by information from the Basque and Huelva archives. The report published by the Basque delegation to the penitentiary of El Puerto in July 1939 gives details of the large-scale gradual transfers of some four thousand Basques from prisons in the Basque Country and El Dueso to Andalusia, thereby constituting "a nucleus of Basques."[68]

The report estimates that, "over a period," large contingents of Basques had been transferred from the north; by July 1939, there were some 540 in Seville, 200 in Huelva, 200 in Granada, and 2,000 in El Puerto.[69] Others went to the prisons of Osuna and Cazalla de la Sierra, both in Seville province, which may not have taken many prison transfers; on visiting the latter in June 2009, it appeared very small. According to the Cádiz files of prisoners, one of the busiest days relating to Basque transfers to El Puerto was August 6, 1938, when 228 prisoners (151 from Bizkaia, 56 from Gipuzkoa, 17 from Araba, and 4 from Navarre) were moved there.

---

65. AHPH/PPH, Signatura 07709/006.
66. José Luis Gutiérrez Molina, "Los presos del canal," in *La inmensa prisión*, ed. Molinero, Sala and Sobrequés, 72.
67. Gatica Cote, "Una cárcel de posguerra." See chapter 1.
68. SAF/PSM/CON/7/39.
69. SAF/PSM/ANON/3/40.

There were also around fifty Basque priests who had been transferred to Carmona, Seville.[70] That they were sent to Carmona in 1940 was in part due to the pressure by Cardinal Segura, then Bishop of Seville, who undertook to supervise them. Details of Segura pressurizing the ministry of the interior on behalf of the Basque priests between October and November 1939 can be found in a study by Santiago Martínez, *Los papeles del Cardenal Segura, 1880—1957* (2004).[71]

There is further evidence of the presence of Basque priests in Carmona (who are named) in a photograph taken with Julián Besteiro, former president of the PSOE, the UGT, and the Cortes Genenerales.[72]

Table 5.5 indicates the number of prisoners transferred by the penal authorities in Andalusia in 1939.[73]

---

70. See Euzko Apaiz Talde, *Historia General de la Guerra Civil en Euskadi*, vol. 8, *El clero vasco ante los tribunales* (San Sebastián: L. Haranburu, 1982). Also see photo of Basque priests with Julián Besteiro: http://urkullu.files.wordpress.com/2009/07/carmonal-7.jpg (accessed May 20, 2010).

71. See Martínez Sánchez, *Los papeles del Cardenal Segura, 1880–1957*.

72. The Basque priests included José Sanchez Campos, Juan Aguirre Lazcano, Gregorio Fernández Acha, Luis Aguirre Vergara, Vicente Bátiz Bilbao, Eugenio Legarra Magueregui, Aquilino Ayerdi Goicoechea, Juan Aldecoa-Otalora Beitia, Modesto Arana Fulain, Vicente Sainz Rodríguez, Jose Pío Jauregui Plaza, Santos Arana Bergareche, Manuel Oruzar Eguiluz, Castor Marañón Muguruza, Manuel Lladós Arzuaga, Florencio Barrenechea Garraitabarrena, Áldama Guinea, Mariano Ereño Dañobeitia, Bernabe Acha Sasia, Santiago Villanueva Aramburu, Federico Zorrozua Arrandia, Daniel Torrontegui Mendiburu, Rafael Uronaguena Garro, Candido Nogueras Mateo, Fernando Marcuerquiaga Itza, Lino Aquesolo Olivares, Gregorio Fernández González, Honorio Urgoita Esturo, Saturnino Ganchegui Lascurain, Juan Zabaleta Arrizabalaga, Ignacio Arechabaleta Bengoechea, Eugenio Larrañaga Landaburu, Victoriano Larranagan Landa, Sinforiano Traspuesto Guerra, Ezequiel Guisasola Artamendi, Nazario Sarasola Acarregui, Juan Marquegui Maya, Ángel Iturbe Alberdi, Federico Orbea Bergareche, José María Dañobeitia Arruza, Florentino Sagarra Mendezona, José Antonio Loinaz Otaño, Santiago Onaindia Baseta, Damián Celaya Acarregui, José Domingo Ugarechea Urquieta, Fermín Goti Basterra, Román Jauregui Urizar, Enrique Arriaga Aguera, Domingo Aguirre Ocerin, Julio Ugarte Vicuña, Ramón Oruzar Laca, and Justo Atucha Atucha. I am very grateful to Peter Anderson for his help in this matter.

73. Alicia Domínguez Pérez, *El verano que trajo un largo invierno. La represión política-social durante el primer franquismo en Cádiz (1936–1945)* (Cádiz: Quorum, 2005), 122.

Table 5.5. Prison transfers in Andalusia 1939.

Alicia Domínguez Pérez, *El verano que trajo un largo invierno*, 122.

Prison	Number moved
Penal Pto Sta María	542
Vapor Miraflores (a prison ship)	325
Fábrica Torpedos San Fdo.	200
Prisión y Campo Prisioneros Sevilla	63
(reconstruction of Dos Hermanas)	39
Depósito Olvera	38
Cortijo Vicios Jerez	19
Cárcel Algeciras	19
Castillos de S. Sebastián y Sta. Catalina	13
Depósito Villamartín	

Table 5.6 illustrates the use of El Puerto as a local Andalusian prison with a major intake from nearby Cádiz and surrounding area.[74] This includes the provincial prison in Cádiz (332), the Castillo prison in Santa Catalina (23), the Casería de Ossio prison in San Fernando (21), the municipal prison in La Línea de la Concepción (11), and the municipal warehouse in Algar.

In addition to Cádiz, the use of Jerez de la Frontera (47) and Seville (54) meant that some 51 percent of the prison intake from the province of Cádiz ensured that El Puerto played an important penal role in Andalusia. When one sets this against the 31 percent of prisoners sentenced for "civil war crimes" in the province of Cádiz, as against 81 percent in the Basque Country, it explains how El Puerto came to cater for different categories of inmates from the extreme north and south of Spain, with all the ramifications that this involved.

The theme of localism relating to inmates from the province of Cádiz was reinforced when it came to the matter of transferring prisoners from El Puerto, although some 765 prisoners remained in situ and appear to have served their sentence there.[75] Of the 224 transferred, almost three quarters were simply moved to another prison in Cádiz. This comprised a combination of political and nonpolitical prisoners, with a majority from the latter category. This might have been a factor that affected favorable release conditions for those prisoners from Cádiz province.

---

74. AHPC/PSM, Legajos 29246–29477.
75. Ibid.

Table 5.6. The use of El Puerto Cádiz province: Inmates transferred to El Puerto de Santa María from local prisons. Archivo Histórico Provincial de Cádiz.

Location	Number
Prisión Provincial de Cádiz	332
Prisión Provincial de Sevilla	54
Prisión de Partido de Jerez de la Frontera	47
Prisión Militar de Hacho (Ceuta)	27
Prisión Castillo de Santa Catalina (Cádiz)	23
Prisión Casería de Osio de San Fernando	21
Prisión Partido de San Roque	19
Prisión Fábrica de Torpedos	14
Prisión Provincial de Madrid	13
Prisión Provincial de Málaga Prisión de Partido de Algeciras Prisión de Partido de Ceuta	12
Prisión Municipal de La Línea de Concepción (Cádiz)	11
Prisión Provincial de Granada Depósito Municipal de Sanlucar de Barrameda	8
Depósito Municipal de Algar (Cádiz)	7
Depósito Municipal de Algeciras Prisión Provincial de Las Palmas	6 6
Depósito Municipal de Chiclana de Frontera	5
Prisión Provincial de Murcia Prisión de Partido de Melilla	4
Colonial Penitenciaria del Dueso (Santoña) Depósito Municipal de El Puerto de Santa María Prisión Europea de Tetuán Prisión Militar de Escopetas de Algeciras	3
Prisión Escuela de Madrid Prisión Provincial de Santander Prisión Provincial de Las Comendadores (Madrid) Prisión Central de Guadalajara Prisión de Partido de Algeciras	**2**
Others prisons include Santander, León, Albacete, Gijon, Alicante, Valencia, Pamplona, Cartagena, Huelva, Donostia-San Sebastián, Zaragoza, Almería, Castellón, Badajoz, Puerto Real, and Jaén	1

Table 5.7 illustrates the policy of containing transfers within Andalusia of prisoners from Cádiz province.[76] Once again, the Cádiz prisons are all important, but the provincial prison of Casería de Ossio (San Fernando, Cádiz) replaces the provincial prison in Cádiz as the major outlet.

Table 5.7. Numbers of prisoners transferred out of El Puerto locally.
Archivo Histórico Provincial de Cádiz

Location	Number
El penal Casería de Osio (San Fernando, Cádiz)	108
Prisión Provincial de Cádiz	25
Prisión Provincial de Madrid	11
Castillo de Santa Catalina de Cádiz	8
Sanatorio Penitenciario de Cuéllar	4
Prisión Provincial de Sevilla	3
Prisión de Puerto Real Conde de Peñalver (Madrid)	2
Other prisons include: 1ª Agrupación de Colonias Penitenciarias, Sanlúcar Barrameda, Banderín Enganche Legión (Sevilla), Regimiento Cádiz no.41, Batallón de Trabajadores no 8 (Algeciras), Batallón disciplinario de Marruecos, Villamartín, Cuartel regimiento de Infantería, Hospital Penitenciaria Yeserías (Madrid), Juzgado Militar no.1 Puerto Real, Manicomio Penal de El Puerto de Santa María, Burgos, Guadalajara, Cortico de Vicos (Jerez), Prisión Escuela de Madrid, Prisión Porlier de Madrid, Prisiones Provinciales de Cádiz, Madrid and Sevilla, Ceuta, Alicante, Talavera de la Reina (Toledo)	1 1

Transfers took place between June and October 1937, and in these cases of temporary confinement, some prisoners were again transferred to the nearby prisons of Casería de Ossio and the provincial prison in Cádiz.[77] Yet again, there was later evidence of inconsistencies and a lack of congruence in sentencing. For example, there were a few cases in which

---

76. Ibid.
77. Ibid.

the provincial prison of Huelva was involved and a Basque prisoner, Julian Chertudes Torres, from the Desertu/Desierto district of Erandio, Bizkaia, was imprisoned on a charge of *usurpación de funciones* (usurpation of functions) for merely five days in November 1943.[78]

In another highly unusual transfer, Andrés Domínguez Pérez from La Línea de la Concepción (Cádiz province), who had been convicted for *rebelión militar*, was transferred to the nearby penal mental asylum in El Puerto de Santa María on March 25, 1938, even though he had served eight months in El Puerto.[79] Even here, inmates regarded as criminal were partly treated for remedial action: "the prisoner in the lunatic asylum had to serve time in two institutions.

One provided treatment for mental problems; the other socialization in order that he would no longer present a threat to state security."[80] The comparison between the transfer of Basque and Cádiz prisoners is stark and makes clear that the Nationalist prison authorities had a different political agenda for the former. By far the vast majority of Basque captives were transferred from the prison of El Dueso and served up to four years and six months in El Puerto. Some 96.5 percent of the Basques served their prison sentences in the latter prison.

This reluctance to move Basques to a northern prison could also have been determined by their length of sentences for serious "crimes," influenced by their reputation as "red separatists." Gabriel Jackson writes that "the Basques attracted enormous opprobrium in some quarters and . p375. . the Carlists and the Insurgent military regarded the Basque Nationalists as traitors p375 . . a centralizing military dictatorship punished them for having taken the side of the Republic in [sic] behalf of regional autonomyp384."[81]

Table 5.8 illustrates that very few Basque prisoners were transferred north from El Puerto before they had completed their (reduced) sentence.[82]

---

78. AHPH/PSM, Signatura 07595/001. For a similar offense, two El Puerto inmates, José Soto Rivas and Juan Antonio Aguirre, had been sentenced to between one and two years. See AHPC/PSM, Legajos 29399 and 29401.
79. Ibid.
80. Federico. Castejón, *Comentarios científicos-prácticos al Código Penal de 1870*, vol. 2, *Tratado de la responsabilidad* (Madrid: Reus, 1926), 281–82.
81. Gabriel Jackson, *The Spanish Republic and Civil War, 1931–1939* (Princeton: Princeton University Press, 1972), 375, 384.
82. AHPC/PSM, Legajos 29246–29477.

Table 5.8. Basque transfers north from El Puerto out of Andalusia.
Archivo Histórico Provincial de Cádiz

Location	Number
Araba	
Prisión de Vitoria, Prisión de Yeserías (Madrid)	1
Navarre	
Prisión Hospital de Madrid	2
Prisión Principal de Donostia-San Sebastián	1
Gipuzkoa	
Prisión Principal de San Sebastián	4
Prisión de Cádiz	3
Prisión Principal de Madrid	1
Bizkaia	
Prisión Principal de San Sebastián	8
Prisión de San Sebastián	7
Prisión de Bilbao	3
Prisión de Santander	2
Prisión Cortijo de Vicos (Jerez), Hospital Penitenciario de Madrid, Prisión de los Escalapios (Bilbao), Prisión de Vitoria, Prisiones Pricipales de Zaragoza y de Guadalajara, Talleres Penitenciarias de Alcalá Henares	1

Northern local prisons were hardly used for transfer purposes. Where the few local Basque prisons were utilized, there was a heavy reliance on penal establishments around Donostia-San Sebastián. But this was accounted for less than 4 percent of the total prison intake. This lack of transfers north would have compounded the climate of uncertainty that enveloped the lives of prisoners and reinforced their feeling of isolation. In the circumstances, it is perhaps surprising that the only suicide case among the prisoners' files I could find involved a Basque prisoner, Cándido Urrutia Ajuria from Bilbao, who had been convicted for *adhesion a la rebelión*. His death was officially recorded as a suicide, after thirty months in El Puerto, on June 6, 1940.[83]

---

83. AHPC/PSM, Legajo 29267.

The Cádiz archives only relate to Basque transfers out of Andalusia once they have arrived in El Puerto. However, the Basque archives in Bergara also mention transfers within Andalusia, such as the four hundred Basque and leftist prisoners moving from El Puerto to Seville on December 14, 1938.[84] This included three hundred Basque nationalists, seventy-five socialists and republicans, and twenty-five communists and CNT members, as well as sixty-five from Asturias and thirty-five from Santander.[85] In view of the political organization within El Puerto, my view would be that the prison authorities moved them in December 1938 in an attempt to nip this in the bud. That they were unsuccessful was evidenced by the discovery of the activities of the Rubial organization in October 1940.[86] This lack of success may be partly explained by the fact that although there were Basque transfers out of El Puerto, there were between the peak years of late 1938 and 1941 a very definite nucleus of Basque prisoners there. The Basque report of July 1939 [87] suggests that the presence of 2,000 Basque inmates by summer 1939 meant that if the Francoist penal authorities wished to stifle Basque political activity, they would have to substantially dismantle their numbers in El Puerto. This they would not, or could not do, for a variety of reasons.

The failure to keep records on large-scale transfers could be due to a variety of reasons. Perhaps the most likely explanation is that the penal authorities may have decided simply to transfer files wholesale to the recipient prisons, thereby losing a record in the prison of origin. This actually happened in a number of other cases in which prisoners' details from El Puerto ended up in Sanlúcar and files from El Dueso are now in Cádiz.[88]

Finally, an examination of the decisions of the prison authorities concerning the different conditions of release for prisoners from El Puerto between 1936 and 1949 again raises interesting questions concerning the

84. SAF/PSM/ANON/3/40.
85. The Basque reports in July 1939 and March 1940 contain detailed information about transfers within Andalusia while the Cádiz archives relate to Basque transfers to and from Andalusia. A combination of intelligence reads: a) August 1938, arrival of 228 Basques in El Puerto; b) May 1939, arrival of Ramón Rubial; c) December 1938, 400 Basque activists moved to Seville prison; and d) October 1940, Rubial organization discovered, Rubial moved. Prison authorities act to crush political organization within.
86. See chapter 1 regarding Basque political organization in El Puerto.
87. SAF/PSM/ANON/7/39.
88. Large-scale transfers within Andalusia do not always appear to have been shown on individual prisoner's files. See introduction on statement regarding movement of prisoners to the new prison complex at Centro Penitenciario Puerto 1 and problems with transfers of *fichas* (index cards).

consistency of the Francoist penal system. In the case of prisoners from Cádiz province, there were twenty-six different conditions of release as opposed to sixteen different conditions recorded for Basque prisoners. These deviations in turn centered on another sixteen variations of *libertad/libertad condicional* (liberty/conditional liberty). The terminology is confusing and was often used interchangeably. Many prisoners would have made strenuous efforts to secure a certificate of *libertad /libertad definitiva* (liberty/definitive liberty, see figure 5.1) as this meant that the released prisoner would have more freedom of movement, including the flexibility of seeking employment elsewhere without having to report to the police every week.

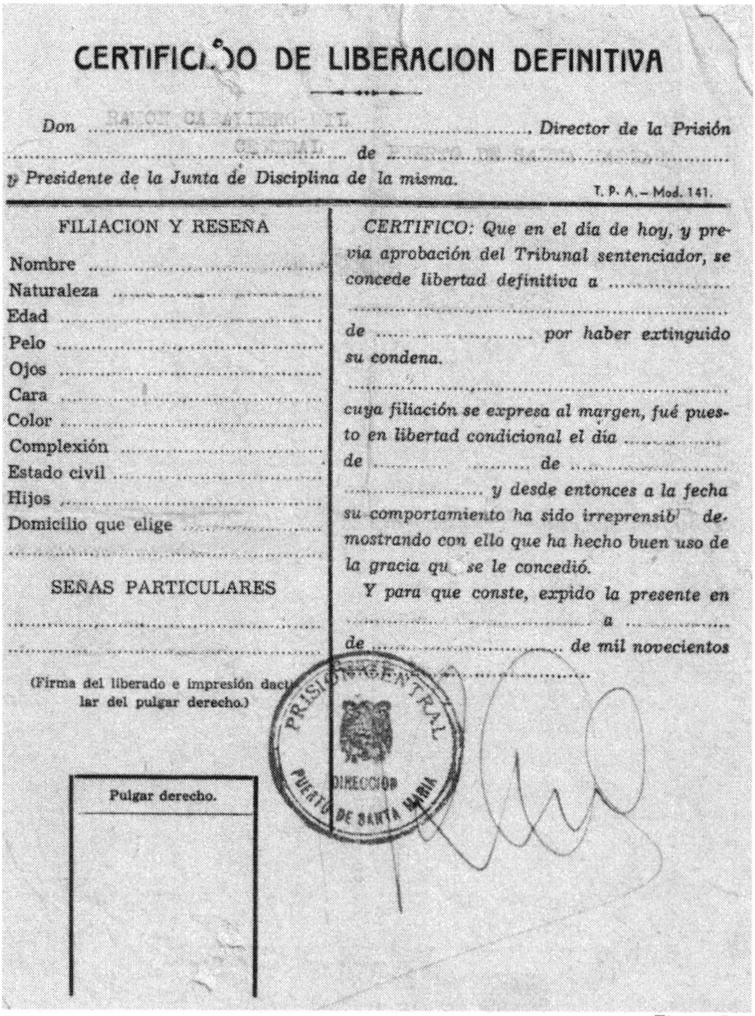

CERTIFICADO DE LIBERACION DEFINITIVA

Don .... *Director de la Prisión* .... *de* ....
y Presidente de la Junta de Disciplina de la misma.

T. P. A.—Mod. 141.

FILIACION Y RESEÑA

Nombre ....
Naturaleza ....
Edad ....
Pelo ....
Ojos ....
Cara ....
Color ....
Complexión ....
Estado civil ....
Hijos ....
Domicilio que elige ....

SEÑAS PARTICULARES

(Firma del liberado e impresión dactilar del pulgar derecho.)

Pulgar derecho.

CERTIFICO: Que en el día de hoy, y previa aprobación del Tribunal sentenciador, se concede libertad definitiva a .... *de* .... *por haber extinguido su condena.*

.... *cuya filiación se expresa al margen, fué puesto en libertad condicional el día* .... *de* .... *de* .... *y desde entonces a la fecha su comportamiento ha sido irreprensible demostrando con ello que ha hecho buen uso de la gracia que se le concedió.*

Y para que conste, expido la presente en .... *a* .... *de* .... *de mil novecientos* ....

Figure 5.1

The sentencing policy (figure 5.2) usually led to one of two final outcomes when it came to the category of release, providing the person was not sentenced to be executed. The first related to some form of release involving *libertad /libertad definitiva/ libertad por prisión atenuada* (house arrest).

INSTRUCCIONES

1.ª Irá directamente al lugar que se le ha designado, que es _____

_____, provincia de _____, donde permanecerá hasta que se le conceda la libertad definitiva si observa buena conducta.

2.ª No podrá salir del lugar que se le haya designado sin autorización del Director que suscribe. Si se ausentare sin dicho permiso, le será revocado el beneficio concedido con el efecto de su reingreso en la Prisión.

Si tuviere necesidad de cambiar de residencia, lo solicitará del Director de este Establecimiento y esperará a que su solicitud se resuelva, para evitar la revocación de la gracia que disfruta.

3.ª Tan pronto como llegue al lugar de su destino, se presentará al Director o Jefe de la Prisión, y, si no la hubiere en la localidad, a la Autoridad gubernativa, y le exhibirá el presente documento, al objeto de identificar su persona y para que le sirva de recomendación y garantía.

4.ª Queda obligado a dirigir por correo, el primer día de cada mes, un conciso informe referente a su propia persona, escrito por sí mismo. Este informe lo presentará al Director o Jefe de la Prisión o a la Autoridad gubernativa de la localidad, para que lo vise y lo remita al Director de esta Prisión.

En este informe expresará el jornal a remuneración señalada a su trabajo, así como las economías y ahorros que haya podido hacer.

Si quedare sin ocupación, lo manifestará a este Establecimiento, consignando el motivo, para practicar las gestiones posibles a fin de proporcionarle otra nueva, si su proceder lo merece.

Habrá de ser veraz en sus informes, y con todo interés se le recomienda que evite las malas compañías y todo lo que pueda conducirle a una vida relajada o a la comisión de nuevos delitos.

La Junta de Disciplina de esta Prisión, así como las Autoridades superiores y las de la provincia en que va a residir, se interesan vivamente por su suerte; podrá contar con la ayuda y consejo de dichas Autoridades y de esta Junta, y en esta Prisión hallará siempre un lugar de retiro y protección en caso de desgracia.

_____ de _____ de mil novecientos _____

V.º B.º
EL PRESIDENTE,   EL SECRETARIO,

Figure 5.2

The third relates to some form of *libertad condicional/ libertad condicional provisional/ sin o con destierro* (with or without exile, figure 5.3).

CERTIFICACION DE LIBERACION CONDICIONAL

Don .... Director de la
Prisión .... de .... y Presidente
de la Junta de Disciplina de la misma.

FILIACION Y RESEÑA	CERTIFICO: Que la Junta de Disciplina

FILIACION Y RESEÑA

Naturaleza (pueblo y provincia)
Edad
Estado civil
Hijos
Delito
Condena
Tiempo extinguido
Tiempo que le falta por extinguir

SEÑAS PARTICULARES

(Firma del liberado e impresión dactilar del pulgar derecho)

Pulgar derecho

CERTIFICO: Que la Junta de Disciplina de este Establecimiento, en sesión de hoy, ha dado cumplimiento a la Orden ministerial de .... de .... del corriente año, por la que se concede la libertad condicional al penado ...., atendiendo a su buena conducta. El liberado fijará su residencia en ...., provincia de ...., y estará bajo el patrocinio y vigilancia de las Autoridades locales del pueblo en que va a residir o de aquel a que por necesidad se traslade, hasta que se le conceda la libertad definitiva por su buena comportamiento, o reingrese en la Prisión de procedencia por su mala conducta. Se le entrega en concepto de ahorros, socorros de marcha, etcétera, la cantidad de .... pesetas .... céntimos.

Y para que conste, y de conformidad a lo mandado, se expide la presente en ...., a .... de .... de mil novecientos ....

(Firma)

Figure 5.3

Mirta Núñez Díaz-Balart writes:

> In order to qualify for conditional liberty under the Nationalist penal authorities the following conditions had to be met: time redeemed, good conduct, and an assessment by the respective prison . . . this privileged parole was not possible before the completion of religious instruction, a minimum of basic literacy, and other minor requirements such as being deloused.[89]

Libertad condicional/ provisional con destierro (exile) made life extremely difficult for a released prisoner, since he was paroled in a strange area, away from home, unknown, and criminalized, and where he often

---

89. Núñez Díaz-Balart, *Los años del terror,* 82.

met with a hostile reception. Indeed, as Michael Alpert writes, this condition of release "merely continued the punishment for their families."[90] There were several examples in El Puerto in which a prisoner was released on condition of internal exile. Felix Abascal Bilbao from Durango had a record of military involvement, albeit a somewhat checkered one, but not markedly different from others who were released without internal exile.[91] It is not obvious to see why he merited release with internal exile. A thirty-three-year-old fitter, he served with Marxist militias, fled to France from the Irun front, and then returned to Barcelona. From there he went to Eibar, where he worked in an ammunitions factory. Affiliated to the UGT, he was considered to be an extremist. Like so many other Basques, he was charged with *adhesión a la rebelión* and sentenced to thirty years' imprisonment. He began his sentence in Laredo in August 1938, was transferred to El Dueso, and then to El Puerto; he was finally released on *libertad condicional provisional con destierro* (exile) in July 1941 at a distance of 250 kilometers (155 miles) away from home in Zaragoza. After supportive letters from the local heads of the Falange and Civil Guard, the restriction of exile was lifted in November 1941. Later, in July 1943, there was a softening of rules concerning internal exile when the Ministry of Justice stipulated that, while prisoners in this category were banned from living in their immediate locality, they could reside in their home province.[92]

The second Basque case involving internal exile was that of Saturnino Bejino Pajarín from Andoain, Gipuzkoa. His case was highly unusual in that he was one of the few inmates that I found who was recalled to prison for bad behavior, and then moved to six other locations. Bejino Pajarín, aged forty-one, a scrap dealer, was charged with *auxilio a la rebelión* and sentenced to twelve years and one day.[93] Admitted to El Dueso on December 9, 1937, he was transferred to Huelva on December 5, 1938 (after a year in El Puerto) and then released on January 28, 1941 on the condition of *prisión atenuada en domicilio* (house arrest). He was, however, admitted to the provincial prison in Donostia-San Sebastián on December 29, 1942 for *mala conducta* or bad behavior. He was denounced by the mayor of his home town, Andoain, for not having shown repentance, persisting with Marxist ideas, and generally for being a dangerous and unsatisfactory member of the local community. Readmitted to the provincial prison of Huelva on March 7, 1943, he was released on May 12, 1943, but re-

---

90. Alpert, *The Republican Army in the Spanish Civil War 1936–1939*, 302.
91. AHPC/PSM, Legajo 29326, Causa número 126/37.
92. *BOE*, July 17, 1943.
93. AHPH/PPH, Signatura 07709/013.

mained in internal exile in Burgos until he was finally freed with *libertad definitiva* on October 25, 1948. His case provides a good example of a prisoner having to serve an extra seven years under the much more difficult conditions of internal exile for not having demonstrated sufficient evidence of remorse.

However, in certain other cases it appears that the Francoist prison authorities adopted a harder approach to those who fell within the category of continued parole eligibility. Suspect ex-prisoners could also be recalled to prison if their behavior was considered to be unacceptable. Gómez Bravo gives examples of further grounds for denial or withdrawal of parole as late as 1948 and 1950.[94] In 1948, Miguel Higuera was denied parole on grounds that he was an "evildoer." His father and brother had been executed for the assassination of a Civil Guard and then hanging a cowbell round his neck. In !950, Rafael Carbonell, a prisoner in El Puerto, was released on October 9 that year and reported for "immoral conduct" three days later. Police were informed that he had been living in a house with a Hilaria García, "a woman of lax morals" who had shared her house with another man with whom she conducted marital life. One suspects that the Nationalist authorities were also interested because the man in question had been an officer who had been expelled from the Francoist air force. This case (which led to withdrawal of *libertad condicional*) is a good example of the refusal of the Nationalist authorities to allow released prisoners a normal life. It also gives an indication of their insistence on "purification" and "morality," which paradoxically led to the establishment of houses for *mujeres extriviadas* or "fallen women." The Franco regime condoned *casas de tolerancia* (brothels) until 1956. Extreme poverty led to the enormous growth of prostitution in the 1940s, which operated alongside a much publicized "purification" policy.

Table 5.9 illustrates the widely inconsistent conditions of release by category from El Puerto in the years 1941 to 1953 in the province of Cádiz and the Basque Country.[95] The later dates relate to convictions sometime after the Civil War.

Table 5.9. Different policy of release of prisoners in Cádiz and the Basque Country (mp = mainly political mainly, mnp = mainly nonpoltical, p = political, np = nonpolitical).Archivo Histórico Provincial de Cádiz.

94. Gómez Bravo, *El exilio interior*, 192. Also see Gómez Bravo, "The Origins of the Francoist Penitentiary System, 1936–1948)."
95. AHPC/PSM, Legajos 29246–477.

Conditions of release	Areas	Crime	Number	Span of dates of release
Libertad	Cádiz	mnp	158	March1937/July 1946
	Bizkaia	mp	45	Sept 1939/Sept1940
	Gipuzkoa	mp	19	March1940/October 1950
	Araba	mp	3	May/June1941
	Navarre	p	3	August 1940/Sept1946
Libertad condicional	Cádiz	mnp	134	June1940/June 1951
	Bizkaia	mp	72	Sept 1940/May 1953
	Gipuzkoa	mp	25	Sept1940/ June1950
	Araba	p	8	June 1941/June 1950
	Navarre	np	7	Sept1940/March 1949
Libertad definitiva	Cádiz	mnp	83	August1942/Sept 1951
	Bizkaia	np	12	August1939/June 1946
	Gipuzkoa	np	6	January1945/Feb 1950
	Araba	np	2	March 1946/ May1950
	Navarre	np	4	April1945/Sept 1948
Libertad condicional provisional sin destierro (provisional release without exile)	Cádiz	p	88	June1941/Sept 1943
	Bizkaia	p	20	June/Sept 1941
	Gipuzkoa	p	6	June/Sept 1941
	Araba	p	2	August1941/June 1943
	Navarre	p	5	May/July1941
Libertad condicional con destierro (provisional release with exile)	Cádiz	p	63	July1941/Feb 1943
	Bizkaia	p	4	June/ August 1941

	Araba	p	2	July 1941
	Navarre	p	1	August 1941
Libertad por prisión atenuada	Cádiz	p	45	August1940/Dec 1942
	Bizkaia	p	355	August1940/Aug 1941
	Gipuzkoa	p	140	August1940/Oct 1941
	Araba	p	42	July1940/Jan 1943
	Navarre	p	23	August1940/July 1941
Libertad condicional provisional	Cádiz	p, np	28	June1941/Nov 1942
	Bizkaia	p	42	May1941/March 1942
	Gipuzkoa	p	13	May/July 1941
	Araba	p	2	June/Nov 1941
	Navarre	p	5	May/Sept 1941
Prisión atenuada en su domicilio (prison confinement at home completed)	Bizkaia	p	41	July1940/March 1943

Perhaps the most significant conclusion to be drawn from this chapter is further confirmation of the ad hoc attitude of the Nationalist authorities toward penal policy and indeed the military tribunals concerning sentencing. This was reflected in the wide difference of conditions of release that varied between prisoners from Cádiz province and the Basque Country. *Libertad condicional* was granted for nonpolitical prisoners from Cádiz province (134) whereas Basque political prisoners received a similar parole condition (105). *Libertad condicional con destierro* (exile) was handed to a sizeable number of Cádiz prisoners (63), but no more than a handful of Basques. (7). *Prisión atenuada en domicilio* was a Basque condition of release (81), but simply did not exist for those from Cádiz. Other irregularities are demonstrated by the continuing use of military tribunals for non-Civil War "crimes." For example, in Gipuzkoa a prisoner was released on *libertad* in October 1946 after having been convicted for *estafa* (black-market dealings) in March of the same year. In Cádiz province a prisoner was released on *libertad* in July 1946 after being convicted for *abusos dishonestos* (indecent assault) in October 1945. Occasionally,

Republicans were still charged with one of the Spanish Civil War offenses, *excitación de rebelión*; one such person from Cádiz province was charged as late as November 1945, but was released some seven months later.

However, a comparison of the files of prisoners of El Puerto from the two areas does show that nonpolitical prisoners inevitably obtained more favorable conditions of release. Nevertheless, this was not automatic and, especially in the nonpolitical area, was always at the fickle largesse of the Francoist prison authorities. As Núñez Díaz-Balart writes: "The released prisoner always had the sword of Damocles over his head. If during the conditional period of parole he failed to complete any aspect of what was required or the authorities judged that he had breached them or was guilty of bad behavior, he would have to return to prison."[96]

Further evidence of pressure on prisoners released on *libertad condicional* is provided by Vicenta Garnica Laserra, who related that released prisoners were even induced to change friends. This interest in the former prisoners did not cease after fulfilment of *libertad* requirements, since after her death, Vicenta's great granddaughter found a document among her belongings that contained a request from a military judge about Vicenta's social activity.[97]Morever her official documentation indicated that her real date of birth was April 14 but at the age of fourteen her relatives had changed the date of her birthday to April 5. This was to avoid any form of celebration that coincided with the proclamation of the Second Republic on April 14.

Another interesting aspect relating to liberty after release was provided by a member of the 1936 Durango Association.[98] A young girl named Libertad moved to Atxondo, Bizkaia, after the war with her other grandparents as her father, uncle, and grandfather had all been executed. When five-years-old, she was playing with other children who called her by her name. On hearing this, her remaining grandfather rushed into the street and declared that, "From now on, this girl is called Mari Tere." She has been known by that name ever since.

The Nationalist penal policy constituted a major pillar of Francoist repression and, as may be seen, the charges and sentences were variable and even erratic. In my view, there seems to have been a different policy of penal punishment between prisoners from Cádiz and the Basque Country as regards political "crimes." As has been mentioned earlier, local jails in the province of Cádiz had a large input in El Puerto, but as far as

---

96. Núñez Díaz-Balart, *Los años del terror,* 82.
97. Email from María González Gorosarri, December 17, 2008.
98. Ibid.

output was concerned only the prison of Casería de Ossio in San Fernando, with 108 transferees, comprised any numbers of prisoners resembling that transferred out of El Puerto.

The examples drawn from the prisoners' files of El Puerto highlight the discrepancies in sentencing of the eighteen military tribunals ranging from Andalusia to the Basque Country, the differing policies adopted by Nationalist penal authorities in the transfer and movement of prisoners, and the apparent lack of cohesion relating to conditions of release. Gómez Bravo considers that, "a probation system was put into operation in a manner more characteristic of the nineteenth century than the middle of the twentieth century."[99] One could argue that there were certain similarities with the nineteenth-century probation system in England and the Netherlands, based on a harsh prison structure, centered on the belief that wrongdoing merited atonement by punishment that compensated for the crime, and accompanied by severe revocation restrictions. Many of these factors were present in Franco's system of conditional release between 1937 and 1949.

---

99. Gómez Bravo, "The Origins of the Francoist Penitentiary System, 1936–1948."

6

The End of the Odyssey

> A esos hombres que en su muerte
> encontraron l...A esa Historia que late
> en la memoria de los vivos.

—Alejandro Pérez Guillén, Benalup- (Casas Viejas)

This final chapter seeks to highlight important aspects of the Francoist penitentiary system between 1936 and 1949 as they affected Basque prisoners of El Puerto penitentiary. In order to illustrate different outcomes, a comparison has often been drawn with the treatment of inmates from Cádiz province, the other majority group in this prison. El Puerto provided evidence wherein Basque and Cádiz prisoners had been convicted on different charges and sentences with disparate conditions of release.

Moreover, as the examples in chapter 5 indicate, there were a plethora of "nonpolitical" charges, such as infringement of tax laws and embezzlement, which enabled military tribunals to intervene in many aspects of everyday life. Whatever the perspective of the reader, there was no doubt that "while it is certain that Franco did not invent the prisons, he extended their use in an extraordinary manner in a way previously unknown in contemporary Spanish history."[1]

Life for prisoners was based on an institutionalized terror that bore no resemblance to the message of Franco to Republicans that had promised "*perdón, pan y paz*" (pardon, bread, and peace). On the contrary, prisons served as one of the most important purging instruments of Na-

---

1. Gómez Bravo, *El exilio interior*, 15.

tionalist repression.[2] El Puerto played an important role in the Francoist penal system in Andalusia between 1936 and 1949 for a variety of reasons, in part due to its relative size and isolation. Indeed, after 1981, the movement of the prison to nearby Sanlúcar de Barrameda ensured that the new Puerto complex was to become one of the most sizeable prison institutions in Spain.

Archival data obtained from Cádiz province and the Basque Country has raised further questions concerning the coherence and consistency of the Nationalist penal system during this period, a view confirmed by relatives of Basque prisoners in El Puerto. This concluding chapter returns to the lack of conformity as proved by the wide range of different charges and sentences for not dissimilar "crimes," followed by diversified conditions of release. The Basque dimension in El Puerto was all pervasive, not only because it provided evidence of flaws in penal policy, but because it introduced a consonance that the prison system itself lacked.

The problem of an increasing prison population had been one of the many confronting Nationalist penal authorities in which the director of prisons, Cuervo, had responsibility for shaping these institutions into retaliatory instruments, based on a kind of religious and punitive retribution. This was always reinforced with the message of promised redemption allied to a revengeful military form of discipline.[3] The overcrowding, epidemics, and increasing costs had reached a zenith in 1940, when the Ministry of Justice stated that there were 270,719 Republican prisoners.[4] Accompanied by growing unrest, this was a crucial year in the collapse of the Nationalist prison system, which forced large-scale releases. As has been mentioned earlier, this caused a revision to the penal system that was influential to this case study and particularly affected release and parole conditions relating to Basque prisoners in El Puerto. Official records show that of the 124,423 prisoners held in the regime prisons by the end of

2. Prison repression was not confined to El Puerto and Spain. The Nationalists ensured that around 1,500 Spanish refugees ended up in Nazi concentration camps such as Auschwitz, Dachau, and Buchenwald. In Mauthausen, Spanish prisoners comprised the second largest contingent, where between 6,000 and 7,000 were to die. See Richards, *A Time of Silence*, 83. Also see David W. Pike, *Spaniards in the Holocaust: Mauthausen, Horror on the Danube* (London: Taylor & Francis, 2000).

3. Máximo Cuervo, "Fundamentos del Nuevo Sistema Penitenciario Español," Universidad Central, lecture given on October 28, 1940.

4. *Memorias y Boletín de la Dirección General de Prisiones de enero de 1940, julio de 1943 y diciembre de 1945. Breve resumen de la obra del Ministerio de Justicia para la pacificación espiritual de España*, Madrid, Ministerio de Justicia, 1946. See also Julián Casanova, *República y Guerra Civil*, vol. 8, *Historia de España* (Madrid: Marcial Pons, 2007), 407–8.

1942, 80 per cent were detained for 'crimes of rebellion.[5] In El Puerto the vast majority of Civil War prisoners from Cádiz province and the Basque Country had been released between 1941 and 1942

In the period 1937 to 1943, many of the penal decisions of the Nationalists appear to have been reactive rather than proactive. The sheer number of cases, allied to a stifling bureaucracy, determined the enormous number of all prisoners detained in all types of incarceration units, including concentration camps (Miranda de Ebro in Burgos was the last to close in 1947), male provincial prisons, male central and workshop prisons, female prisons, and prison hospitals. These large numbers of imprisoned Republicans, allied to the problems of maintaining discipline and security in the many types of prisons, had led to enormous problems for the Nationalist penal authorities. For example, unforeseen large numbers of Republican prisoners had been captured following defeats at Santander (August 1937), Aragón (April 1938), the Ebro River (November 1938), and Catalonia (January 1939). The response had involved conversions of a large number of buildings overnight. The Church had emerged as one of the major providers of these makeshift prisons, in some cases adapting monastery accommodation (as was the case with El Puerto); other buildings were used for the first time. Preston contends that the Francoist prison system was "chaotic, improvised and utterly arbitrary."[6] This view is supported by Gómez Bravo, who writes that "from the start of 1939 the [prison] situation in general already was chaotic . . . the list of prisoners throughout the country was interminable."[7]

My view is that, while this prison system itself proved to be surprisingly durable, the enormous prisoner intake, allied to a lack of central control of tribunals, made improvisation inevitable. Dominated at all times by an obsession to control and punish the defeated, a perfect fusion of terror and the harshest ideological elements in the army and the Church went a long way to dehumanize the Nationalist prison system.[8] Nevertheless, the scale of the situation gave rise to a capricious bureaucracy; one of best examples occurred in 1945, when 481 records of sentences of prisoners were mislaid by the Nationalist penal authorities themselves. Despite a special investigation by the Ministry of Justice, details of twenty-eight records

---

5.   Eiroa San Francisco, *Viva Franco*, 263.
6.   Preston, *The Spanish Civil War*, 308.
7.   Gutmaro Gómez Bravo, "La política penitenciaria del franquismo y la consolidación del Nuevo Estado," *Anuario de Derecho Penal y Ciencias Penales* 61 (2008), 175–77.
8.   Gómez Bravo, "The Origins of the Francoist Penitentiary System, 1936–1948."

had still not been located two years later.[9] In the case of El Puerto, some of the Basque relatives accused the penal authorities of deliberate inefficiency in delaying the release of members of their families (see chapter 3). Vicente Pujana Galíndez's daughter, Miren, complained that every time her father was due for release, his application was continually mislaid.[10] My research suggests that the contents of individual prison records themselves indicate a lack of a systematic organization at best, at worst a system of confusion and inconsistency relating to trials of the accused.

The Nationalist penal policy, as far as the Basques were concerned, gives rise to the issue of whether their allocation to a variety of penal institutions after sentence was part of a consistent policy or, simply, an ad hoc reaction to events as they unfolded between 1937 and 1938. Basque prisoners were initially allocated to El Dueso, Burgos, and Larrinaga (this included a large number of *gudari* officers), and then many were transferred to Andalusian prisons. Others could find themselves interned in a plethora of other retentive institutions such as prison ships, concentration camps, and labor battalions. In addition, not all Basque *gudaris* were captured at Santoña. Some escaped to fight in the Asturias campaign, others to fight in Aragón and around the Valencia in September 1937, and some Basque soldiers were involved in the later defense of Madrid. Once captured, all were regarded as political prisoners and after conviction were sentenced and often transferred within an improvised and arbitrary penal system.

In my view, the rationale of Nationalist penal policy was not always easy to follow because many of the prison files and reports of court proceedings leading to conviction are sparse in the extreme, whereas others are merely repetitive, with the absence of individual trials making the task of the researcher that much harder. Ironically, the most detailed and lengthy prison report was that of Mario González Zaera, a corrupt Galician Falange head who had unsuccessfully tried to help Hedilla to challenge Franco for the Falange leadership.[11] This report lists the former's misdemeanors at great length, including widespread corruption in local commerce, defrauding of the people, personal enrichment, and the exercise of absolute power over life and property. Sentenced to death for treason, later commuted to a lengthy sentence, González Zaera was admitted to El Puerto on April 14, 1942.

---

9. Ruiz, *Franco's Justice*, 123.
10. Email from Miren Pujana Bolibar, March 3, 2010.
11. AHPC/PSM, Legajo 29266.

Perhaps one of the best indications of arbitrariness on the part of the Francoist penal authorities was the policy adopted concerning Basque imprisonment. Large numbers of Basques were transferred to prisons in Andalusia, mainly in the time from the summer of 1938 to the summer of 1939. The confidential report of a Basque prison delegation in July 1939 cited that around two thousand Basques were sent to El Puerto;[12] this was a larger number than all the other Basque prisoners in the rest of the prisons in Andalusia put together. Before 1938, the Nationalist penal authorities had hardly ever transferred Basque prisoners to El Puerto.[13] The change in policy whereby so many Basque prisoners were transferred to the extreme south may have been a deliberate attempt to constrain Basque nationalism; alternatively, it was simply a pragmatic response to accommodate the numbers of captives after the fall of Bilbao.[14] The prison accommodation situation was greatly worsened by the large-scale Basque surrender at Santander.[15]

If this was a deliberate move to imprison Basques in large numbers in a distant prison, the repercussions were unforeseen. Whereas it may be said to have succeeded in isolating prisoners from their families, the net result was to concentrate a large number of Basque prisoners in a single prison. In part, it could be argued that this changed policy indicated a lack of political awareness on the part of the Nationalist penal authorities. El Puerto contained a prison population some 80 percent of whom had been convicted on the most serious charges against the Franco regime. This meant that these Basque captives were mainly regarded as political prisoners. On the other hand, the transfer of some three hundred Basque activists in December 1938 out of El Puerto could have been an attempt to forestall activists. If so, it proved unsuccessful.

The political nucleus clearly remained within the prison and the outcome was an organized part hegemonic unit consisting of Basque nationalism allied to socialism.[16] This was led until October 1940 by the Basque PSOE leader Ramón Rubial, assisted on the prison committee by other Socialist prisoners from the north including Rubial and Gorostiza[17] from

---

12. SAF/PSM/CON/7/39.
13. AHPC/PSM, Legajo 29334. The only case I could make out was that of a prisoner from Navarre convicted for sedition and sent to El Puerto on November 18, 1936.
14. Preston, *Franco*, 280.
15. Martínez Bande, *El final del frente norte*, 97–104.
16. SAF/PSM/ANON/3/40. One Basque prisoner spoke of "news that may nourish our spirit – from the Basque Country and for the Basque Country we are always ready and prepared for you, the PNV authorities, and the government of our Basque Country.".
17. See Chapter 1.There were two Gorostizas in El Puerto. Both from Bizkaia.

the Basque Country and others from Asturias and Santander..[18]It was perhaps unfortunate for the prison authorities that in Rubial they had a leading Basque and country wide Socialist leader in El Puerto. In fact Preston writes "Ramón Rubial attempted to organize the [Socialist] party in prison."[19]

Although one can reasonably accuse the Nationalist penal authorities of inconsistency and arbitrariness in the matter of sentence and release conditions, the same allegation cannot be made about their vetting process relating to prison staff following the fall of the Basque Republic.[20] A very thorough investigation took place concerning each prison, including the names and addresses of all prisoners held, relating to the situation before and after the Civil War regime that extended to food, cells, and visits; and to all staff from the director to auxiliaries, whether they were appointed by the Spanish government or the Basque Republic.[21] This was part of the "red terror" investigations and the Brotherhood of Ex-Prisoners was widely used.[22] It would appear that a purge of possible Republican prison sympathizers had a much higher priority than had the desirability of ensuring consistency within the Nationalist penal system.

The policy of isolating Basque prisoners was further reflected in the major difference in the prison transfer policy between captives from Cádiz province and the Basque Country. The latter were very rarely transferred, but when they were, it was usually to other Andalusian prisons. As mentioned earlier, a large number of Basque prisoners were transferred from El Puerto on December 14, 1938 to the provincial prison of Seville, alongside others from northern Spain; the Basque contingent included Basque nationalists, Socialists, Republicans, Communists, and CNT members.[23] The additional length of prison time Basques served in El Puerto, allied to a transfer back north of only 3.5 percent, clearly suggests a policy to keep them isolated as well as incarcerated for as long as possible. In my view, the Nationalist policy adopted toward transferring Basque prisoners proved to be of dubious value, and the initial movement of 5,400 prisoners

18. See Bernardo Díaz Nosty, ed., *Ramón Rubial. Un compromiso con el socialismo 1906–86* (Madrid: PSOE, 1986).
19. Preston, The decline and resurgence of the Spanish Socialist Party during the Franco regime, *European History Quarterly*, 1988 11 (2) 207-208.
20. SAF/PSM: Judge Advocate report on repression in the Basque Country, October 1939. See also *Informaciones* 24-April 7, 1939.
21. See chapter 2.
22. Ibid. Set up in 1939 by organizations representing former Nationalist prisoners, *Informaciones* 24 (April 6, 1939) carried accounts of Nationalist experiences while in Republican jails.
23. SAF/PSM/ANON/3/40.

from April 1938 onward to El Puerto, Seville, Huelva, Granada, Carmona, Osuna, and Cazalla de la Sierra may well not have solved the problem for the prison authorities.[24]

One major aspect of such disparity of methods of penal control in El Puerto was the way the authorities dealt with the problem of religion within the prison context itself. The theme of the Basque Church repeatedly intervening in favor of the Basque nationalists on account of their conservatism and exemplary Catholicism is regularly cited;[25] but this factor alone must have been a source of severe embarrassment to the El Puerto prison authorities. This appears to be a fairly regular occurrence wherein Basque prisoners in El Puerto habitually challenged and pressurized the prison authorities for improved provision of Mass, both in content and availability; this drive in order to obtain access to priests for other pastoral support seems to have had some success. An interesting power struggle in this area has been highlighted by reference to the collective petitions from Basque prisoners in the two Basque reports in 1939 and 1940.[26] It would appear that their exemplary Catholicism enabled them to repeatedly question the authenticity of the religious stance of the prison authorities, bearing in mind the professed sanctity of the Nationalist cause and the myth of Franco as the Catholic Crusader. However, this attitude was not shared by all Basques in this prison as some refused to go to Mass.[27] There were instances when it seemed that Basque pressure was successful since the prison authorities were persuaded to make priests more available, to turn a blind eye to the observance of the Aberri Eguna, and to unofficially condone the teaching of the prohibited Euskara within the Basque prisoners self-help group.

Anything to do with Basque traditions or the language had been banned since the fall of the Republic. Any departure from this policy could be construed as evidence of success of an unusually strong group pressure, not always present in other prisons at this time. However, this pressure was not always successful. For example, Basque prisoners in El Puerto were not able to prevent Mass being used for Francoist propaganda and were punished for protesting. There was great offense caused by homosexual prisoners (dressed in a variety of garbs with make-up) being based in the same cells as heterosexuals, for the amusement of guards.

24. SAF/PSM/CON/7/39.
25. Aguilar, "The Memory of the Civil War in the Transition to Democracy," 10.
26. SAF/PSM/CON/7/39; SAF/PSM/ANON/3/40.
27. See contrary evidence given by relatives of Vicente Pujana and Serapio Echeandia, former prisoners of El Puerto.

Protests were of little avail. The prisoners had questioned what kind of Catholicism would permit this type of behavior. Núñez Díaz-Balart writes about the policy whereby some prison guards deliberately set out to offend the Catholic propensities of some prisoners, "degradation of heterosexuals would be a victory for the institutions," which could well have been the case in El Puerto.[28] Nevertheless, no amount of exemplary Catholicism could detract from the impact of the Nationalist penal policy of imprisoning Basque prisoners so many miles from home.

The way collective trials were conducted throughout Spain provides evidence of what Ruiz considers to be the "chaotic, decentralised nature of military justice."[29] His particularly bad example of the case of fifty-seven condemned to death on August 3, 1939 in Madrid in a collective trial is worth citing again.[30] A large number of examples are provided by the prison archives that reveal the many inconsistencies in both charge and sentence before the prisoners arrived in El Puerto. This is not entirely surprising as a range of inmates from Cádiz province in this prison had been convicted on ninety-eight different charges (again, in some cases, for not very different "crimes"). Some sentences were indeed arbitrary, capricious, and inconsistent. Moreover, other prisoners had been sentenced following a charge in which the military tribunal had not taken a great deal of notice of the stipulated sentence. Conxita Mir identifies the problem brought about by the individualism of these tribunals and observes that, "Military Tribunals were the basic instrument of repression, but despite its manifest importance, their guiding principles and procedures of implementation remain unknown."[31]

Examples of military tribunal sentences illustrate the arbitrary, if not chaotic, decentralized system leading to erratic military justice at this time. A Cádiz tribunal heard a charge of *auxilio a la rebelión* in March 1939 against Manuel López Sierra and sentenced him to thirty years, a far longer period than stipulated by the maximum sentence of twenty years.[32] His problems arose when he was heard saying "*¡salud!*" (greetings (comrades)!) instead of "*¡arriba España!*" (long live Spain!). This is one of the worst excesses I could find. Other cases, in which similar hostile remarks were made, provoked different responses from different tribu-

---

28. Núñez Díaz-Balart, *Los años de terror*, 33.
29. Ruiz, "A Spanish Genocide? Reflections on the Francoist repression after the Spanish Civil War," 186.
30. Ruiz, *Franco's Justice*, 107.
31. Conxita Mir, "Violencia política, coacción legal y oposición interior," *Ayer* 33 (1999), 132.
32. AHPC/PSM, Legajo 29351.

nals. Francisco Serrano Perula, also charged with *auxilio a la rebelión*, was sentenced in March 1937 in Seville to twelve years and one day imprisonment.[33] Lorenzo González Vilches was charged with *excitación a la rebelión* for insulting remarks but was only sentenced to six years and one day in Ceuta on March 31, 1939, the minimum period stipulated for the offense.[34] Sebastián Pantoja Puerto, a recent Falange member, was charged with *adhesión a la rebelión* for giving a Republican salute.[35] The Cáceres tribunal sentenced him to eight years in November 1937, well under the stipulated minimum of twenty years. Antonio García Benítez a black marketeer (with a previous prison sentence for robbery) was charged with selling coffee and not delivering the goods.[36] He was sentenced in El Puerto de Santa María to two years and four months in June 1940, an indication of the way disparities operated between real criminal offenses and the "political crime" of serving as a soldier that attracted the maximum of thirty years' imprisonment.

A study of prisoners' files suggested a different outcome to that of several historians in issues relating to prisoners from the Basque Country and Cádiz province. The first example concerns the number of prisoners released on conditions of external exile, in which José Manuel Sabín writes that, in 1943, 25 percent of paroled prisoners were placed in internal exile.[37] My research revealed that only 4 percent from Cádiz province and 1 percent of Basque prisoners came into this category.[38] The second example relates to membership of Freemasonry, which carried a thirty-year maximum sentence, but twelve years and one day is quoted as the most common sentence for membership.[39] Those sentenced for this "crime" in El Puerto were very largely from Andalusia and actually served between one and seven months, albeit in 1942. Earlier, some of those sentenced in Andalusia had faced a harsher sentence than the maximum stipulated, with executions for twenty-four Freemasons in Algeciras and twelve in La Línea de la Concepción, followed by eighty in Málaga, as late as October 1937.[40] The third example dispels the commonly held belief, cited by Andrés de Blas[41] and based on the contributions of a Francoist general and a

33. Ibid., Legajo 29357.
34. Ibid., Legajo 29319
35. Ibid., Legajo 29289.
36. Ibid., Legajo 29347.
37. Sabín, *Prisión y muerte en la España de postguerra*, 209.
38. AHPC/PSM, Legajos 29246–29474 (Cádiz); Legajos 29246–29476 (País Vasco).
39. Ruiz, *Franco's Justice*, 219.
40. Preston, *The Spanish Holocaust*, 489.
41. Andrés de Blas."La izquierda española y el nacionalismo. El caso de la transición." (Madrid: Fundación Pablo Iglesias, *Leviatán 31*, 1988) 71-85.

military historian Ramón Salas Larrazábal[42] and Eugenio Ibarzabal,[43] that after 1943 there were no (Basque) nationalist prisoners in Franco's jails.[44] Archival research indicates that there were Basques still imprisoned after 1943, although the vast majority of cases found were unrelated to the Civil War. For example, there were thirteen Basque prisoners in the provincial prison of Huelva until 1949;[45] there were also fifty-three in the penitentiary of El Puerto until 1950.[46] If there were some sixty-six Basque prisoners detained in the two above prisons after 1943, it was quite likely that there were more held in other Andalusian prisons after this date.

However, these cases were subsumed within the mantle of the all-enveloping prison system of Franco, "where more died from disease [in prison] than from execution."[47] The victors sought not merely surrender, but permanent demoralization and impoverishment of the defeated in all aspects of postwar Spanish life. Basic survival instincts were always paramount as extracts from prison diaries between 1939 and 1943 from Larrinaga, Burgos, and El Puerto indicated. All made mention of the overcrowding, lack of sanitation and medical care, executions, suicides, tuberculosis, typhus, lice, scabies, bugs, and dysentery.[48] All these diaries regularly mention the weather and hunger with regular entries such as "*sin novedad*" (nothing new), "*día triste*" (a sad day), "*día frío todo el dia*" (cold all day today), "*Comunión*" (Communion), and "*he dormido precioso y sin diarrea*" (I slept great and no diarrhea). Others often refer to the lentil tablets of "Dr. Crespo" (a remedy for everything), "*por la noche oímos gritos desgarradores*" (last night we heard harrowing shouts), and "*los desgraciados han recibido garrottevil*" (the wretches have been given the *garrotte vil*).

Constant indoctrination ensured that "in prisons, massive efforts were made to break not only the bodies of prisoners but also their minds."[49] This was borne out by treatment of former prisoners since release was followed by stringent conditions; those who survived in a reasonable condition were often employed at an exploitive wage, having to move to gain

42. See also Salas Larrazábal, Ramón, *Pérdidas de la Guerra* (Barcelona: Editorial Planeta 1977).
43. See also Ibarzabal Eugenio (ed.) *Cincuenta años de nacionalismo vasco1928-1978* (Bilbao: Ediciones Vascas 1978).
44.
45. AHPH/PPH, Signaturas 07516/021–07620/032.
46. AHPC/PSM, Legajos 29258–29346.
47. Preston, *The Spanish Holocaust,* 509.
48. Mendizabal, *Gudaris y rehenes de Franco (1936–1943),* 227–399.
49. Preston, "Crimes of Franco," The Len Crome Memorial Lecture, Imperial War Museum, London, March 12, 2005.

employment. Some were too ill to work. Many were fined or had assets foreclosed under the Law of Political Responsibilities of 1939. These penalties were passed on to their relatives in the event of death. Others were not allowed to resume their previous occupations.

The state of impoverishment of many released prisoners has already been mentioned but is worth laboring as it was one of the most punitive after effects on prisoners and their families. Not until March 1943 were pensions granted to men (and their dependents) who had served in the Republican army.[50] But even this minor concession did not apply to those cases in which loss of pension rights was involved in the original sentence.[51]

An ex-prisoner, Luis Díaz, adequately summed up the position with a letter that found its way to the British Embassy in 1949: "I am pretty certain that we are still wearing shackles. We not only wear them while in prison but also now, under this state of invigilated freedom . . . we are permanently and perpetually purged out of our professions or taken out of our hometowns. Nothing is allowed to us in Spain."[52] Evidence gathered from relatives of prisoners in El Puerto confirms that former prisoners lived under a dark shadow. Even when released, they continued to be punished and were never accepted as equal citizens. In reality, their sentences never ended. Reconciliation was never considered. All lived under the sword of Damocles, threatened with recall to prison in the event of unacceptable conduct, existing under a system of tremendous uncertainty and fear: "That state of terror, the continuation of the state of war, transformed Spanish society, destroyed entire families, and inundated everyday life with coercive and punishment practices."[53]

In 1977, even Ramón Serrano Suñer, the brother-in-law of Franco and a highly prominent member of the Franco regime until August 1942, confessed that in the Spanish Civil War, the policy of punishing Republicans for "the crime" of military rebellion was to "turn justice on its head."[54] This confession was particularly significant as Suñer was the driving force behind the creation of the Bellón Commission.[55] This Commission, with the help of the Causa General or judicial investigation process, had helped

50. *BOE*, March 2, 1943.
51. Alpert, *The Republican Army in the Spanish Civil War 1936–39*, 328, 333, 348. This also applied to senior Republican soldiers such as Vicente Rojo, Fernández Villabrille, and Seismundo Casado, whose sentences included loss of rank and pension.
52. Gómez Bravo, "The Origins of the Francoist Penitentiary System, 1936–1948)."
53. *Morir, matar, sobrevivir*, ed. Casanova, Espinosa, Mir, and Moreno Gómez, xi.
54. Serrano Suñer, *Entre el silencio y la propaganda*, 245.
55. *BOE*, December 22, 1938.

to "establish" the "illegitimacy and criminality" of the legally elected Republican government in 1936.[56]

An unhappy legacy of the Spanish Civil War was that the contribution of those who fought for the legitimate government was rarely, if ever, recognized. Defeated Republicans were permanently criminalized and the convictions by illegal military tribunals still stand. Spain has made no attempt to heal its divisions through a post-Apartheid South African style reconciliation process and the Amnesty Law of 46/1977 states that crimes committed during the Franco era—that is, by the regime itself— OK would not be prosecuted.[57] Although Spanish law now permits "a certificate of personal recognition and reparation," few have been issued and they are written in such a way as to preclude compensation claims. All those from the Basque Country and other parts of Spain who defended a democratically elected government, the Spanish Republic, were never honored with plaques and monuments in churches with glowing epitaphs such as "*caídos por Dios*" (died for God) "*por España*" (for Spain). Their memory deserves to be preserved.

This work is an attempt, albeit in a small way, to do so.

---

56. *BOE*, May 4, 1940.
57. *BOE*, October 17, 1977.

Bibliography

Primary Sources

Andalusia

Cádiz

Archivo Histórico Principal de Cádiz: el penal de El Puerto de Santa María.

Legajos Cádiz 29246–29476; Basque Country 29246–29453.

El Puerto de Santa María

Archivo Histórico Municipal de El Puerto de Santa María: Sección Sanidad, Partes de Cementerio, 1936–1941. Legajo 1941.

El Centro Municipal de Patrimonio.

Padrón de Habitantes 1935, 1940, and 1945.

Huelva

Archivo Histórico Provincial de Huelva: la Prisión Provincial de Huelva.

Signaturas 07516/021–07620/032, 07510/ 062.

Basque Country

Artea

Archivo del Nacionalismo. Sabino Arana Fundazioa.

El penal de El Puerto de Santa María: *Informe confidencial de la situación de los presos vascos en El Puerto de Santa María*, julio 1939.

Informe sobre la persecución de los vascos durante y después de la Guerra Civil.

Informe por un preso vasco de la situación en El Puerto de Santa María, marzo 1940.

Bergara

Irargi, Centro de Patrimonio Documental de Euskadi/Euskadiko Dokumentu Ondarearen Zentroa

El penal de El Puerto de Santa María Yes

Una carta de Saturnino de Gantxegi a Elisa de Linazasoro.

Letter to Duchess of Atholl from Secretary of Basque Government in
London.

Letter from Sir Archibald Sinclair to C.R.Atlee, Noel Baker, and Duchess
of Atholl.

Letter from George Lansbury to Count Ciano.

Letters from David Lloyd George to José Ignacio Lizaso, Basque delegate
in London.

Letter from Robert Vansittart to London Basque delegation.

Document headed *Prisioneros de Santoña condenados a muerte.*

Report by Judge Advocate 6th Region urging more Basque repression.

Listados de Documento de Sacerdotes Vascos Fusilados.

La represión en Guipúzcoa 1939.

Afiliaciones de los fusilados en Guipúzcoa 1939.

Sesión del Ayuntamiento de Durango Augusto 1936.

Bilbao

Prisión Provincial de Bilbao

Causa número 13.629.

Interviews and Personal Correspondence

Interviews in the Provincial Historical Archive in Cádiz with Manolo Ravina Martín (Director) May 21, 2007, June 5, 2008, and June 12, 2009.

Interview in Durango with Basque newspaper *Deia*, October 4, 2009.

Interview in Durango with Asunción Gerediaga Garamendi, September 8, 2009.

Interview in Berriz with Jabier Gorosarri, September 9, 2009.

Interview in Berriz with Yolanda Echaburu Alzaa, September 9, 2009.

Interview in Mungia with María del Carmen Ruiz de Aguirre and Irantzu Bustina, June 8, 2012.

Letters from José Luis Arrondo, Durango, August 18, 2009 and March 15, 2010.

Letter from Joxemari Mendizabal Sarasua, Donostia, May 1, 2010.

Letter from María del Carmen Ruiz de Aguirre, Amorebieta, November 11, 2009.

Emails from the archivist of the Municipal Historical Archive of El Puerto de Santa María, June 20, 2008 and October 26, 2009.

Emails from the director of theProvincial Archive of Cádiz, February 5, October 2, 2009; November 7, 2011; and May 16, 2012.

Emails from the director of the Historical Archive of Huelva, October 16 and 18, 2009; April 5, 2010; May 2, June 24, and November 26, 2011. Yes

Email from the secretary of Basque children of the 37 Association Natalie Benjamin December 8 2009.

Emails from María González Gorosarri, Galdakao, August 15, November 14, and December 17, 2008; March 9, and April 4 2010; and December 9, 2011.

Emails from Miren Pujana Bolibar, July 10, 2009; March 3, 2010; April1, and April 7, 2010.

Emails from Andoni Barrera, September 7, 23, 2009.

Emails from Martín Aurrekoetxea, October 4, 16, and 18, 2009.

Emails from Joseba Arruza Goitia, October 5 and 8, 2009.

Email from Joseba Andoni Bikandi Arana, October 5, 2009.

Emails from Rafa Mendibil Sobrón, October 30, 2009.

Emails from Irantzu Bustinza, October 4, 21, November 8, 15, and 29, 2009; January 24, March 5, April 1, and May 23, 2010; and July 16, 2012.

Email from Arantzazu Garay, October 6, 2009.

Email from Mikel Arieta-Araunabeña, October 22, 2009.

Emails from Begoña Torrontegui, October 14 and November 13, 2009.

Emails from Galder Unzalu Etxabe, October 3 and 5, 2009.

Email from Pedro Barruso, April 20, July 23, 2009; and April 5, 2010.

Email from Fernardo Romero Romero, May 26, 2010 and September 17, 2012.

Email from Todos los Nombres, Andalusia, April 2, 2009.

Emails from Eduardo Jauregui, Coordinator, Nationalism Archive, Sabino Arana Foundation, September 9, 2008, January 26, 2009, March 2, 2010, and January 22, 2013.

Emails from Roberto Kerexeta, Irargi, Euskadi, July 15, 2009 and March 2010.

Newspapers, Magazines, and Periodicals

Almajar

American Journal of Public Health

Ayer

Auria

Cuadernos Para El Diálogo

Deia

Diario de Cádiz

Egin

El Diario Digital

El Mundo

El País

European History Quarterly

Euzkadi

Gaceta Sanitaria (Sociedad Española de Salud Pública y Administración Sanitaria)

German History

Informaciones

International Journal of Iberian Studies

La Gaceta del Norte

La Vanguardia

Leviatán

Redención

Revista de Historia Contemporánea

Revista Mundo Gráfico

Revista de Historia de El Puerto de Santa María

Times Literary Supplement

War in Spain

West European Politics

Personal Documents

Extracts from prison diary of Jenaro Ruiz de Aguirre, 1937–1940, while in El Dueso and El Puerto de Santa María prisons.

Public Documents

Archivo General de la Administración, Justicia.

Archivo General de la Administración, Presidencia.

Archivo General Militar, Ávila, Zona Roja.

Archivo Histórico Nacional, Causa General.

Archivo Militar de Madrid, Consejo de Guerra.

Boletín Oficial de Estado.

Boletín Oficial de la Junta de Defensa Nacional.

Dirección General de la Administración Local del Gobierno Vasco.

Documentos inéditos para la Historia del Generalísimo Franco, Fundación Nacional Francisco Franco.

Instituto Nacional de Estadística de España.

Memorias y Boletín de la Dirección general de Prisiones.

Ministerio de Justicia, Dirección de prisiones, Carmona.

Ministerio de Educación Nacional.

Ministerio de Trabajo y Seguridad Social.

The National Archives, Kew (UK), Archives of the British Foreign Office.

Political Affairs Committee, Parliamentary Assembly, Council of Europe. Document 0737, March 2005.

Padrón de Habitantes, El Puerto de Santa María.

Report on the Administration of Justice in Basque Country during the Civil War.

Sesión del ayuntamiento de Durango.

Published Collections

Documentos inéditos para la historia del Generalisimo Franco. Vol. 2. Madrid: Fundación Nacional Francisco Franco, 1992.

Contemporary Accounts

Brenan, Gerald. *The Face of Spain. The Spanish Labyrinth: An Account of the Social and Political Background of the Civil War.* Cambridge: Cambridge University Press, 1993, (First published 1943).

Fernández Asiain, Eugenio. *El delito de rebelión militar. Estudio sistemático del delito, comentado, concordado y anotado.* Madrid: Instituto Edit. Reus, 1943.

Franco, Francisco. *Palabras del Caudillo, 19 abril 1937–31 diciembre 1938.* Barcelona: Seix y Barral, 1939).

Koestler, Arthur. *Spanish Testament.* London: Victor Gollancz, 1937.

Pérez del Pulgar, José Agustín. *La solución que España da al problema de sus presos políticos.* Valladolid: Librería Santarén, 1939.

Secondary Sources

Acosta Bono, Gonzalo, José Luis Gutiérrez Molina, Lola Martínez Macías, and Ángel del Río Sánchez. *El canal de Los Presos (1940–62): Trabajos forzados. De la represión política a la explotación económica.* Barcelona: Crítica, 2004.

Alba, Victor, *Transition in Spain: From Franco to Democracy.* Translated by Barbara Lolito. New Brunswick, NJ: Transaction Books, 1978.

Águila Tejerina, Rafael del, *Ideología y fascismo.* Madrid: Centro de Estudios Constitucionales, 1982.

Aguilar, Paloma. *Memoria y olvido de la guerra civil española.* Madrid: Alianza Editorial, 1999.

———. *Memory and Amnesia: The Role of the Spanish Civil War in the Transition to Democracy.* New York: Berghahn Books, 2002.

Alted, Alicia. *La voz de los vencidos: el exilio republicano de 1939.* Madrid: Aguilar, 2005.

Alpert, M., *The Republican Army in the Spanish Civil War, 1936–39.* Cambridge: Cambridge University Press, 2007.

Anderson, Peter. *The Francoist Military Trials: Terror and Complicity 1939–45.* New York: Routledge, 2010.

Arco Blanco, Miguel Ángel del. *Hambre de Siglos: mundo rural y apoyos sociales del franquismo en Andalucía oriental (1936–51).* Granada: Comares, 2007.

Arenillas de Chaves, Ignacio. *El proceso de Besteiro.* Madrid: Revista de Occidente, 1976.

Aulestia, Gorka, *Improvisational Poetry for the Basque Country.* University of Nevada, 1995.

Azaola, José Miguel de. *Vasconia y su destino.* Vol. 1. *La Regionalización de España.* Madrid: Revista de Occidente, 1972.

Ballbé, Manuel. *Orden público y militarismo en la España constitucional 1812–1983.* Madrid: Alianza Editorial, 1983.

Barruso, Pedro. *Verano y revolución. La guerra civil en Guipúzcoa (julio-septiembre de 1936).* San Sebastián: R&B Editores, 1996.

Beevor, Antony. *The Battle for Spain: The Spanish Civil War, 1936–1939*. London: Penguin, 2006.

Benegas, José María. *Ramón Rubial. Reflexiones* Madrid: Pablo Iglesias, 2011.

Bowers, Claude. *Misión En España: En el umbral de la Segunda Guerra Mundial, 1933–1939*. Translated by Juan López S. Barcelona: Grijalbo, 1977.

Britton, R.K, *The Poetic and Real Worlds of César Vallejo*. Eastbourne: Sussex Academic Press., *2016*

Callahan, William J. *The Catholic Church in Spain, 1875–1998*. Washington, DC: Catholic University of America Press, 2000.

Caro Cancela, Diego. *La Segunda República en Cádiz. Elecciones y partidos politicos* Cádiz: Diputación Provincial, 1987.

Casanova, Julián. *República y Guerra Civil*. Vol. 8, *Historia de España*. Madrid: Marcial Pons, 2007.

———. *The Spanish Republic and Civil War*. Translated by Martin Douch. Cambridge: Cambridge University Press, 2010.

Casanova, Julián, Francisco Espinosa, Conxita Mir, and Francisco Moreno Gómez. *Morir, matar, sobrevivir:* La *violencia en la dictadura de Franco*. Barcelona: Crítica, 2002.

Castejón, Federico. *Comentarios científicos-prácticos al Código Penal de 1870*. Vol. 2. *Tratado de la responsabilidad.*Madrid: Reus, 1926.

Clark, Robert P. *The Franco Years and Beyond*. Reno: University of Nevada Press, 1979.

Cenarro, Ángela. *La sonrisa de la Falange: Auxilio Social en la Guerra Civil y en la posguerra*. Barcelona: Crítica, 2005.

Chueca, Josu. *Gurs: el campo vasco*. Tafalla: Txalaparta, 2007.

Cobo Romero, Francisco. *Conflicto rural y violencia política: el largo camino hacia la dictadura, Jaén 1917–50*. Jaén: Universidad de Jaén, 1998.

Commission Internationale Contre le Régime Concentrationnaire. *Livre blanc sur le système pénitentiaire espagnol*. Paris: Le Pavois, 1953.

Cuevas, Tomasa, Presas. *Mujeres en las cárceles franquistas*, Barcelona: Icaria, 2005

Díaz Nosty, Bernardo, ed. *Ramón Rubial. Un compromiso con el socialismo 1906-86* (Madrid: PSOE, 1986).

Dobson, Miriam, and Benjamin Ziemann, eds. *Reading Primary Sources: The Interpretation of Texts from 19th and 20th century History.* Abingdon: Routledge, 2009.

Domingo, Alfonso. *El canto del búho: la vida en el monte de los guerrilleros antifranquistas.* Madrid: Oberon, 2002.

Ealham, Chris, and Michael Richards, eds. *The Splintering of Spain: Cultural History and the Spanish Civil War, 1936–1939.* Cambridge: Cambridge University Press, 2005.

Domínguez Pérez, Alicia. *El verano que trajo un largo invierno. La represión política-social durante el primer franquismo en Cádiz (1936–1945).* Cádiz: Quorum, 2005.

Eiroa San Francisco, Matilde. *Viva Franco: hambre, racionamiento, Falangismo: Málaga, 1939–1942.* Málaga: M. Eiroa San Francisco, 1995.

Espinosa, Francisco. *La Guerra Civil en Huelva.* Huelva: Diputación Provincial, 1996.

———. *La Justicia de Queipo: Violencia selectiva y terror fascista en la II División en 1936: Sevilla, Huelva, Cádiz, Córdoba, Málaga y Badajoz.* Barcelona: Crítica, 2006.

Euzko Apaiz Talde. *La Historia General de la Guerra Civil en Euskadi.* Vol. 8. *El clero vasco ante los tribunales.* San Sebastián: L. Haranburu, 1982.

Fernández, Carlos. *Antología de 40 años (1936–1975).* Sada, La Coruña: Edicios do Castro, 1983.

Fraser, Ronald. *Blood of Spain: The Experience of Civil War, 1936–1939.* London: Allen Lane, 1979.

Fusi Aizpurúa, Juan Pablo. "The Basque Question 1931-7." In *Revolution and War in Spain, 1931–1939*, edited by Paul Preston London: Routledge, 1993.

Galarza, R., *Diario de un condenado a muerte*, San Sebastián 1977).

García Venero, Maximiano. *Historia del Nacionalismo Vasco*. Madrid: Editorial Nacional, 1969.

Gómez Bravo, Gutmaro. *El exilio interior. Cárcel y represión en la España franquista 1939–50*. Madrid: Taurus, 2009.

González Gorosarri, María, and Eduardo Barinaga. *No lloréis, lo que tenéis que hacer es no olvidarnos. La cárcel de Saturraran y la represión franquista contra las mujeres, a partir de testimonios de supervivientes*, Donostia: Ttarttalo, 2008.

Graham, Helen. *The Spanish Republic at War, 1936–1939*. Cambridge: Cambridge University Press, 2002.

———. *The Spanish Civil War: A Very Short Introduction*. Oxford: Oxford University Press, 2005.

Gutiérrez Molina, José Luis. *La idea revolucionaria: el anarquismo organizado en Andalucía y Cádiz durante los años treinta*. Madrid: Madre Tierra, 1993.

———. "Los presos del canal." In *Una inmensa prisión. Los campos de concentración y las prisiones durante la guerra civil y el franquismo*, edited by Carme Molinero, Margarida Sala, and Jaume Sobrequés. Barcelona: Crítica, 2003.

Gutiérrez Arosa, Jesús. *La Guerra Civil en Eibar y Elgeta*. Eibar: Eibarko Udala/ Ayuntamiento de Eibar, 2007.

Guzmán Martín, Sebastián. *Luces y Sombras de la historia de Chipiona. Segunda República, Guerra Civil y represión militar*. Chipiona: Ayuntamiento de Chipiona, 2007.

Hernández Holgado, Fernando. *Mujeres encarceladas. La prisión de Ventas: de la República al franquismo, 1931–1941*. Madrid: Marcial Pons Historia, 2003.

Ibarzabal, Eugenio (ed.) *Cincuenta años de nacionalismo vasco 1928-1978*. Bilbao: Ediciones Vascas, 1978.

Irujo, Xabier. *Expelled from the Motherland: The Government of President Jose Antonio Agirre in Exile, 1937–1960*. Translated by Cameron Watson and Jennifer Ottman. Reno: Center for Basque Studies, University of Nevada, Reno, 2012).

Jackson, Gabriel. *The Spanish Republic and the Civil War, 1931–1939*. Princeton: Princeton University Press, 1972.

Joaniquet, Aurelio. *Calvo Sotelo. Una vida fecunda, un ideario político, una doctrina económica.* Madrid: Espasa-Calpe, 1939.

Jiménez-Landi, Antonio. *Breve historia de la Institución Libre de Enseñanza 1896–1939.* Madrid: Tébar, 2010.

Juliá, Santos, Julián Casanova, Josep María Solé, and Tomás Villaroya. *Víctimas de la guerra civil.* Madrid: Temas de Hoy, 1999.

Junod, Marcel. *El tercer combatiente, Comité Internacional de la Cruz Roja.* Geneva: CICR, 1985.

Lannon, Frances. *Privilege, Persecution and Prophecy: The Catholic Church in Spain, 1875–1975.* Oxford: Clarendon, 1987.

Leitz, Christian. *Economic Relations between Nazi Germany and Franco's Spain, 1936–1945.* Oxford: Clarendon, 1996.

López, Juan. *Una misión sin importancia.* Madrid: Editora Nacional, 1972.

Irazabal Agirre, Jon. *1937 martxoak 31 Durango 31 de marzo de 1937.* Abadiño: Gerediaga Elkartea, 2001.

Martínez Bande, José Manuel. *El final del frente norte.* Madrid: San Martín, 1972.

Martínez Cordero, Manuel. *El Penal de El Puerto de Santa María 1886–1981.* Cádiz: Diputación de Cádiz, 2005.

Martínez Sánchez, Santiago. *Los papeles del Cardenal Segura, 1880–1957.* Barañáin: EUNSA, 2004.

Matthews, James. *Reluctant Warriors: Republican Popular Army and Nationalist Army Conscripts in the Spanish Civil War, 1936–1939.* Oxford: Oxford University Press, 2012.

Mendizabal, José Manuel (ed.) *Gudaris y rehenes de Franco (1936–1943). Diarios de José Manuel Mendizabal "Mañul", José Luis Lasa y Fernando Agirre* et al, Irún: Alberdania, 2006. He has written to me stressing that he is not the author but the editor and that he wishes full publicity to be given to the authors.

Mitchell, David J. *The Spanish Civil War.* New York: F. Watts, 1983.

Molinero, Carme, Margarida Sala, and Jaume Sobrequés, eds. *Una inmensa prisión. Los campos de concentración y las prisiones durante la guerra civil y el franquismo.* Barcelona: Crítica, 2003.

Moreno Gómez, Francisco. *Córdoba en la posguerra. La represión y la guerrilla, 1939–1950.* : Córdoba, Francisco Baena 1987

———. *La resistencia armada contra Franco. Tragedia del maquis y la guerrilla. El centro-sur de España, de Madrid al Guadalquivir.* Barcelona: Crítica, 2001.

Muñoz Rodríguez, Antonio. *Vejer de la Frontera.* Cádiz: Diputación Provincial De Cádiz, 1996.

Núñez Calvo, Jesús Narciso. *Francisco Ochoa Cossi: 1898–1936. El último Presidente de la Diputación de Provincial de Cádiz en la Segunda República. Una muerte sin esclarecer.* Cádiz: Diputación de Cádiz, 2005.

Nicólás Marín, Encarna. *La Libertad encadenada.España en la dictadura franquista 1939-75.* Madrid: Alianza Editorial, 2005.

Núñez Astrain, Luis. *The Basques: Their Struggle for Independence.* Translated by Meic Stephens. Cardiff: Welsh Academic Press, 1997.

Núñez Calvio, Jesús, Mercedes Rodríguez Izquierdo, Fernando Romero Romero, and Pedro Pablo Santamaría Curtido. *Memoria rota. República, Guerra Civil y Represión en Rota.* Rota, Cádiz: Ayuntamiento de Rota, 2008.

Núñez Díaz-Balart, Mirta. *Los años del terror: La estrategia del dominio y represión del General Franco.* Madrid: La Esfera de los Libros, 2004.

Núñez Díaz-Balart, Mirta, Manuel Álvaro Dueñas, Francisco Espinosa Maestre, and José María García Márquez. *La gran represión: Los años de plomo de la posguerra (1939–1948).* Barcelona: Flor del Viento, 2009.

Ortiz Heras, Manuel. *Violencia política en la II República y el primer franquismo. Albacete, 1936–50.* Madrid: Siglo XXI de España, 1996.

Orwell, George. *Homage to Catalonia.* London: Penguin, 2000. As you know there are a variety of dates for this book which was first published in 1938, I have a Penguin Modern Classics edition which was reprinted in 2000.

Ardo San Gil., Juan. *Crónica de la Guerra en el Cantábrico: Las Fuerzas Navales Republicanas 1936–1939.* San Sebastián: Txertoa, 2011.

Payne, Stanley G. *Basque Nationalism*. Reno: University of Nevada Press, 1975.

———. "Gobierno y oposición (1939–1969)," in *La Época de Franco, 1939–1975*, coordinated by Raymond Carr. Madrid: Espasa Calpe, 2007.

Pérez Castroviejo, Pedro Mª. *Clase obrera y niveles de vida en las primeras fases de la industrialización vizcaína*. Madrid: Ministerio de Trabajo y Seguridad Social, 1992.

Pike, DavidW. *Spanairds in the Holocaust: Mauthausen, Horror on the Danube*. London: Taylor & Francis, 2000.

Preston, Paul. *¡Comrades! Portraits from the Spanish Civil War* London: Fontana, 1999.

———. *Franco: A Biography*. London: Fontana.

———. *The Politics of Revenge: Fascism and the Military in Twentieth-Century Spain*. London: Unwin Hyman, 1990.

———. *The Spanish Civil War: Reaction, Revolution and Revenge*. London: Harper Perennial, 2006.

———. *We Saw Spain Die: Foreign Correspondents in the Spanish Civil War*. London: Constable & Robinson, 2008.

———. *The Spanish Holocaust: Inquisition and Extermination in Twentieth-Century Spain*. London: HarperPress, 2012.

Puzzo, Dante A. *Spain and the Great Powers, 1936–1941*. New York: Columbia University Press, 1962.

Raguer, Hilari. *Gunpowder and Incense: The Catholic Church and the Spanish Civil War*. London: Routledge, 2007.

Ribeiro de Meneses, Filipe. *Franco and Spanish Civil War*. New York: Routledge, 2005.

Richards, Michael. *A Time of Silence: Civil War and the Culture of Repression in Franco's Spain, 1936–1945* Cambridge: Cambridge University Press, 1998.

Rodrigo, Javier. "Campos en tiempos de Guerra." In *Una inmensa prisión. Los campos de concentración y las prisiones durante la guerra civil y el franquismo*, edited by Carme Molinero, Margarida Sala, and

Jaume Sobrequés.Barcelona: Crítica, 2003.

———. *Cautivos. Campos de concentración en la España franquista 1936–1947*. Barcelona: Crítica, 2005.

Rodríguez Jiménez, José Luis., *Historia de Falange Española de las JONS*. Madrid: Alianza Editorial, 2000.

Romero Romero, Fernando. *Socialistas de Torre Alháquime: de la ilusión republicana a la tragedia de la Guerra Civil 1931–1946* (Torre de Alháquime, Cádiz: Ayuntamiento de Torre Alháquime; Ubrique, Cádiz: Tréveris, 2009.

Ruiz, Julius. *Franco's Justice: Repression in Madrid after the Spanish Civil War*. Oxford: Clarendon Press, 2005.

Sabín, José Manuel. *Prisión y muerte de la España de postguerra*. Madrid: Anaya & Mario Muchnik, 1996.

Salas Larrázabal, Ramón. *Historia del ejército popular de la República*, vol. 1. Madrid: Editora Nacional, 1974.

Salas Larrazábal, Ramón. *Pérdidas de la Guerra*. Barcelona: Editorial Planeta, 1977.

Sánchez Guerra, Rafael. *Mis prisiones*. Buenos Aires: Claridad, 1946.

Serrano Suñer, Ramón. *Entre el silencio y la propaganda. La historia como fue: Memorias*. Barcelona: Planeta, 1977.

Suárez, Ángel. *Libro Blanco sobre las cárceles franquistas 1939–1976*. Paris: Ruedo Ibérico, 1976.

Sueiro, Daniel. *La verdadera historia del Valle de los Caídos*. Madrid: Sedmay, 1976.

Southworth, Herbert. *Guernica! Guernica! A Study of Journalism, Diplomacy, Propaganda, and History*. Berkley: University of California Press, 1977.

Suárez, Xosé Manuel. *Armas para la República. La Aventura del 'Mar Cantábrico'*.El Ferrol: Embora, 2006.

Talón, Vicente. *Memoria de la Guerra de Euskadi de 1936*. Vol. 1. *De la paz a la guerra*. Barcelona: Plaza & Janés, 1989.

Thomas, Hugh. *The Spanish Civil War*. London: Penguin, 1977.

Thompson, Paul. *The Voice of the Past: Oral History*. Oxford: Oxford University Press, 1988.

Vargas Alonso, Francisco Manuel. *Bermeo y La Guerra Civil: La Batalla de Sollube*. Donostia: Eusko Ikaskuntza, 2007.

Verhoeven, Claudia. "Law and History." in *Reading Primary Sources: The Interpretation of Texts from 19th and 20th century History*, edited by Miriam Dobson and Benjamin Ziemann. Abingdon: Routledge, 2009.

Vilar, Juan Bautista. *La España del exilio: Las emigraciones políticas españolas en los siglos XIX y XX*. Madrid: Síntesis, 2006.

Vilar, Sergio. *Protagonistas de la España democrática. La oposición a la dictadura 1931–1969*. Paris: Ediciones Sociales, 1969.

Vincent, Mary. *Spain 1833–2002: People and State*. Oxford: Oxford University Press, 2007.

Vinyes, Ricard. *Irredentas. Las presas políticas y sus hijos en las cárceles de Franco*. Madrid: Temas de Hoy, 2002.

———. "El universo penitenciario durante el franquismo." In *Una inmensa prisión. Los campos de concentración y las prisiones durante la guerra civil y el franquismo*, edited by Carme Molinero, Margarida Sala, and Jaume Sobrequés. Barcelona: Crítica, 2003.

Articles/ Study Days

Acosta Bono, Gonzalo, and Fernando Romero Romero. "Todos Los Nombres, Todas Las Fosas: Dos Proyectos para La Recuperación de la Memoria Histórico en Andalucía." *Almajar. Revista de Historia Arquelogía y Patrimonio de Villamartín y la Sierra de Cádiz*, no.3 (2006): 123–141.

Aguilar, Paloma. "The Memory of the Civil War in the Transition to Democracy: The Peculiarity of the Basque Case." *West European Politics*, vol. 21, no. 4 (October 1998):5–25.

Alonso Carballés, Jésus J. "El primer exilio de los vascos 1936–9."*Revista de Historia Contemporánea* 35 (2007): 683–708.

Anderson, Peter. "In the Interests of Justice? Grass-roots Prosecution and Collaboration in Francoist Military Trials, 1939–45." *Contemporary European History* vol. 18, no. 1 (2009): 25–44.

———. "Singling Out Victims: Denunciation and Collusion in the Post-Civil War Francoist Repression in Spain, 1939–1945." *European History Quarterly*, vol. 39, no. 1 (2009): 7–26.

Barruso, Pedro. "La represión en las zonas republicana y franquista del País Vasco durante la Guerra Civil." *Historia Contemporánea* 35 (2007): 653–81.

Constenla, Tereixa. "How Franco Banked on Victory." *El País* (English edition), June 13, 2012.

Cuervo, Máximo. Article in first publication of no.1 *Rendición* (April 1, 1939).

———. "Fundamentos del Nuevo Sistema Penitenciario Español." Universidad Central, conferencia pronunciada el 28 de octubre de 1940.

Cura, Isabel del, and Rafael Huertas. "Public Health and Nutrition after the Spanish Civil War: An Interventuion by the Rockerfeller Foundation." *American Journal of Public Heath*, vol. 99, no.10 (2009): 1772–1779.

De Blas Guerrero, Andrés. "La izquierda española y el nacionalismo. El caso de la transición." *Leviatán*, no. 31 (1988): 71–85.

Gatica Cote, Daniel. "Una cárcel de posguerra: La prisión central de El Puerto de Santa María en 1940: Los prisioneros gaditanos." *Revista de Historia de El Puerto de Santa María.* Sumario no. 35 (2005). The article is obtainable in full under the heading *Una cárcel de posguerra La prisión Central de El Puerto de Santa María en 1940: los prisioneros gaditanos.* Pages are not easily to isolate as the whole article is relevant. 1-47. Or the web page address is as follows: http://www.sbhac.net/Republica/Externos/comunicIII-3.pdf

Gómez Bravo, Gutmaro. "El desarrollo penitenciario en el primer franquismo (1939–45)" *Hispania Nova. Revista de Historia Contemporánea*, no.6 (2006). Online journal.

———. "La política penitenciaria del franquismo y la consolidación del Nuevo Estado." *Anuario de Derecho Penal y Ciencias Penales* 2008.

————. "The Origins of the Francoist Penitentiary System, 1936–1948." *International Journal of Iberian Studies*, vol. 23, no. 1 (2010): 5–21. González- Zapata, Laura Inés, et al. "Famine

in the Spanish Civil War and Mortality from Coronary Heart Disease: A Perspective from Barker's Hypothesis." *Gaceta Sanitaria,* vol. 20, no.5 (2006): 360–367.

Guzmán, Eduardo de. "1940: Juicio y condena de Miguel Hernández," *Nueva Historia* 15 (1980): 78–87.

Leitz, Christian. "Hermann Goering and Nazi Germany's Economic Exploitation of Nationalist Spain, 1936–1939." *German History* 14, no. 1 (1996): 21–37.

Preson, Paul. "An Awareness of Guilt." *Times Literary Supplement,* June 29, 2001

————."The Crimes of Franco." *Study Day BFI Southbank* (January 19, 2008).

"The decline and resurgence of the Spanish Socialist Party during the Franco regime" *European History Quarterly,* 11 (2) (1988) 207-8.

Richards, Michael. "The Limits of Quantification: Francoist Repression and Historical Methodology." *Hispania Nova. Revista de Historia Contemporánea,* no.7. (2007). Online journal.

Rodrigo, Javier. "Internamiento y Trabajo Forzoso: Los Campos de Concentración de Franco." *Hispania Nova. Revista de Historia Contemporánea* no.6 (2006). Online journal.

Romero Romero, Fernando, and Pepa Zambrana Atienza, "La represión en El Gastor durante la Guerra Civil." *Almajar,* no.3 (2007): 143–159.

Romero Romero, Fernando. "Torre Alháquime 1936: A todos se les aplicó el bando de la guerra." *Cuadernos Para El Diálogo,* no. 39 (March 2009):22–33.

Ruiz, Julius. "Seventy Years On: Historians and Repression During and After the Spanish Civil War." *Journal of Contemporary History,* vol. 44, no. 3 (2009): 449–472.

————. "A Spanish Genocide? Reflections on the Francoist repression after the Spanish Civil War." *Contemporary European History,* vol. 14, no. 2 (2005): 171–191.

Thompson, Paul. "The Voice of the Past: Oral History," in, *The Oral History Reader*, edited by Robert Perks and Alistair Thomson. London: Routledge, 1998.

Urquijo, Mikel. "La memoria negada: la encrucijada de la vía institucional en el caso del Gobierno Vasco y las víctimas del franquismo," *Hispania Nova. Revista de Historia Contemporánea*, no.6 (2006). Online journal.

Internet Sources

Ramón Rubial Fundazioa. *Historia y Memoria*. "La cárcel y represión franquista 1937–56." www.ramonrubial.com/represión.asp

(Accessed February 20, 2010).

Listado fusilados procedentes de la prisión central y del hospital San Juan de Díos del Puerto de Santa María. www.forumperlamemoria. org/?LISTADO-DE-FUSILADOS-PROCEDENTES (Accessed February 3, 2010).

Basque priests at Carmona with Julián Besteiro

http://urkullu.files.wordpress.com/2009/07/carmonal-7.jpg

(Accessed May 20, 2010).

Index

A Arnoia, 184

Abadiño (Abadiano), 100, 106, 109, 114, 133

Abando y Oxinga, Julián de, 95

abandono de destino (abandoning his post), 187

Abanto-Zierbena (Abanto y Ciérvana), 61

Abascal Bilbao, Felix, 225

Aberri Eguna, 83, 126, 176, 237

abusos dishonestos (indecent assault), 228

Acosta Bona, Gonzalo, 52,

Adell Gargallo, Elias, 180

Adhesión a la rebelión, 13, 46, 109, 119, 142, 145, 147, 161–62, 164–65, 169–71, 183, 185–86, 200, 202–3, 205, 209–10, 225, 239

adhesión military, 142, 145, 147, 163

Agirregoitia, Mateo de, 88

Agrupación Enfermeras, 180

Aguirre Lertxundi, Fernando, 126

Aguirre, Felipe, Don, 107

Aguirre, Fernando, 69, 126

Aguirre, José Antonio de, 91

Agustín Anapistate, Jesús, 144

Aiara (Ayala), 119

Aidatz Alberdi, Agustín, 130

Aitzol First Company, 69

Ajuriagerra, Juan, 70

Alanís de la Sierra, 70

Alcalá de Guadaíra, 172–73

Alcalá de Henares, 17

Alcalá de los Gazules, 28

Alcalá del Río, 158

Alcalá-Zamora, Niceto, 47

Alcázar of Toledo, 69

Alcázar, 69, 147, 163

Aldea Feliz, Santos, 20, 187,

Algodonales, 141, 194

Algorta, 170

Alhaurín el Grande, 195

Alkartzeak Battalion, 121

Aller, 169

Allue Herranz, Antonio, 169

Almirante Cervera, 161, 163

Almodóvar del Campo, 201

Alonso Carballés, Jesús, 258

Altos Hornos de Vizcaya, 38, 163

Altura Garitano, José, 157

Alvarez, Pedro 53

Amayur Battalion, 66–67

amenazas (threats), 206

Amnesty, Law of, 46,197, 242

Amorebieta, 8, 12, 100, 120–24, 132–33, 245

Amuategui Battalion, 63

Amurrio, 62, 71, 119

Anapistate, Agustín, 144

Andalusia, 7–9, 13, 17, 19, 21–22, 27, 28, 30, 36–38, 42, 45–47, 53, 55, 66, 69, 71, 93, 98, 102, 110, 137, 142, 153–54, 158–59, 165, 171–72, 181, 198, 194, 196, 203, 206, 213–16, 218, 220–21, 232, 234–36, 239, 243, 246

Antxia, Lucio, 115

ANV (Acción Nacionalista Vasca, Basque Nationalist Action), 67, 106,

Aquilera Jaén, José, 142–43

Araba (Álava), 8, 17, 21, 35, 42, 47–48, 51, 58, 64, 160, 163

Araba Batallion, 63

Aralar Batallion, 67

Arana Goiri Batallion, 63, 175

Arana, Sabino, 8, 17, 30, 62–63, 82, 163, 119, 175–76, 243, 246, 254

Archbishop of Burgos, 59, 73

Archivo General Militar, 167, 248

Arcos de la Frontera, 53, 143, 176

Areilza, José María de, 64–65

Arenas FC, 88

Arenzana Ramón, Celestino, 186

Arieta-Araunabeña, Gregorio, 128

Arjona, Father, 41

Armour, Norman (US ambassador), 19

Arriba España, 121, 146,

Arrien Utriaga, Juan, 174

Arrieta Calleja, Martín, 174

Arrigorriaga, 163–64, 169

Arrondo Elgea, Santiago, 114

Arruti Gurmendi, Santiago, 164

Arruza Bilbao, León, 117

Arruza Goitia, Joseba, 8, 117, 246

Artea, 12, 243

asesinato (murder), 207, 211–12

Askatasun Eguzkia, 126

Asla, Modesto, 119

Assault Guards (a Spanish police force created during the Second Republic), 137, 167

Association for the Martyrs of Paracuellos de Jarama y Torrejón de Ardoz, 90

Association for the Recuperation of Historical Memory, 21

Astizaran Leturia, Marcelino, 143

Asturias, 106, 139, 163–64, 176, 179, 221, 234, 236

Asua, 119

Attlee, Clement, 93

Atxondo, 229

Auditor de Guerra, 139

Aurrekoetxea Unzueta, Martín, 8, 117

auxilio a la rebelión, 69, 126, 131, 147, 172, 183, 202–3, 205, 210, 238

Auxilio de Invierno, 104

Auxilio Social, 104, 109

Ave María Purisíma, 44

Azaña, Manuel, 46, 51, 70, 83, 101, 147, 198

Azkoien (Peralta), 95

Bab-Tazza, 148

Badajoz, 22, 44, 141, 185, 188, 217, 252

Bailén Regiment, 186

Bajo Guadalquivir Canal, 214

Bakio, 100, 128

Banco de Crédito de la Unión Minera, 117

Bandera, 148

Barakaldo, 61, 115, 143–44, 157

Barcelona, 19, 20, 22, 42, 77, 82, 146, 158–160, 225, 249–52, 254–55, 257–58,

Barreiro López, Antonio, Don, 158

Barriga Galán, Fernando, 51, 53, 196–97

Barrio de San Roque, 195

Basque Archive in Bergara, 59, 73

Basque Army, 69, 116–17, 120, 166, 212

Basque bertsolaris, 49, 82

Basque Catholics, 59

Basque Country, 88, 90, 98–99,

107, 117, 136–37, 142, 151, 156, 188, 204, 209–10, 213–14, 216, 226, 228–30, 232–33, 236, 239, 242

Basque military police, 145

Basque Nationalist Party (PNV), 57, 66, 106

Basque Nationalists, 58–59, 63, 73, 89, 100, 120, 129, 221, 236–37

Basque prisoners, 9, 12, 13, 17, 19, 23, 31, 34, 38, 40–41, 43–45, 49, 57, 59–60, 67, 69–72, 74–79, 83, 86, 92–93, 95, 98–99, 102–03, 107, 110, 112, 116–17, 119, 124, 126, 129–30, 134, 137, 144–45, 157, 178, 200, 203–4, 209–10, 212–14, 219, 221, 232, 234–37, 239–40

Basteguieta, Antonio, 213

Basurto hospital, 164, 179, 183

Battalion of Machine Gunners, 197

Battle of Brunete, 184

Battle of Irun, 63

Battle of Sollube, 157, 164

Battle of the Ebro, 185, 150

Batzoki of Santurtzi, 174

BBB (the Bizkaian provincial committee of the Basque Nationalist Party), 66

Beevor, Antony, 251

Beita, Teodoro, 186

Bejino Pajarín, Saturnino, 225

Bellón Commission, 14, 241

Benaoján, 28, 53

Benarrabá, 148

Bengoa, Carmelo, 115

Benjamin, Natalie, 87

Bergara, 8, 12, 59, 66, 73, 75, 88–

89, 91, 157, 178, 221, 244
Bermeo, 157, 174
Bernota López, Elías, 180
Berreteaga district (Loiu), 119
Berroga, Pedro, 79, 81
Besteiro, Julián, 18, 47, 141, 215,
Bilbao, 19, 38, 45, 48–49, 58, 61,
    63–64, 66, 69, 71–73, 77, 83, 87,
    92, 94, 98, 100, 102–3, 108, 110,
    114–27, 130–35, 141, 143–45,
    153–57, 163–80, 183–84, 220,
    225, 235, 244
Bilbao, Esteban, 19, 115
Bioko, 82
Bishop of Seville, 73, 91, 215
Bizkaia, 18, 48–49, 60–63, 65–66,
    69, 71, 74–75, 78, 95, 98, 106,
    119, 128, 151, 157, 163–64,
    169–170, 174, 183, 208, 214,
    219–20, 22–29, 235
Bizkaian Provincial Council, 18, 69
Black Arrows, 174
Bolinaga, Father, 44, 124
Bolivar Batallion, 67
Books on Communism, 177
Bootellos Campos, Don Luis, 55
Borrego Runiera, Julián, 148
Bowers, Claude, 92
Brenan, Gerald, 44
Brigada 8, 123
brigadas (prisoners' confinement
    areas), 33
Brotherhood of Ex-Prisoners, 90,
    91, 236
buena conducta, 145
Buesa Arguinchoa, Ramón, Don,
    Colonel, 178
Burgos prison, 18, 44, 92

Burgos, 18, 20, 44, 59, 66, 68, 72,
    73, 92, 110, 124, 128, 145, 168,
    170, 183–84, 218, 226, 233–34,
    240
Bustinza, Irantzu, 8, 120

Caballero, Ramón, 94
Cáceres tribunal, 239
Cáceres, 141, 185, 188, 239
Cadavieco, Avelino, 48
Cádiz prison, 13, 157, 218, 219,
    228, 231,
Cádiz, 182, 185, 192, 194, 197,
    199, 203–6, 209–10, 212, 214,
    216–22, 226–29, 231–33, 236,
    238–39,
caídos por Dios, 242
Calvente Apanda, José, 178
Cañadas Penas, José, 158
Canarias (ship), 137, 158–59, 187
Canary Islands, 18, 69–70, 98, 124,
    160, 187
Cancer, 32
Cantabria, 66, 100, 110, 143, 145,
    158
Cantabrian Sea, 158
Cape Trafalgar, 29
Capitán Casero Batallion, 144
Capuchin friars, 197
Cara al Sol, 67, 68, 110
Carabineros, 54
Carbonell, Rafael, 226
Carlist, 58, 60, 67, 89, 100, 106,
    110, 112, 117, 131, 219
Carmelite Convent in Amorebieta,
    87
Carmelites, 123, 124
Carmona, 215, 237, 248,

Carrera García, Emilio, 144–45
Carrillo Jurado, Diego, 173
Cartagena, 137, 141, 161–62, 217
Casa del Pueblo, 147, 165, 169, 174
Casanova, Julián, 18, 20, 27, 206
casas de tolerancia (brothels), 226
case of Zacarías Mora Rodríguez of Puertollano, 149
Casería de Ossio in San Fernando, 230
Casería de Ossio prison in San Fernando, 216
Castile La Mancha, 23, 49
Castillo de San Francisco, Las Palmas de Gran Canarias, 187
Castillo prison in Santa Catalina, 216
Castro Urdiales, 66, 72
Catalonia, 23, 45, 94, 107
Catholic Church, 87, 154, 192,
Catholicism, 40, 45, 89, 91, 156, 237–38
Causa General, 14, 241
causa número (indictment number), 171
Cazadores del Serrallo Battalion, 185
Cazalla de la Sierra, 70, 102, 214, 237
CEDA (Confederación Española de Derechas Autónomas, Spanish Confederation of Autonomous Right-wing Groups), 100
cemeteries for the living, 34
Ceniceros Dufós, María, 180
Centro de Patrimonio

Documentalde Euskadi/ Euskadiko Dokumentu Ondarearen Zentroa, 91
Centro Penitenciario Militar de Dos Hermanas, 47
Cerrajuena, Echaque, 183
certificado de libertad, 108
Ceuta, 185–86, 217–18, 239, 141, 145–50, 177–78
chapel of *Nuestra Señora*, 109
Chinchilla, 18, 162
Chipiona, 52–53
Christian resignation, 44
Churchill, Randolph, 141
Ciano, Count, 106
Cicero, 145
Ciempozuelos front, 150
Cinturón de Hierro (Ring of Iron), 144
Cipriano de Rivas, 45–46
City Hall of Ibiza, 161
Ciudad Condal, 160
Ciudad de Cádiz (ship), 160–61
Ciudad Real, 149, 201
Civil Governor, 23, 90, 125, 209
Civil Guard, 23, 45, 54, 89, 100, 109, 111–12, 116, 119, 125, 139, 149, 152, 165, 171–73, 188, 190, 196, 204, 209, 225–26
Clark, Robert P., 68, 74
Clemente Pantaleón, Alberto, 187
CNT (Confederación Nacional del Trabajo, National Workers' Confederation), 66
cobardía ante el enemigo, 188
coffee in Fernando Pó, 81, 82
Cohen Bentata, Isaac, 177
Coll Broadvent, Salvador, 81–82,

157–59, 187
Collado, Esteban, 149
Comerera, Juan, 46
Commander of Engineers, 145
Communion, 41–42, 87, 107, 240
Communist Party, 142, 148, 172–73, 176, 178
Communists, 58–59, 73, 221, 236
Companys, Luis, 45
Comunión, 239
Conde Hernando, Juan, 179
condicional/libertad condicional provisional/sin o con destierro (with or without exile), 41, 47, 49, 105, 107, 111, 114, 121, 131, 138, 150, 222, 224–26, 227–29
Congil, José, 48
Consejo General Vasco (Basque General Council), 49
Constitutional Rights Court (Tribunal de Garantias), 46
Controller of Prisons, 44
Convent of Adorers in Ondarreta, 71
Convent of Mount Carmel in Vitoria-Gasteiz, 71
Convent of Paul in Vitoria-Gasteiz, 71
Convent of San Carlos, 195
Córdoba, 28, 36, 89, 166, 201, 209
Corpus Christi, 42
Cruz Orozco, Juan, 119
Cuellar prison, 47
Cuervo Radigales, Máximo, 17, 201, 232
Czech military equipment, 63

Daily Mail, 141

Day of the Basque Homeland, 83, 126
Dean of Canterbury, 101
deberes cívicos religiosos, 103
Defense Committees, 60, 73, 90
Defense Council, 13–14, 36
Deia, 106
Denuncia, 89–91, 138–39, 198, 200
Depuración, 170
deserción al frente de enemigo, 186
Desertu/Desierto district of Erandio, 219
Diaz Estevez, Juan, 142
Díaz Vázquez, Victoriano, 189
dinero en peculio, 193
Diputación de Cádiz, 22, 27, 55
Diputación Provincial, 22, 28, 172, 213
Donostia-San Sebastián, 8–9, 61, 63, 71, 88, 98, 100, 125–27, 130, 133, 166, 176, 178, 182–83, 217, 220, 225
Dos Hermanas, 47, 119, 214, 216
Dueso, 20, 23, 66–69, 71–72, 75, 82, 102, 109–10, 112, 114–15, 119, 121–26, 128–30, 214, 217, 219, 221, 225, 234, 248
Duke of Seville, 141
Dukes of Medicaneli, 27
Durango Defense Committee, 101
Durango, 104–6, 108–9, 111–12, 114–15, 125, 131, 133, 167, 169, 225, 229
Durruti Battalion, 71

Ebro River, 233
Echaburu Alzaa, Yolanda, 8, 109
Echaburu Irastorza, Isidro, 102

Echaque Cerrajueria, Fernando, Dr., 183

Echeandia Apriz, Serapio, 102, 132, 133, 138

Eibar, 144, 156, 167, 225

El Barracal, 196

El Burgo, 195, 197

el día de la Merced, 30

el día de Reyes, 30

El Dueso (Santoña), 23, 66.72, 119, 217

El Ferrol, 159

El Gastor, 28, 51, 53

El Mundo Gráfico, 46

El País, 23

El Puerto prison, 165

El Rincón del Medik, 177

El Saco (the sack), 26, 52

El Tribunal Especial para la Represión de la Masonería y del Comunismo, 152

Elgeta, 144

Elorena, Eugenio, 159

Emakume Abertzale Batza, 124,

Enbeita, Balendin, 49

Equatorial Guinea, 82

Erandio, 8, 12, 48, 100, 119, 128, 144, 219

Ermua, 62

Escolapians, 131

Escribano Garrido, Antonio, 187

Espera, 53

Espetxean, 128

Espinosa, Francisco, 22, 135

Espinosa, Manuel, 172, 177

Espinosa-Cartelle, 184

estafa (black-market dealings), 228

estraperlo (black market activities), 209

Etxabe Aldai, Jesús, 8, 130–31, 133, 246

Etxano, 115

Eusko Gudariak, 69

Euzkadi bajo el régimen de Franco: la represión en Guipúzcoa, 88

Euzkadi, 63, 72, 88

Euzko Gudarostea, 63

Evolución lodge, 154

excitación a la rebellion, 145

Excitación a la rebellion,

excitación e inducción a la rebelión, 202

Falange Española Auténtica (Authentic Spanish Falange), 209

Falange institution, 104

Falange of Candás, 139

Falange, 172, 185, 188–90, 195–97, 209, 225, 234, 239,

Falangistas, 104

fall of Málaga, 195

fall of Santander, 65, 72, 74, 106, 112, 143, 200, 203

falsedad de documentos (false documents), 206

Federación Anarquista Ibérica (FAI), 165

Federation of Spanish Tobacco, 172, 178,

Fernández Asiain, Eugenio, 14, 202

Fernández Gómez, José María, 55

Fernando Lopéz, Fernando, 147

Fernando Pérez, Luis, 168–69, 171, 172

Fiat Paul, Abel, 154
Fichas, 23
Fiesta de la Merced, 41
First Battalion of the Socialist
    Militias, 46
First Military Region, 52
Foro por la Recuperación de la
    Memoria de El Puerto de Santa
    María (Forum for Recovering
    Historical, Memory about El
    Puerto de Santa María), 52
Franco regime at Montjuic, 46
Franco regime, 88–89, 110, 138,
    145, 157, 183–84, 188–89, 199,
    201, 226, 235, 241
Franco, Nicolás, 189
Francoism, 14, 138,
Francoist economic repression, 95
Francoist propaganda, 40, 44, 237
Francoist terror, 152
Francoist, 13, 17, 20, 40, 44, 65, 74,
    89, 94–95, 97, 111, 116–17, 126,
    137, 139, 141–42, 152, 169, 197,
    198, 200–3, 212, 221–22, 226,
    229, 231–33, 235, 237, 239
franquistas falsas, 111
Freccie Nere, 174
French zone of Morocco, 185
Fuentes, José, 48

Gaceta del Norte, 66, 87
Galarza, Ramón, 113
Galdakao (Galdácano), 8, 61
Gamboa Larrondo, Pablo, 110,
    119, 138
Gámez Parra, Dolores, 53
Gandiaga, Expósito, 167
Gantxegi, Saturnino, 77, 156,

Garay Hormaza, Peli, 128
Garay, Arantzazu, 8, 128
Garbisu Llaguno, Eduardo, 183
García Benítez, Antonio, 152, 197,
    239
García Borreguero, Alfonso, Dr.,
    179
García Braojos, Fernando, Don,
    146
García Torres, Manuel, 27
García, Hilaria, 226
García, Manuel, 27, 35
Garnica Lasera, Vicenta, 131
garrotte vil, 72, 240
gastric ulcers, 32
Gatica Cote, Daniel, 37
Gatica, Daniel, 37, 214
Geneva Convention of 1929, 72
Geneva, 23, 34, 46, 72
Getafe, 155
Getxo (Guecho), 61, 70, 170
Gipuzkoa, 48, 60–67, 69, 78,
    88–89, 95, 98, 124, 130, 132,
    143–44, 151, 156–57, 167, 169,
    174–75, 178, 183, 214, 220, 225,
    227–28
Giral, José, 47
Girón, Francisco, 149
Gironella Ronquillo, Don,
    Captain, 161
Gobierno Civil (central
    government representative in
    the provinces), 182
Goienkale Barracks, 100
Gomara Fernández, José, 167
Gómez Bravo, Gutmaro, 9, 21, 36,
    98, 226, 230, 233
Gómez Guerra, Juan, 172

Gómez Requejo Rodríguez, Eduardo, 188–190
Goñi firm, 175
Gonzálelz Palacios, Anastasio, 180
González Cruz, Ramiro, 172
González Gorosarri, María, 8, 12, 97
González Vilches, Lorenzo, 147, 239
González Zaera, Mario, 234
Gordexola Battalion, 145
Gorosarri Gojenola, Ángel, 60, 101–2, 105–6, 131
Gorosarri, Jabier, 8, 105, 106
Gorosarri, Kepa, 8
Graham, Helen, 14, 58
Granada provincial prison, 46
Grazaelema, 165
Grimau, Julián, 19
Guadalquivir Canal, 17, 214
gudaris (Basque soldiers), 72–73, 94, 112, 128
Gudaris y Rehenes de Franco, 66
Guggenheim Museum, 49
Guimón Rezola, Julián, Dr., 102–3, 107, 178–79, 181, 197
Gutierrez Silva, Father, 40–42
Guzmán Martín, Sebastián, 52
Guzmán, Eduardo, 141

Hacho Fort prison, 146
Hacho prison, 178
Hamburg, 63
Hamed Ben Mohamed, 186
Hedilla, Manuel, 189
Heli de Tella, General, 209
Herbette, Jean, 92
Heredia, José, 149

Hermanas de la Caridad, 77
Hidalgo Martín, Julián, 185
Higuera, Miguel, 226
Hijos de Mendizabal, 115, 131
Hinojosa del Duque, 20
Hispano American Bank , 177
Historical Memory Act of 2007, 198
Holy Sacrament, 43
honor tribunals, 154
Hospital de San Antonio, 77
Hospital of As Lagoas, 184
Huelva, 7, 17, 82, 102, 117, 142, 152, 165, 168, 204, 206, 213–14, 217, 219, 225, 237, 240, 243, 245, 252
Huesca, 168–69

Ibarra, 69, 126
Ibarrola Echeverria, José, Dr.,
Ifni Snipers' Battalion, 187
Iglesias Martínez, Jenaro, 176–77
Ikasle Abertzaleen Batza (Basque Nationalist Students' Association), 130
Infantry Regiment, 150
infracción de la Ley de Tasas (infringement of tax laws), 212
injuria al ejército, 145, 148–49
Institución Libre de Enseñanza (Free Educational Institute), 168
Institute of Santoña, 71
Iñurrieta Inguida, Felix, 167
Invierno, Auxilio de, 104
Irargi (Basque Document Archive), 8, 88–89, 91, 244, 246
Irasuegui, Cruz, 124

Irazabal Agirre, Jon, 254, 112
Irazabal, Alfredo, 121
Isla de San Simón, 116, 119
Itxarkundia, 67
Izquierda Republicana, 142–44,
    152, 154, 184–85, 194

Jagi-Jagi faction, 175
Javier Rodrigo, 15, 2, 200, 74
Jerez de la Frontera, 216, 217, 27,
    28, 53, 142, 149, 156, 190
Jesuits, 131
Jiménez Amaya, Antonio, 5, 53
JONS (Juntas de Ofensiva
    Nacionalista Sindicalista,
    Unions of the National-
    Syndicalist Offensive), 104
José Villegas, 165
JSU (Juventudes Socialistas
    Unificadas, United Young
    Socialists), 49
Judge Advocate on technicalities,
    141
juez instructor, 139
Justice for God and Spain, 198

Kirikiño Battalion, 115
Koestler, Arthur, 249
Kortezubi, 214

La Almeda, 172
La Campaña, 148
La Espiga de Oro, 177
La Gaceta del Norte, 66, 247
la horda roja, 59, 73
La Línea de la Concepción, 28,
    216, 219, 239
la Plaza Barria, 117

La Rioja, 144
La Sauceda district of Cortes de la
    Frontera (Málaga), 143
La Tarde, 87
La Valencia, 148
La Vanguardia Española, 47
Langurica Eizaguirre, Juan
    Antonio, 170–71
Laredo, 66, 70, 72, 225
Largo Caballero, 144
Larrea, Gregorio, 100
Larrinaga, 66, 68, 72, 83, 103, 110,
    113–14, 116, 119, 128, 234, 240
Larrondo, 110, 119, 138,
Las Hormigas farm, 196,
Las Palmas, 217, 14, 160, 187
Laudio (Llodio), 119,
Law for the Repression of
    Freemasonry and Communism,
    14
Law of Archives 1985, 22
Law of Political Responsibilities of
    1939, 241
Law of Purging the Publicly
    Employed, 14
League of Nations, 46
Legutio (Villareal in Spanish), 145
Leitz, Christian, 73, 254, 260
Lenago-il Battalions, 67
León, José, Father, 123–24
Lerroux, Alejandro, 45, 100, 198
letter of Cañadas Penas, 158
Levante, 29
Liberal Party, 93
*libertad /libertad definitiva/
    libertad por prisión atenuada*
    (house arrest), 223
libertad condicional (parole), 74,

105, 107, 114, 138, 150, 222, 224–29

Libertad condicional/provisional con destierro (exile), 224

libertad definitivo, 112, 222–23, 226–27

libertad/libertad condicional (liberty/conditional liberty), 105–8, 111–12, 114, 138, 150, 222–26

Libro Blanco sobre las cárceles franquistas, 20

Liendo, 145

Lladós Virós, Juan, 45, 47

Logroño, 157, 185–87

Loiu (Lujua), 12

López López, Cirulo, 82, 165

López Macías, Juan, 51, 192

López Sierra, Manuel, 145–47, 238

López Tamayao, Juan, 168

López y López, Luis, 188, 190

Loring, Jorge, 42

los novios de muerte (the bridegrooms of death), 44

Loyola Battalion, 175

Lozano, Don Justo de, 87

Luhí, Juan, 46

Luis Arrondo Uriarte, José, 8, 114

Luis Caso de Cobos, 168

Luis Gutiérrez Molina, José, 214, 250, 8

Luis Hidalgo, José, 35

Luisa Goicoechea Guezurraga, María, 180

Luisa Quintana, María, 86

Madres Irlandesas Order (Congregation of Jesus), 116

Madrid, 9, 19, 20, 22, 28, 36, 45–48, 59, 67, 147, 150, 153–54, 157, 169, 176, 184, 203, 208, 214, 217–18, 220, 234, 238, 248–50, 253–58

mala conducta, 145, 225

mala educación, 38

Málaga prison, 18

Málaga province, 197

Manuel Martínez Bande, José, 106, 213

Manuel Mendizabal, Joshe, 128

Manzanas, Melitón, 127

Mar Cantábrico, 137, 158, 159, 257

Margarita, 163, 89, 131

Mari Eskubi, Juan, 105

Mari, Joshe, 125, 69, 92, 98

María Deu, José, 47

María Galarza Zulueta, José, 183

María Galíndez, José, 100

María Otxoa, José, 71

Marín Salguero, Pedro, 5, 53

Martin, Rodolfo (Minister of the Interior at the Civil Guard [Guardia Civil]), 23

Martínez, Florencio, 144

Martínez, Santiago, 215

Marxists, 148

Mata Ratón, Agustín, 149

Matilde Eiroa San Francisco, 18

Matthews, James, 16, 166–67, 180, 185

Maunday, 44

Meabe Battalion, 144

Medalla Militar (Military Medal), 47

Medina Guerra, Diego, 5, 195

Medina Guerra, Juan, 5, 53, 195

Meixengo Pereira, José, 184
Méjico militias, 36, 195
Melilla, 4, 36, 217
Mendibil Manrique, Jesús, 119, 133
Mendibil Sobrón, Rafa, 8, 119
Mendizabal Sarasua, Joxemari, 8–9, 70, 83, 92, 98, 125, 128
Meningitis, 32
Miajadas road, 188
Milicianos, 106, 195–97
Military Academy of Artillery, 145
Military Code of Justice, 203
Military Delegation for Public Order in Seville, 22
military tribunal in Ceuta, 100
military tribunals of Franco, 9, 140
Millán Astray, Julio, 27
Ministerio Fiscal (Attorney General), 187
Ministry of Interior 73
Mintegui Uriguen, Ruperta, 124
Miota, Pedro, 100
Miraflores, 325, 172
Mohamed Ben Hamed Ramu, 177
Mola, Emilio, General, 60, 63, 101
Molinero, Carme, 19, 21
Monarchists, 100
Monasterio de la Victoria, 27
Montejaque, 28, 53
Montero Cabañas, Juan, 187
Morales Geva, Roque, 5, 53
Morales Guerra, Roque, 195
Morejón Pizarro, Bartolomé, 148
Moreno, Antonio, 149
Morteros de Euskadi, 66
Mount Hacho, 148
Mount Isuskitza, 186–87

Movimiento Nacional, 165
mujeres extriviadas (fallen women), 226
Mundaka, 88
Mundo Obrero, 149
Mungia (Munguía), 12
Muñoz Espinosa, José, 177
Muñoz Rodríguez, Antonio, 171
myth of Franco as the Catholic Crusader, 237

National Movement of Barcelona, 23
Nationalist and Fascist anthems, 17
Nationalist Army of the South, 53
Nationalist Battalion, 65
Nationalist elite force, 44
Nationalist penal policy, 4, 20, 200, 229, 234, 238,
Nationalist penal system, 34, 200, 232, 236
Nationalist policy of imprisoning Republicans, 18
Nationalist propaganda, 41
Nationalist *Regulares* (regular army), 188
Nationalists, 15–16, 20, 27, 34, 50, 52, 55, 58–59, 60, 63–66, 73–74, 88–89, 97, 100, 103–5, 114, 116, 120, 123, 132, 148, 159, 165, 168, 172, 174–75, 186–88, 196, 202, 209–10, 219, 222, 232–33, 236–37
Navarra (Basque ship), 158
Navarre, 15, 46, 58, 60–63, 65, 95, 106, 213–14, 220, 227, 228
Navarro Oliver, Serafín, 82, 161,

163
nephritis, 32
Nevia Ossorio, Ramón, Don,
    Admiral, 161
Nieto Álvarez, Francisco, 149
Nogales Rivera, Rafael, 166
Nuevo Estado, 38, 68, 89, 137, 147,
    206
número de causa, 139
Núñez Calvio, Jesús, 52
Nuñez de Castro Caudil, Ramón,
    177
Núñez Díaz-Balart, Mirta, 20, 78,
    102, 206, 224, 229, 238

Ocaña (Toledo) prison, 18
Ochoa Cossi, Eduardo, 55
Ochoa Cossi, Francisco, 22, 55
Ochoa Ruiz, Antonio, 173, 178
October Revolution of 1934, 164
Oion (Oyón), 60, 62, 84, 86
Olvera, 28, 51, 53, 194
Omaza, Ruperto, 174
Ondarreta (Donostia-San
    Sebastián), 71, 125, 127, 176
Ondazarate (sanatorium), 76
Oriamendi (Carlist anthem), 67
Ormaiztegi, 157
Orozko, 119, 178, 183, 184
Ortuella (as part of Greater
    Bilbao), 61, 174, 175
Ossio, Casería de, 159, 216, 218,
    230
Osuna, 102, 214, 237
Otxandio (Ochandiano), 8, 12,
    112, 133
Ourense Republicans, 184

Pact of Santoña, 18, 66, 69, 94, 112
pacto de olvido, 21, 99
Padín, Félix, 71
Padrón General de Habitantes, 37
Padura, 67
Pamplona-Iruñea, 46, 62, 63
Pantoja Puerto, Sebastián, 185, 239
Pantoja Puerto, José, 185
Pardo San Gil, Juan, 158
Parejo Arrecha, Clemente, 151
Parroquia de Santiago, 173
Pasaia (Pasajes, 88, 125,
Patria, 34
Payne, Stanley G., 72, 78
Pedroso, Manuel, 146, 158
Pena González, Valeriano, Don,
    168
Peña Rey, Manuel, 184
Penitentiary of Dueso, 71
perdón, pan y paz (pardon, bread,
    and peace), 231
Pérez Álvarez, Pedro, 196
Pérez Andrés, Francisco, Dr., 179
Pérez Benítez, Miguel, 143
Pérez del Pulgar, José Agustín, 17
Fernando Pérez, Luis, 17, 143,
    153–54,
Ruiz Pérez, Joaquín, 167
Pizarro, Morejón, 148
Placencia de las Armas, 169
Plaza de Unamuno, 117
Pneumonia, 32, 75
PNV (Partido Nacionalista Vasco,
    Basque Nationalist Party), 18,
    45, 57–60, 66, 69, 74, 100–2,
    105–7, 113, 116–17, 119–25,
    129, 133, 144–45, 174–75, 179
Political Responsibilities

legislation of 1939, 105
Pons Abelló, Álvaro, Captain, 82, 159–161
Popular Front coalition, 131
Popular Front Committees, 90
Popular Front, 46, 58, 60, 90, 101, 131, 164–192, 195–196
Port of Barcelona, 46
Port of Gijón, Austria, 168
Portugalete, 61, 170, 174,
post-Apartheid South African style reconciliation, 242
Prado, Sanchéz, 148
President of the Generalitat (the Catalan government), 46
Primo de Rivera, Pilar, 104
Príncipe De Viana, 176
Prior of Santo Domingo, Father, 192
prisión atenuada en domicilio (house arrest), 225, 228
Prisión del Fuerte, 46
prison of Ocaña, 23
province of Córdoba, 201
Provincial Historical Archive, 7, 11, 23–24, 50, 99, 159, 204, 213
Provincial Priest of the Carmelites, 123–124
Provincial Prison of Bilbao, 131
PSOE (Partido Socialista Obrero Español, Spanish Socialist Workers' Party), 48–49, 58, 144, 147, 163, 165, 174, 176, 196, 198, 215, 235
Puente de Vallecas, 36
Puerto de La Sía, 145
Puerto de Santa María, El, 19, 27, 36, 48–49, 62, 65, 69, 74–75,

92, 94, 98, 103, 111, 120, 124, 146, 148, 152, 159, 161–62, 166, 168–69, 178, 182, 187, 190, 192, 194, 197, 214, 240
Pujana Bolibar, Miren, 8, 112
Pujana Galíndez, Vicente, 112, 133, 234
Pujol, Ruiz, 146

Quartermaster Corps, 121
Queipo de Llano, 53, 173
Quintana, Juan, 86

Radical-Ceda regime of Alejandro Lerroux, 198
Radio Sevilla, 173
Ramón Serrano Súñer, 14, 189, 241
Ramos, Rafael, 145
Real Madrid Football Club, 47
Rebelión de la Sal Battalions, 63
rebelión military, 202, 209, 241
Rebellion, 13–14, 19, 46, 60, 66, 68, 141–42, 145, 151, 203
reclusión perpetua, 71
Red Army, 170,
Red Cross, 23, 92
Redemption of Sentences, 17
Redención (journal), 17
Redición, 47
Redondo, Onésimo, 104
reeducation and re-catholicization, 15–17
Regulares, 157, 188
Reino Caamaño, Carlos, 184
Republican, 14, 18–34, 45, 47, 55, 58, 60, 62, 63–67, 72, 74, 77–78, 86, 89–91, 97–106, 109, 111, 114, 117, 120, 133, 135–52,

154–61, 164, 166–67, 169, 171,
177, 184–88, 194–97, 202–3,
206, 212, 221, 229, 231–33, 236,
239, 241–42
Republican-controlled Spain, 155
Requetés (Carlist militiamen), 58,
60, 67, 100, 106, 186
Reverend Mother Superior
Amparo, 76
Revolutionary Movement of
Erandio, 48
Rezola Arana, Luis, 82–83, 175–76
Richards, Michael, 20, 41, 63
Rivas Cherif, Cipriano de, 46
River Guadalete, 26
Rivera Mallaina, Don Carlos, 54
Rockefeller Foundation, 36
Rodrigo, Javier, 15, 21, 74, 200
Rodríguez Delgado, Luis, 173
Rodríguez Izquierda, Mercedes, 52
Rodríguez Pérez, Sebastián, 188
Rodríguez, Isidoro, 27
Rohstoff-Waren-Kompensation
Handelsgesellschaft (ROWAK),
73
Rojas, José, 148
Rojo Ugarte, Ignacio, 100
Roma (ship), 87, 161
Romero Romero, Fernando, 8, 52,
194
Ronda, 28, 53, 195, 197
Rosa de Luxemburgo Battalion,
184
Royo, Romualdo, 70
Rubial Cava, Ramón, 45, 48, 75,
87, 221, 235–36
Ruescas Pérez, Antonio, 153–154
Rugama, Don Ramón de, 87

Rugateiro Bozada, José, 172
Ruiz de Aguirre Mintegui,
Carmen, 120
Ruiz de Aguirre, Jenaro, 8, 120,
128
Ruiz Guzmán, Hidalgo, Dr., 35
Ruiz Pérez, Joaquín, 167
Ruiz Valle, Dionisio, 156
Rusia Batallion, 66, 112

Sabino Arana Battalion, 116–117
Sacerdotes Vascos Fusilados
(Executed Basque priests), 59,
73
Sacred Heart of Jesus church, 155
Safón Carvert, Emilio, Sergeant,
177
Salazar, Luis, 148
Saldana, Sixta,158
San Andrés Battalion, 130, 157
San Fausto, 112
San Fernando, 75, 159, 169, 192,
216, 230
San Francisco, Eiroa, 18–19, 209
San José de la Valle, 142
San José, Padre Román de, 87
San Juan de Aznalfarache, 171–72
San Pedro Alcántara, 195
San Pedro de Cadeña, 68
San Roque, 47, 195
Sánchez Guerra, Rafael, 36, 45, 47
Sánchez Sánchez, Alejandro, 177
Sanlúcar de Barrameda, 23, 28, 32,
151
Sanlúcar, 54, 221, 232
Sanmartín, José, 177
Santamaria Curtido, Pedro Pablo,
52

Santa María Ruiz, Serafín, 159

Santander, 18, 47, 63, 65, 72, 74, 87, 106, 112, 125-126, 131, 143–145, 161, 163–164, 167, 179, 200, 213, 221, 233, 235–236

Santo Domingo de la Cazada, 144

Santoña, 18, 66, 67, 69, 71–72, 109–10, 112, 171, 174, 176, 183, 121, 130, 164, 234

Santutxu, 71

Sanz Bachiller, Mercedes, 104

Saseta Batallion, 67, 125–26

Second Military Region, 25

Secretary General of the President's Office, 47

Segovia (Castile and León), 18

Segura, Cardinal, 73, 91, 215

Seminary of Saturraran in Mutriku, 71

Serrano Perula, Francisco, 147, 239

Serrano Suñer, Ramón, 14, 189, 241

Sestao, 144, 163

Setenil de la Bodegas, 53

Setién Garrido, Cesário, 164–165

Seville, 8, 17, 22, 24, 27, 36, 44, 47, 70, 91, 102, 119, 145, 147, 150–152, 158, 166, 168, 172–173, 178, 214–216, 221, 236–237, 239

Sierra de Cádiz, 28, 194

Sinclair, Archibald, Sir, 93

Sixta Saldana, 158

Soccoro Rojo Internacional (International Red Aid, commonly known by its Russian acronym MOPR), 137

Soraluze, 169

SOV (Solidaridad de Obreros Vascos, later renamed Solidaridad de Trabajores Vascos, STV), 164, 174

Soviet Separatists, 59, 73

Spanish based Hispano-Marroqui de Transportes (HISMA), 73

Spanish Casa del Pueblo (PSOE), 174

Spanish Civil War, 11–12, 25, 27, 37, 65, 74, 92, 97, 99, 106, 109, 136–37 139, 151, 158, 176, 185, 197, 200, 202, 204, 229, 241–42

Spanish Constitution of 1978, 97

Spanish Foreign Legion, 44, 137, 149, 166, 168, 173

Spanish Freemasonry, 153

Spanish Legion, 27,148,166

Spanish National Statistics Institute, 19, 60

Spanish Parliament, 47, 115

Spanish Republican Parliament, 74

Stalin, 144

State Security Law,141

Stevenson, R.C., 92, 94

STV (Solidaridad de Trabajadores Vascos, Basque Workers' Solidarity), 130

Sukarrieta Battalion, 109

Talavera de la Reina, 141, 150, 218

tenenecia ilícita (illicit possession), 212

Tetouán, 149, 157, 158, 177, 217

Three Kings' Day, 30

Tinoco Rodriguez, Manuel, 190, 192

Tirado, José, 115
Tobar, Don Laureano, 44, 124
Torre Alháquime, 190,194_197
Torrontegui, Begoña, 8
Torrontegui Elguezabal, Antonio, 129–30
traición (treason), 188, 212
Traverso González, Antonio, 149
Triana, 171, 173, 178, 240
Tribunal de Garantias (Constitutional Rights Court), 46
Tuberculosis, 30, 32, 72, 76–77, 122, 128, 240
Txorierri, 12

Ubrique, 141, 166
UGT (the Unión General de Trabajadores, General Workers' Union), 48
Unamuno, Miguel de, 57, 117
Uníos Hermanos Proletarios (Unite, Proletarian Brothers), 143
United Spain, 65, 67
University of Deusto, 70, 71, 167
Upo Mendi prison, 119
Urbi (Bizkaia), 71
Urduña (Orduña), 8, 12, 100, 103, 119–20, 133, 167, 183–84
Uriate y Larrea de Yurre, Pedro de, 75
Uribasterra Ibarrondo, Adolfo,100
Urkiaga, Don Esteban de, 87
Uruguay, 46
Usabiaga, Marcelo, 70
usurpación de funciones (usurpation of functions), 207, 208, 212, 219

Vadillo Cuevas, Juan, 180
Valencia, 20, 28, 36, 47, 82, 141, 148, 158–59, 185, 217, 234
Valladolid, 104, 141, 158–59, 161
Valle de los Caídos, 17, 214
Vallejo de Mena, 168, 170
Valverde, 141, 165
Vaticanist Gibraltar, 78
Vázquez Álvarez, Manuel, 184
Vega Caballero, Antonio, 51, 53
Vejer de la Frontera, 171–72
Velasco (ship), 171
Venezuela, 129
Veracruz, 158
Vías y Obras de los Ferrocariles del Norte, 119
Vicar General of the Diocese of Andalusia, 154
Vicente Ballester Battalion, 143
Vichy Government to the Gestapo, 46
Vilches Guerra, Manuel, 196
Villaba Rubio, Antonio, 149
Villalba de Losa (Burgos), 183
Villaluenga del Rosario, 155–56
Villamartín, 8, 28, 52–53, 194, 216, 218
Villanueva Moreno, José, 150
Villate Arena, Teodimiro, 170
Vincent, Mary,9, 59, 99
Vinyes, Ricard,19, 20, 131, 202
Virgen de Begoña, 144
Virgen de la Merced, 45
Virgen del Valle, 142
Vitoria-Gasteiz, 61, 71, 120, 124, 141, 144, 186, 187

Workers' Battalion, 184

Yagüe, Juan, 148
Young Socialists, 49, 143, 196

Zabala, Don Juan de, 88
Zaldibar, 102–5, 133, 138
Zapadores Battalion, 144
Zaragoza, 20, 70, 130, 168, 217,
    220, 225
Zarautz, 8, 12, 100, 107, 130–31,
    133, 163–64
Zaro Alava, Casáreo, 163
Zeruko Argia, 176
Zimmerman Ruiz, Carlos, 45–47
Zuloga, Ignacio, 156

47474132R00169

Made in the USA
Middletown, DE
26 August 2017